MW00461287

God Save
Benedict Arnold

Also by Jack Kelly

Valcour

The Edge of Anarchy

Heaven's Ditch

Band of Giants

Benedict Arnold

(National Archives and Records Administration)

God Save Benedict Arnold

The True Story of America's Most Hated Man

Jack Kelly

ST. MARTIN'S PRESS
NEW YORK

First published in the United States by St. Martin's Press,
an imprint of St. Martin's Publishing Group

www.stmartins.com

Maps by Joy Taylor

Designed by Meryl Sussman Levavi

Library of Congress Cataloging-in-Publication Data

Names: Kelly, Jack, 1949– author.
Title: God save Benedict Arnold : the true story of America's most
    hated man / Jack Kelly.
Other titles: True story of America's most hated man
Description: First edition. | New York : St. Martin's Press, 2023. |
    Includes bibliographical references and index.
Identifiers: LCCN 2023031027 | ISBN 9781250281951 (hardcover) |
    ISBN 9781250281968 (ebook)
Subjects: LCSH: Arnold, Benedict, 1741–1801. | American
    loyalists—Biography. | Generals—United States—Biography. |
    United States. Continental Army—Biography. | United
    States—History—Revolution, 1775–1783.
Classification: LCC E278.A7 K455 2023 | DDC 973.3092 [B]—
    dc23/eng/20230712
LC record available at https://lccn.loc.gov/2023031027

Our books may be purchased in bulk for promotional,
educational, or business use. Please contact your local
bookseller or the Macmillan Corporate and Premium Sales
Department at 1-800-221-7945, extension 5442, or by email at
MacmillanSpecialMarkets@macmillan.com.

First Edition: 2023

10   9   8   7   6   5   4   3   2   1

Contents

PART FOUR: DOWNFALL—1780

List of Maps

Author's Note

MOST AMERICANS KNOW ONE THING ABOUT BENEDICT Arnold: He betrayed his country. Arnold's treason was real and serious. If he had, as planned, surrendered to the British the important fort at West Point, it's possible that American patriots would have faced defeat in the war for independence.

But Arnold was a hero as well as a traitor. As soon as the conflict broke out, he understood that a revolution was underway, not just a dispute over taxation. He provided backbone to the armed rebellion during its first critical years. He helped push toward a dramatic change, one that would be labeled a "new order of the ages" (the words, in Latin, are printed on the dollar bills in our pockets).

Late eighteenth-century America was favored with many bold thinkers. Jefferson's Declaration of Independence, Madison's enduring Constitution, and the words of people like Thomas Paine and Benjamin Franklin have long served as the mainstay of our country's values. These men are considered our Founders. Arnold contributed something different to the cause. He offered his country not rhetoric but energy, not rationalization but grit, and an astounding ability to fight.

Our view of the Founding generation has evolved as we have continued to reassess our past in light of new information, changing interpretations, and shifting value judgments. History is never static. To regard the Founders as idols who could do no wrong does not do justice to the truth. In the same way, depicting Benedict Arnold as nothing more than a scoundrel misses the fact that he made some of the most pivotal contributions to the struggle for independence.

When Arnold switched sides, his reputation descended into a black hole. The gravity emanating from his treason has long distorted accounts of his genuine accomplishments. The patriot dominance of Lake Champlain in upper New York State, which thwarted a British counterattack from Canada for two years, was his work. He led the extraordinary march of a patriot army over the Maine mountains to attack the British at Quebec. He stopped an enemy invasion in 1776. The following year, he played a critical part in the momentous victory at Saratoga, the turning point of the entire war. Yet his role in all of these feats has been down-played so as to rob credit from a man who had a change of heart.

The purpose of this book is not to exonerate or excuse Arnold's treason—the stain on his character is indelible. Rather, it is to show the genuine heroism of Arnold's early actions, to give readers a deeper understanding of the complexity of the Founding era, and to illuminate Arnold's enigmatic character.

Arnold was imperfect, disloyal, villainous. He waged war against American patriots. But his treachery does not erase his earlier dedication and courage. It will be up to the reader to decide whether his important contributions to the cause of liberty outweighed his grievous breach of faith.

Like a meteor, the real Benedict Arnold traced a glorious streak across our history before disappearing into darkness. This book offers a new look at the time when he blazed as bright as any star in our national firmament. Americans have hated Benedict Arnold for 250 years. Perhaps the time has come for us to take another look at one of the most vital and paradoxical figures of our history.

On what foundation stands the warrior's pride?

—Samuel Johnson, 1749

Part One

To Arms—1775

Battle of Lexington

(From Joel Dorman Steele and Esther Baker Steele,
A Brief History of the United States, 1885)

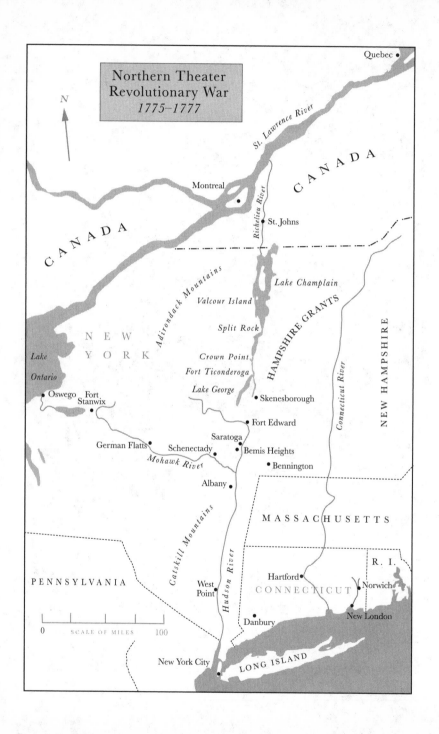

Northern Theater
Revolutionary War
1775–1777

N

Quebec •

St. Lawrence River

Montreal •

Richelieu River

St. Johns •

C A N A D A

C A N A D A

Adirondack Mountains

Lake Ontario

Lake Champlain

Valcour Island

Split Rock

N E W
Y O R K

Crown Point

Fort Ticonderoga

Lake George

HAMPSHIRE GRANTS

NEW HAMPSHIRE

Connecticut River

• Skenesborough

Oswego •

Fort Stanwix •

• Fort Edward

Saratoga •

German Flatts •

Schenectady •

• Bemis Heights

Mohawk River

• Bennington

Albany •

M A S S A C H U S E T T S

Catskill Mountains

Hudson River

West Point •

Hartford •

C O N N E C T I C U T

R. I.

Norwich •

P E N N S Y L V A N I A

New London •

0   SCALE OF MILES   100

• Danbury

New York City •

L O N G   I S L A N D

I

War

THE SUDDEN ARRIVAL OF A HORSEMAN ON A FRIDAY AFTERNOON electrified New Haven. Israel Bissell leapt from his saddle and shouted for the village selectmen. His eyes bulged with news. Citizens came rushing to the green at the center of the prosperous Connecticut seaport. Bissell, his face strained with fatigue, rattled off his brief, shocking story. Fire. Slaughter. War.

Stupid with excitement, he had been riding from Massachusetts since Wednesday morning. Forty miles to Worcester, pushing his horse so hard that the animal dropped dead on arrival. Pounding southward on a fresh mount, he had alerted all those along the dusty roads. Into Connecticut, all night along the coastal post road, throat raw from screaming his warning to every village and farm.

"To arms! To arms!"

He pulled from his shirt a statement by Joseph Palmer of the Massachusetts Committee of Safety. Two days earlier, on April 19, British general Thomas Gage had sent a thousand redcoats marching westward from Boston. At Lexington they confronted "a company of our colony militia in arms, upon whom they fired without any provocation and killed six men and wounded four others."

The words flashed through the crowd. Repeated in shouts and whispers, they ignited New Haven's streets and taverns and markets with fear. "I have spoken with several persons," Palmer wrote, "who have seen the dead and wounded." Images of blood spilled into the minds of the people. Fear quickly turned to rage.

Bissell had set off too early to know the outcome. The short firefight at Lexington had exploded into a blaze at Concord, a conflagration on the road back to Boston. Fire had consumed homes, bayonets had pierced innocent flesh. "A BLOODY BUTCHERY BY THE BRITISH," the first newspaper account howled. In fact, well-organized patriot militiamen had shot dead seventy of the king's soldiers and wounded many more.

In a day, the world had changed.

IN NEW HAVEN, the news quickly arrived at a prominent mansion on Water Street, "by far the grandest" residence in the town of five thousand souls. The house, with its mahogany paneling, English wallpaper, and sweeping central stairway, was not yet completed that April afternoon. The peach, plum, and cherry trees that filled four acres of orchards were just coming into leaf. The new stables housed some of the finest riding and carriage horses in the region.

The owner, Benedict Arnold, was a fifth-generation American of Puritan stock. His great-great-grandfather, also Benedict, had been governor of Rhode Island—a thousand mourners had attended his funeral a century earlier. His name was handed down through a line of Arnolds but the family wealth was not. The fourth Benedict, a cooper's apprentice, had settled in Norwich on the eastern edge of Connecticut, married well, climbed the social ladder, and made himself a prosperous merchant and trader. When he succumbed to depression, bad luck, and drink, he left his son, the current Benedict, to start over from scratch.

As soon as word of the violence reached him, Arnold rushed to the town green on a slick stallion. He was greeted with relief by the townspeople. Here was a man to take charge during this daunting time. His eyes, poised between anger and anticipation, swept their faces as he listened to the details. His verdict was simple: They must act. Must march to Boston and join the fight. Must leave today, tomorrow at the latest.

Few in New Haven could match him in enthusiasm. Another man might have weighed the risks. At thirty-four, Benedict Arnold had a lot to lose: a prosperous international trading business, a large retail store, ships and wharfs along the waterfront, a wife he loved, three young sons on whom he doted. "He has had great luck at sea of late," a neighbor observed. Arnold himself would later testify: "I was in easy circumstances. I was happy in domestic connections and blessed with a rising family."

Yet Arnold could smell the future. Something fundamental was about to happen, something that could not only alter his life but shape the destiny of the country. He had always felt an irresistible urge, almost a mania, to climb, to acquire, to become somebody. Here was an opportunity even grander, a chance to play a role in history, a chance for immortality. He never hesitated.

Risk was nothing new to Arnold. In business, he had seen his fortunes heave up and down on the stormy commercial seas that followed the French and Indian War. Blessed with a vast store of energy, he had worked, calculated, gambled, and prevailed.

The previous December, Arnold and a group of New Haven citizens had established a voluntary militia unit. This independent company was in part a social club, in part a means to learn the basics of soldiering. The group included sixty "gentlemen of high respectability." They had received their charter in March and were now officially the Second Company Connecticut Governor's Foot Guard. During the spring they had hired a British Army deserter to drill them in the rudiments of military tactics. They had practiced marching, wheeling, handling firelocks in close formation. They had broken the town's quiet with their cracking volleys.

This was Arnold's only formal military training, but his teenage years had been years of war in the colonies. The armed struggle, the British Army and provincial forces fighting the detested French, had infected his play and fed his young imagination. At sixteen he had joined the Norwich militia for a march to the New York frontier. They hurried north to save Fort William Henry on Lake George. The bastion had fallen before they arrived, and Indians had murdered and peeled the scalps from a portion of the British captives. The militiamen returned home, reminded that war was not play.

Although he lacked combat experience, Arnold was familiar with violence. Never a merchant to supervise his business from a counting house, he personally captained the ships he sent to Canada and the Caribbean. By venturing to remote markets, he could take advantage of local trading opportunities, buy and sell as conditions dictated, and keep a close eye on his merchandise. He loved the sea, where danger and promise defied the pettiness of men.

In an age when piracy was a threat and seaports teemed with rough characters, a ship's captain had to assert himself, with force if necessary. Seamen who failed to obey orders were severely flogged. In a zone dominated by the widespread cruelty of enslavement and the outrages of brigands, a reputation for violence was useful.

At home, Arnold dressed in silk and drank tea from expensive china. Out in the world, he was a muscular, black-haired, sunburnt man. His jaw jutted with the defiance of a professional pugilist; his gaze made other men think twice before opposing him. Arnold was noted for his athletic prowess—one acquaintance described him as "the most accomplished and graceful skater" he had ever seen. Everyone noted his hair-trigger temper and the quickness with which he defended his honor.

In 1766, Arnold and a pack of cronies had publicly seized a former crewman, Peter Boles, who had informed on him for smuggling. They "gave him a little Chastisement," and ordered him out of town. When he ignored the warning, they seized him again, tied him to a whipping post, and flogged him "in a shocking manner." Arnold was arrested and a New Haven magistrate fined him fifty shillings for disturbing the peace—Arnold took the penalty as a point of pride.

Gradually, Arnold's concerns had grown more political. He had been trading in the West Indies when he heard about the incident on March 5, 1770, when redcoats shot five colonists dead in what was called the Boston Massacre. "Good God!" he wrote in a letter to a fellow merchant. "Are Americans all asleep and tamely giving up their glorious liberties?" He scornfully referred to these passive patriots as "philosophers."

In response to the 1773 protest in which citizens heaved tea into Boston Harbor, Parliament had imposed the so-called Intolerable Acts. The legislation shut down the port of Boston, stripped Massachusetts of self-government, and allowed British redcoats to be quartered in citizens' homes. Reverend Samuel Peters, a Connecticut clergyman, spoke out in defense of the acts and in opposition to relief measures for Boston's beleaguered citizens. "Deliver us from anarchy," was his sentiment. He asserted his fear of "the mobs of . . . Benedict Arnold." Arnold led a crowd of mechanics and waterfront men to besiege Peters's house. The minister soon decamped to Boston and eventually to England.

On this momentous day in April 1775, Arnold, who had been elected captain of the Foot Guard, sent word to all members. In a quickly convened meeting, they voted to march to the scene of the action. They would assemble on the town green in uniform the next morning. The war that had loomed over the colonies for years was at hand.

That night, the militia captain hurried to put his affairs in order. He sat with his wife, Margaret, known as Peggy, and his unmarried sister, Hannah. Both were knowledgeable about his business from having overseen affairs during his extended sea voyages. Not knowing how long he would now be absent, he gave them instructions about ongoing dealings and the various amounts owed to and by him.

Peggy was an attractive, quiet, often sickly young woman, and Benedict loved her to distraction. He had known her father, Samuel Mansfield, before the marriage. Both merchants were members of the local Masonic lodge. Mansfield, who also served as high sheriff in New Haven, had partnered with Arnold in a number of business deals. His son-in-law referred to him affectionately as Papa.

Although their wedding was in many ways a coupling of flame and ice, Arnold did not lack a strain of domestic sentiment. On his trading journeys, he wrote to his "dear girl," begging for news of "our dear little prattlers." He reminded her, "How uncertain is life, how certain is death," a lesson handed down from his Puritan mother. She wrote back far less frequently than he wished, and he sometimes begged for a word from her.

Arnold's frequent travel strained their marriage. Away from home for months, he had ample opportunity for sexual encounters. On one occasion an embarrassing rumor of venereal disease followed him home. On another, he tried to placate Peggy by purchasing an enslaved girl in the West Indies as a household servant.

When dawn broke, Arnold donned a ruffled white shirt, a white waistcoat, silk stockings, and black leggings. He slipped into a coat of rich scarlet wool faced with buff-colored silk and adorned with silver buttons. Gaudy dress-up had been part of the fun of the Foot Guard, but the display also signaled that Arnold was a gentleman of means. He felt that his uniform announced his authority, an instinct he shared with an equally zealous Virginia planter. In a few weeks, George Washington, resplendent in his military finery, would be appointed commander of a new "continental" army of patriots.

Just after sunrise, Arnold bid adieu to Peggy and Hannah. He hugged Benedict, seven years old; Richard, six; and little Henry, only three. Leather creaked as he climbed onto his handsome horse and trotted the half mile to the green, where his men were already assembling. Arnold greeted Eleazer Oswald, a lieutenant who would help him manage the group. Oswald was a capable twenty-five-year-old immigrant from England. He was the son of a ship's captain and had been apprentice to a printer. He would stick by Arnold through much of his career.

That Saturday morning, the town was still buzzing with the news from Lexington. Folks gathered to watch the uniformed Foot Guards go through their paces, the drummers pounding out staccato signals of war. The air crackled with excitement. This would be the people's answer to the cruelty of the "lobster backs." The crowd cheered every celebratory volley.

The night before, Arnold had recruited a handful of Yale students more eager for adventure than learning. Now sixty men in all lined up for the 140-mile march to Cambridge. With no time to assemble provisions, the men had to carry their own food in knapsacks.

What they could not do without was gunpowder, ammunition, flints, and additional muskets. The town's supply of arms and its kegs of explosive powder were stored in a stone magazine on the outskirts. Arnold was informed that the selectmen were just then conferring in Beers Tavern, a popular meeting spot just up the street from Yale College. He sent a man there to request that the powder house be opened so that the Foot Guards could arm themselves.

The selectmen had already agreed to remain neutral for the time being. How could they know the real facts until they received more definitive information? Nor were they anxious to join in an uprising against the crown—an act of treason—over a dispute between Massachusetts radicals and the British ministry.

They sent David Wooster outside to confer with the brash captain. Wooster, at sixty-four, was the leading military man of the colony, commander of its regular militia forces. He had served in colonial wars over the past thirty-five years, rising to become a colonel in the British Army before retiring on half pay. He was well aware of the gravity of bearing arms against the king, but he was also an American patriot. Like Arnold, he had participated in driving the Tory Reverend Peters out of town.

Arnold, although of medium height—"There wasn't any wasted timber in him," one acquaintance said—had a posture that suggested a perpetual strut. He confronted the older man in front of the tavern. Wooster perhaps wished himself thirty years younger and fired with Arnold's passion. The younger man respected Wooster's military savvy and experience, but when Arnold insisted he hand over the keys to the powder house, Wooster refused. Arnold threatened to order his men to break open the magazine. He swore that "none but the Almighty God shall prevent my marching!" His actual language was likely saltier than the version filtered through the historical record—the profanity of the era was obscenely imaginative, especially among sailors.

Wooster responded by giving up the keys. The populace cheered. Even today Powder House Day is celebrated every April in New Haven.

The men supplied themselves, formed into ranks, and prepared to move out. Before they left, local pastor Jonathan Edwards Jr. pronounced a blessing over the town's patriotic warriors and over the man whose name meant "blessed."

ENTERING CAMBRIDGE AT the end of a long and hurried march, the Foot Guards looked around in amazement. Even Arnold, who had traveled to London, Quebec, and the West Indies, was impressed by the bustle. The whole region was alive with activity. Camps swollen with men from all over New England stretched in an arc from Winter Hill in the north to Dorchester Heights in the south. They formed a large, rattling settlement: men slaughtered bullocks and baked bread to feed the army; farm boys drilled awkwardly on the parades; smoke from a thousand open fires hung in the air. All eyes were focused on the besieged city of Boston, isolated on a virtual island in the center of the bay and occupied by British troops and their loyalist supporters.

Word of the outrages at Lexington and Concord had sent excited militiamen marching the day they heard. Legend depicts Israel Putnam, the well-known veteran of the French and Indian War, leaving his plow in a field in northeast Connecticut and heading for Boston in his work clothes. John Stark, an independent-minded ranger from New Hampshire, tore south with three hundred men. After Arnold and his troops left New Haven, Connecticut authorities ordered David Wooster to gather six thousand of his state's militiamen to support the cause.

Soldiers were packed into the buildings of Harvard College and sheltered under tents made from ships' sails in clearings along the Charles River. Many simply slept in the open. The Foot Guards, elegant in their uniforms and sharp in their drills, were admired by the men of the more ragged militia units. Arnold was able to secure them quarters in the plush former residence of

Andrew Oliver, a recently deceased lieutenant governor loathed by patriots.

IN CAMBRIDGE, ARNOLD sought out a man called "the greatest incendiary in all America" and met a lost brother. Joseph Warren was, like Arnold, largely a self-made product of the colonial middle class. The men were almost exactly the same age. Both were versed in medicine: Arnold operated an apothecary store where he sold herbal potions, aphrodisiacs, and scurvy cures; Warren had studied the craft of healing at Harvard. As a child, Arnold had helped his inebriated father off the streets and had watched his family's belongings auctioned in bankruptcy—he had become the richest man in New Haven. The youthful Warren had hawked milk on the streets of Boston—he was now a prominent physician there. Both men were tough dandies used to fine clothes and opulent surroundings. Both were rebels.

Warren possessed charm and polish, Arnold displayed a rougher exterior. Warren knew how to play politics to get his way, Arnold preferred to force his will on others by means of his relentless self-confidence. Several weeks after their meeting, Warren would write in a letter, "Danger and war are become pleasing." Arnold agreed.

Like Warren, Arnold sensed that the current hubbub was not just another of the temporary tremors that had been erupting in the colonies during the ten years since the Stamp Act crisis. This time, the people would not heave into action only to subside when London agreed to a compromise. This was different. The shots fired on Lexington Common marked the doorway to a new order.

Not everyone could see it. Even avid patriots spoke of negotiation and reconciliation. At the end of April, Connecticut governor Jonathan Trumbull still hoped to avoid further hostilities. Warren convinced him that violence was unavoidable. "No business but that of war," he wrote, "is either done or thought of in this colony."

"Our all is at stake," Warren proclaimed. "Every moment is infinitely precious." Action was needed. Now he found himself staring into the face of a man for whom action was a reflex. And Arnold had a plan.

2

Fort Ticonderoga

Benedict Arnold had arrived in Cambridge the captain of a sixty-man Connecticut infantry company. He left four days later the colonel of a Massachusetts regiment, a fighting unit that typically included about six hundred men. His mission was critical. Patriot military leaders knew that without cannon the militiamen surrounding Boston could not defend against a determined British attack. Without cannon, they could not pry the enemy from the occupied city.

Arnold's mind had flashed to a solution. He had often traded along the corridor that ran from Montreal down Lake Champlain and the Hudson River to New York City. The forts at Ticonderoga and Crown Point, twelve miles apart on the western shore of Lake Champlain, had served as important outposts before 1763, when the French still held Canada. Arnold told Joseph Warren that 130 cannon, maybe more, lay unused at Ticonderoga and that the fort was in "ruinous condition." It could not hold out an hour against a determined force of fighters. If captured by patriot soldiers, the forts would also stand in the way of any enemy incursion from Canada.

Warren was instantly convinced—they should make the attempt immediately. If they moved quickly, they might confront the forts' defenders before they could be reinforced. He made the raid a priority, rushed it through the Committee of Safety, the executive authority for the provincial assembly. He obtained the agreement of the patriots' military commander, Artemus Ward.

Speed was everything. Warren arranged Arnold's commission as militia colonel and secured one hundred pounds for his expenses, along with ten horses and kegs of precious gunpowder. Several of Arnold's lieutenants, including Eleazer Oswald, would go along to assist him. They would have to enlist local men from western Massachusetts to fill out the regiment.

A few days of hard riding brought Arnold and his aides to the western end of the colony. On May 6, they were busy signing up volunteers from around the frontier hill towns of Stockbridge and Pittsfield. Arnold was surprised when he discovered that another militia force, authorized by Connecticut authorities, was just then gathering to attack Ticonderoga on behalf of the patriots.

The confusion had its origin in a chance meeting while Arnold was leading his Foot Guards to Boston. He had encountered Samuel Holden Parsons, a Connecticut militia colonel, headed back to Hartford to recruit more men. Arnold had mentioned to him the idea of capturing the Lake Champlain forts. Parsons alerted Connecticut revolutionaries, who borrowed three hundred pounds from the colony's treasury to purchase military supplies for such an expedition. They contacted Ethan Allen, a Connecticut native now living in the disputed Hampshire Grants along the east side of the lake. Allen gathered his armed Green Mountain Boys for an attack on Ticonderoga.

Arnold now left his lieutenants behind and charged a hundred miles northward to investigate. A week after leaving the Boston area, on the evening of May 9, he cantered into the township of Shoreham on the coast of Lake Champlain opposite Ticonderoga. He sought out a narrow indentation called Hand's Cove. Approaching the shore, he watched storm clouds swallow the sinking sun. Gusty winds heaved the lake water into an angry chop.

Waiting at the lake's edge were nearly two hundred armed men. Arnold, who was familiar with the region, knew their leader by reputation. Now he met Ethan Allen in person, a strapping man described as a "giant." His resplendent green uniform coat, with its epaulets and gold braid, was nearly as striking as Arnold's own.

Sizing up Allen, Arnold confronted a vehement enthusiast three years older than himself. Allen was said to be a man with "boundless self-confidence and a shrewdness in thought and action equal to almost any emergency." The same could have been said of Arnold.

Allen took pride in the fact that New York's royal governor, William Tryon, had put a hundred-pound price on his head. When Tryon issued a proclamation condemning the Green Mountain Boys' abuses, Allen suggested "the Governor may stick it in his arse."

That sentiment highlighted a sharp distinction between the two men. Allen was a frontier populist, a voluble talker, and a braggart. He was marked by "rough and ready humor" and wild storytelling. Respectability was not his goal. He acted the part of a rustic, but beneath the boorish facade was a political sophisticate, sly, smart, and self-centered.

Arnold aspired to join the very elites whom Allen mocked. Although his frank manner fostered a rapport with laborers and sailors, Arnold was an admirer of the refined and wealthy men who influenced events. He considered himself a gentleman in every sense of the word, a man of honor, of substance.

The Green Mountain Boys commanded by Allen were a group of vigilantes who had been active in the territory between Lake Champlain and the Connecticut River, the land that would later become the state of Vermont. During the colonial period, both

New York and New Hampshire laid claim to the area. The dispute over the so-called Hampshire Grants was entirely separate from the sudden uprising against the crown, but Allen was quick to link his cause with that of the patriots in other provinces.

For several years, Allen's hooligans had intimidated settlers who secured New York titles for their land. They had burned homes, threatened bailiffs, and assaulted the "Yorkers" they saw as enemies. At the same time, Allen was purchasing sixty thousand acres of land from New Hampshire authorities with the hope of selling it at a profit to the farmers moving into the area.

Over the coming two months, Benedict Arnold would battle Allen and his cohorts over who was to take charge of the northern forts. Some histories suggest that their animosity erupted immediately. It's more likely that at Hand's Cove that night the two men struck an uneasy accord. Arnold, who had developed a keen ability to size up men, saw Allen and his followers as bully boys who could coerce civilians but had no concept of military order. He also recognized that they constituted something that he lacked: a squadron of armed men. The first of his own Massachusetts recruits would not be arriving for days. Understanding that the men's lackadaisical discipline could endanger a crucial mission, Arnold asserted himself. He would take command of the planned attack, he told Allen.

Although Allen did not intend to give up his position, he examined Arnold's written orders. They indicated that, unlike Allen, he was acting on the authority of an official body at the heart of the rebellion. The instructions Allen had from Connecticut were sketchier, coming from only a handful of influential men in Hartford. Arnold's uniform, his confidence, and his pompous manner impressed Allen, who might have seen him as someone to blame if the raid misfired.

It was Allen's men who resisted when Arnold tried to make himself their leader. They were a voluntary group of independent frontiersmen. Democracy was their watchword. They had elected their leader just as the New Haven Foot Guards had. Arnold was a stranger and a man whose manner reminded them of the hated Yorker elites. They flatly refused to go ahead if he took charge.

Time was wasting. Allen had already sent a man across the lake to reconnoiter the fort. He had ascertained that the men of the small garrison were still ignorant of the events at Lexington and that their security was lax. Allen and Arnold both understood that at any moment, redcoat reinforcements might arrive by water from Montreal. Or word of an intended attack might put the fort on high alert.

Someone suggested a joint command. The two men agreed. Since Arnold lacked an effective weapon, Allen offered him a blunderbuss, a wide-muzzled naval firearm. They were ready to go. The Green Mountain contingent had been joined by fifty Massachusetts militiamen under James Easton, a forty-seven-year-old tavern keeper. He was assisted by a lawyer named John Brown. Both men hailed from Pittsfield and both would prove a scourge to Benedict Arnold.

All that remained was to await the arrival of the boats Allen had sent men to procure. The delay almost defeated the operation before it began. Darkness fell. By the time some Green Mountain Boys pulled into the cove with a sluggish flat-bottomed scow, a storm was boiling the black water, sending waves lapping over the vessel's sides. The rough one-mile crossing, which required much tacking and maneuvering through rain and wind, took an hour and a half. There was no longer time to return for another squad of soldiers. They would have to take Ticonderoga with the force they had: eighty-three wet, undisciplined partisan fighters.

IT WAS NEARLY four o'clock on the morning of May 10. The incipient revolution was hanging by a thread—the ill-equipped militiamen surrounding Boston were considering pulling back to avoid a British assault.

On the shore of Lake Champlain, the wind was still waving pine boughs, but the sky was clearing. The fading stars winked through gaps in the clouds as Arnold stepped from the overloaded boat. He and Allen arranged their troops in a ragged line and started up the steep trail toward the fort, which overlooked the lake from a bluff. As they hurried along, awakening dawn light began to bring the scene into view. The breeze carried the glimmers of early birdsong and the aroma of budding leaves and of lingering winter rot.

Although stiff and wet, the men mounted the rise toward the storied bastion with bouncing steps. The predawn air was delicious to breathe. They clenched their jaws in excitement. At their head, Arnold cradled the blunderbuss and Allen rested his hand on the pommel of his cutlass, a two-foot-long, razor-sharp fighting blade. Both were pirate weapons, made for killing men in close combat.

The company of soldiers moved up through gnarled trees still dripping rainwater and into the cleared fields of fire. They approached the open plaza outside the gate through the stone parapets. Gaping cannon loomed above them—a blast of grapeshot could kill half their force in an instant.

Allen, Arnold, and many of their men had been brought up on tales and myths of fortresses. They had learned about the citadel of Troy that had defied the mighty Achilles. Preachers had spoken of the walls of Jericho tumbling to the Israelites' trumpets. Sixteen years ago, British general James Wolfe had captured the storied bastion at Quebec. Now it was their turn to become immortal heroes, to take part in one of the epics of history.

This was the pivotal moment. With no cover, they rushed across the open space as quietly as they could. In the tepid light they were frighteningly exposed. An anxious thrill lifted Arnold out of the mundane and into the hurly-burly world.

At the middle of the massive gate was a small door, known as a wicket, where individuals could pass into the fort. Beside it, a sentry box. Inside, a British soldier. Asleep. For the attackers, it was an announcement that security was still lax, surprise still possible.

The startled guard suddenly sensed the specters emerging from the morning mist. He called out a challenge. Lifted his musket. Pulled the trigger. *Click.* The dampness of the night caused a misfire.

The sentry ran inside, shouting an alarm. Another terrified soldier opposed the confusing figures who rushed at him from the dark. He caught a man in the arm with his bayonet. Allen swung the cutlass, which could easily slice through a man's spine. At the last moment, he turned the blade and whacked the soldier on the head with his weapon's flat side.

"No quarter!" he shouted.

The Green Mountain Boys began to fill the air with hoots and screams.

"Huzzah! Huzzah! No quarter!"

They burst into the stillness of the parade ground. Their voices rose in a chorus that echoed from the stone walls. No shots sounded in return. Weak gray light washed over the dream-like scene.

Breaking through the doors, they stormed into the two-story stone barracks. Inside, soldiers were just coming awake. Forty men. Two dozen women and children.

As Allen and his men began to mount the stairs to the barracks' second floor, they were confronted by an English officer, barely dressed and with his trousers in his hand. He shouted questions. Who were they? By what authority had they come bearing arms against the king's troops?

In a later account, Allen inserted the answer he wished he had given. He demanded the fort's surrender, he said, in the name of "the great Jehovah and the Continental Congress." Whether God interested Himself in the affair was open to debate, but the delegates of the Second Continental Congress were just that morning convening their first meeting in distant Philadelphia— they knew nothing of the attack on the king's fort, and when they heard of it they would oppose such a radical action.

After some confusion, Allen figured out that the man he was addressing was not the fort's commander, Captain William Delaplace, but his aide, Lieutenant Jocelyn Feltham. Feltham told him that his superior, who had been asleep beside his wife, was in his quarters dressing. Allen called Delaplace a "damned old rat" and insisted he come out at once and surrender the fort or Allen would "sacrifice the whole garrison."

Benedict Arnold, whom Feltham described as more "genteel," kept Allen from bursting through the door. When Delaplace appeared, Arnold requested that he "deliver up his arms, and he might expect to be treated like a gentleman." The British captain had little choice.

SURPRISE HAD COMPENSATED for lack of experience. In spite of the chaos, shouting, and threats, the whole affair had come off without a shot fired. The Green Mountain Boys gathered up the garrison's muskets, secured the fort's magazine, and locked their prisoners in a storeroom. They felt an immense elation. They had succeeded. One of the principal fortifications in America was theirs.

The storm that had vexed them during the night blew away, leaving behind a fresh spring morning. "The sun rising over Ticonderoga," Allen later recounted, "smiled on its conquerors, who tossed about the flowing bowl, and wished success to Congress, and the liberty and freedom of America."

Gaining the far side of fear, the Green Mountain Boys gave up all pretense of discipline. They were soon joined by those whom they had left behind on the eastern shore. Settlers from the surrounding area, astounded by the sudden act of rebellion, began to drift in to join the excitement.

Order broke down entirely. Soldiers and civilians roamed the fort, pillaging what they could carry. They discovered a ninety-gallon stash of rum and set to drinking. They fired their muskets into the air.

Benedict Arnold strictly forbade plunder or the destruction of private property. He told Ethan Allen to control his men. They were not playing at war. At a time when there was important work to be done, "everything is governed by whim and caprice," Arnold complained.

Allen responded that the joint leadership arrangement was over. He alone was in charge. He allowed the looting to continue. Some of the celebratory musket shots came dangerously close to Arnold, perhaps on purpose. Allen got Edward Mott, a Connecticut militia captain and chairman of an ad hoc "Committee of War," to affirm his authority, writing him out a colonel's "commission" to match Arnold's rank and orders from Massachusetts.

Arnold wrote in his regimental memorandum book that day: "When Mr. Allen, finding he had a strong party, and being impatient to control, and taking umbrage at my forbiding the people to plunder, he assumed the entire command, and I was not consulted for four days."

For Arnold, the discord was an annoyance, but his focus was in another direction. Capturing a dilapidated, undermanned fort was one thing, holding it was another. At any moment a British warship could appear and land enough troops to contest control. He had yet to recruit the men who would fill out his Massachusetts regiment.

On May 12, two days after the capture, Seth Warner, another

leader of the Green Mountain Boys, rowed north from Ticonderoga with a force of fifty men. They landed at Crown Point, twelve miles away, and captured the position from the nine British soldiers assigned to guard it.

In 1759, the British had begun building one of the largest fortresses on the continent at Crown Point to protect against French incursions along the lake. The peninsula was well situated, facing north at one of the narrowest spots on Lake Champlain. In 1773, the fortress caught fire and its powder magazine exploded, leaving a ruin. With the French threat gone, there was then little reason to rebuild. Besides the flimsy barracks, there was little left of the fort, but, as at Ticonderoga, there was a large supply of disused cannon lying around the peninsula.

Four days later, the situation at Ticonderoga was changing. The Green Mountain Boys, many of them farmers, had quickly begun to drift away after the initial excitement. They needed to plant crops and did not relish garrison duty. Meanwhile, Arnold's recruiters sent a hundred newly enlisted militiamen north from Massachusetts. On the way, they took control of a schooner that Allen's men had captured at the estate of Philip Skene, a retired British officer who held a large tract of land near the southern tip of Lake Champlain. The mountain men did not know how to sail the forty-eight-foot boat, but Arnold's people did.

DUBBED THE *LIBERTY*, this two-masted sailing vessel was the American patriots' first warship. When Arnold saw Eleazer Oswald cruise up to the waterfront at Ticonderoga in the boat, he immediately plunged into the next part of his plan. He appointed Boston sea captain John Prout Sloan to be the schooner's captain and ordered the men to fit her out with four medium-sized cannon and six one-inch-bore swivel guns. The very next day, he was sailing north, glad to leave behind the tedious bickering at the forts. He brought along fifty-five men and two bateaux, large rowboats with simple square sails.

Along the way, his flotilla intercepted a mail boat heading south with a British ensign on board. A search discovered detailed information about troop deployments in Canada. Arnold was amazed to learn that British general Guy Carleton apparently had only seven hundred soldiers at his disposal. The whole province was vulnerable to an American incursion—if they moved quickly. The news made their current mission all the more important.

Three days later, the men reached the border of Canada, where Lake Champlain flowed into the lazy Richelieu River. When the breeze died, Arnold left fifteen men on the schooner and contin- ued north with forty of his troops in the bateaux. They rowed all night, Arnold piloting one boat, Oswald the other. They pulled quietly into an inlet a few hundred yards from the barracks at St. Johns, a small British outpost along the river. There they waited, Oswald noted, "in a small creek infested with numberless swarms of gnats and mosquitoes."

At six in the morning, the men crept onto shore and marched toward the barracks. The slack security puzzled Arnold, since he assumed the authorities in nearby Montreal must have received word about the rebel capture of Ticonderoga. When the de- fenders finally realized they were under attack, only twelve men emerged to face the invaders. They quickly surrendered to Arnold's superior force.

Now the patriots went for their real objective, a seventy-ton sloop tied up two miles north of the barracks. This one-masted sailing vessel was armed with a pair of cannon and some swivel guns, but was mainly a supply ship for moving men and materials along the lake. Eleazer Oswald led a squad of men who found the seven-man crew asleep. They easily captured the vessel.

The jubilant Americans quickly gathered together food, mus-

kets, and four additional bateaux. They set sail, getting away from
St. Johns only hours before the arrival of the reinforcements that
their prisoners had told them were headed there from two directions. By noon they were back on Lake Champlain and headed
southward, the sloop and schooner forming a rudimentary navy.

Arnold and his men sailed away from Canada overcome with
a sense of destiny. During the capture of Ticonderoga, Arnold
had depended on Allen and his Green Mountain Boys. This naval
expedition was entirely his own initiative. "Had we been 6 hours
later," he wrote to Joseph Warren, "in all Probability we should
have miscarried in our Design."

By moving quickly, they had captured two forts and the only
warship on the lake and still had not fired a shot. They imagined that their virtue had dissolved all obstacles. How could it
be otherwise? The sun sparkling from the waves was the winking
eye of Providence.

BY EARLY AFTERNOON, they were seventeen miles south of the Canadian border. Lookouts spotted four boats approaching. Arnold
put his own ships on alert, but he soon found that the men pulling
against the wind were crews of Green Mountain Boys. Not to be
left out of the action, Ethan Allen had set sail with a hundred fifty
men. Their bateaux had made good time until that morning, when
the wind swung around from the north. The crews had to haul on
oars to heave the thirty-foot rowboats along the choppy surface.

On approach, Arnold ordered his men to fire the cannon as a
salute to their compatriots. Allen's soldiers answered with musket
fire. Allen's boat bumped alongside the captured sloop, which
Arnold had christened the *Enterprise*. With some of his officers,
Allen climbed aboard the larger ship and congratulated Arnold
on his achievement. "Several loyal Congress healths were drunk,"
Allen noted.

The ever-enthusiastic Allen outlined his plan. He would rush northward along the Richelieu, occupy St. Johns while it remained undefended, and set up a base of operations in Canada. Arnold told him what he had learned: British troops were already on their way to reinforce the town. Allen was sure to encounter a body of regulars there.

"It appeared to me a wild, impracticable scheme," Arnold later wrote. He made the point that even if it succeeded, the occupation of St. Johns would be "of no consequence, so long as we are masters of the Lake."

Allen ignored the advice. He was determined to accomplish what Arnold had not. He did admit that, in his hurry to get underway, he had neglected to stock the vessels with enough food—his men were famished. Arnold had his crew transfer provisions from his ship into the bateaux. Watching the mountain men head off toward Canada, he described them as "mad fellows" intent on a mission they had not properly considered.

As it turned out, Allen's Boys did find St. Johns occupied by redcoats. They decided to deploy on the opposite, eastern, side of the river. Fatigued from having sailed and rowed heavy boats more than a hundred miles over the past four days, they made camp and went to sleep. Allen neglected to post the proper sentries. At first light, they were rudely awakened by two hundred British infantrymen firing at them with cannon and muskets. They leapt into their boats so quickly that they left three men behind. They rowed up the river, abandoned the mission, and headed back to Ticonderoga.

This little debacle confirmed Benedict Arnold's initial impression of Allen. "It happened," Arnold wrote, "as I expected."

3

ঔ৶

Public Calamity

I N 1636, ROGER WILLIAMS, CAST OUT OF THE PLYMOUTH COLONY because of his liberal views on religion, lived his first winter in exile with the nearby Wampanoag peoples to the south. He then founded a new colony, the Providence Plantations, later Rhode Island. Williams advocated for religious freedom, "liberty of conscience," and separation of church and state. He questioned the validity of the king's colonial charters, which claimed possession of lands occupied by indigenous peoples.

Rhode Island remained a haven for religious dissidents when the first Benedict Arnold settled there after emigrating from England with his parents. As a young man, he learned to speak several indigenous languages. He rose to prominence and succeeded Williams as the colony's governor in 1663. Following his term in office, this original Benedict settled in Newport, engaged in trade and land speculation, and soon became the wealthiest citizen of the colony. His example would serve as a beacon to his great-great-grandson.

The family's wealth dissipated over three generations. Benedict's father started life with no inherited land. Instead, he served as apprentice to a cooper, shaping barrel staves. He moved across the border from Rhode Island to Norwich, Connecticut, a seaport seventeen miles up the Thames River from the coastal city of New London. There he married Hannah Waterman King, the widow of a sea captain for whom the elder Arnold may have worked. Hannah was related to the Waterman clan, founders of Norwich, and to the Lathrops, who were among the town's most successful merchants.

In the eighteenth century, each of the thirteen colonies touched at least an arm of the sea, and every major city had access to salt water. Fishing and trade sent large fleets seaward. Aided by his wife's capital and connections, Arnold's father became a successful merchant, commanding ships in the West Indies trade. He became known in Norwich as Captain Arnold. During his formative years, young Benedict went along on these journeys and reveled in the ensuing adventures.

In 1752, at age eleven, Arnold set off toward a bright future. He traveled fifteen miles north from Norwich to be tutored by Dr. James Cogswell, a congregational minister and scholar. After training in mathematics, grammar, Latin, and Greek, he would go on to Yale, the largest college in the colonies, to receive the classical education that defined a gentleman.

While he was at school, he was shielded somewhat from dire trouble at home. Death shadowed the family. His sisters, Mary and Elizabeth, died in a 1753 diphtheria epidemic at ages eight and four. He himself had been named in honor of his mother's firstborn, Benedict, who had died in infancy. His little brother Absalom had not made it past age three. Only Benedict and his sister, Hannah, survived. "Deaths are multiplied around us," his mother wrote to him. She reminded him to be ready to die at every moment.

The next year, she advised him that his father was in a "poor state of health." Perhaps shaken by the loss of his children, Captain Arnold had slipped more deeply into alcoholism. His business declined. By 1755, the family could no longer afford to keep their fourteen-year-old son in school. He would have to endure seven years of servitude as an apprentice, learning a trade. His mother's Lathrop relatives agreed to take him in and train him in the apothecary business.

His father's downfall was one of the key passages of Benedict Arnold's youth. During the year 1756, when he was fifteen, the elder Arnold was slipping further into addiction, often drinking himself into unconsciousness. Benedict was assigned to seek him out in a tavern or on the street and help him home, a searing task for any child.

Misfortunes multiplied. In the summer of 1759, his mother died. The following spring his father was arrested on the humiliating charge of public intoxication. He was said to be "disabled in the use of understanding and reason." At the Norwich Congregational Church, where the family had long been respected members, authorities admonished the elder Arnold for "drunkenness in diverse instances."

Young Benedict was stung by the pious disregard of the leading families, who were so quick to treat a broken, luckless man with scorn and condemnation. For the rest of his life, he was acutely sensitive to any insult or show of disrespect.

IN THE SPRING of 1775, Arnold brought his touchy personality into an environment where confused lines of authority and the jealousy of other ambitious men would erupt into squabbling. The discord often turned personal.

He returned to Ticonderoga with a glow of accomplishment, but also with an urgent need to prepare for the inevitable enemy counterattack. Arnold understood intuitively that a raid or a battle was a brief interruption in the course of a war. The real work of fighting was to dig, to fortify, to gather intelligence, to plan for contingencies.

Others had different priorities. While Arnold was trying to restore order and prevent looting at Ticonderoga, Ethan Allen was sending John Brown to Philadelphia bearing the first British flag captured in the conflict. The lawyer sang the praises of Allen to the delegates. James Easton carried Allen's message to the Provincial Congress of Massachusetts.

Allen made little or no mention of Arnold in his reports. His account to Congress began, "I have to inform you with pleasure unfelt before, that on break of day of the tenth of May, 1775, by the order of the General Assembly of the Colony of Connecticut, took the Fortress of Ticonderoga by storm." Easton, he said, acted "with great zeal and fortitude," and John Brown was "an able counselor, and was personally in the attack." His Boys were "agreeably disappointed" that the enemy had not put up more of a fight. Overnight, the outlaw with a price on his head became the hero of Ticonderoga.

Arnold claimed that Easton was "the last man that entered the fort" after having hidden nearby "under the pretense of wiping and drying his gun." His own contribution remained largely unknown to the congressional delegates. He complained to his friend Joseph Warren that Allen's men were "in the greatest confusion and anarchy, destroying and plundering private property, committing every enormity, and paying no attention to publick service. . . . Colonel Allen is a proper man to head his own wild people, but entirely unacquainted with military service."

Arnold considered himself the only duly authorized officer on the scene and wrote, "I think it my duty to remain here against all opposition, until I have further orders." He understood that he was himself a military neophyte—throughout the controversy over command at the fort, he repeated his willingness to "be honorably acquitted of my commission" so that "a proper person might be appointed." But he would not relinquish command to a proven incompetent.

Allen was an egoist and a determined self-promoter. He loved action but had little feel for strategy and tactics. His contributions to the dispute over who was in charge of the forts were compounded by the patriots' organizational confusion during the early days of the rebellion. Who had authority in the colonies? Who could issue military orders? Who would pay the costs? All this was yet to be sorted out.

Patriots in Massachusetts naturally took the lead. Warren's Committee of Safety had ordered the seizure of the forts. So had an ad hoc group of politicians in Hartford. New York authorities had yet to make a decisive move, although the posts were in their territory. As soon as Massachusetts officials learned that Connecticut was willing to send troops to Ticonderoga, they tried to hand over responsibility to their neighboring colony in order to focus their resources on the precarious situation around Boston.

In the meantime, the contention at Ticonderoga dragged on. In late May, two weeks after the fort's capture, a visitor noted that "Colonel Arnold has been greatly abused. . . . Had it not been for him, everything would have been in the utmost confusion and disorder."

It would take a full month for the Continental Congress to set up a unified military command. The delegates' first impulse was that Allen, Arnold, and the others had gone too far in seizing the king's forts and artillery. On May 18, while Benedict Arnold was preparing to attack St. Johns, Congress approved a resolution to hand the forts back to the British. Patriots were defending their rights, not attacking the crown. The armed men there, they decreed, should pull back to the south end of Lake George, forty miles below Ticonderoga. They could move the valuable cannon there, but they should keep an inventory so that the guns could be handed back to the crown "when the restoration of the former harmony between Great Britain and these colonies . . . shall render it prudent."

It would take politicians more than a year to declare the colonies independent. Aggressive, war-minded men like Arnold and Joseph Warren saw things differently. When Warren heard of the capture of Ticonderoga, he wrote, "Thus a War has begun."

An absence of organization, overlapping jurisdictions, and innate caution aggravated the situation. So did the time it took for communications to travel through the rugged interior. Arnold was astonished when he received the congressional order to abandon the forts on May 29, eleven days after it was issued. He immediately scribbled a fervent reply.

"The report of Ticonderoga's being abandoned," he wrote, "has thrown the Inhabitants here into the greatest Consternation." If the insurrectionists pulled out, they would leave local citizens "at the mercy of the King's Troops & Indians." Militarily, he wrote, "Ticonderoga is the Key of this extensive Country." By the time his letter reached Philadelphia, the delegates had already thought better of their timidity and rescinded their May 18 resolution.

THE CONFUSION OVER command partly resolved itself. As the number of Allen's Green Mountain Boys dwindled, recruits arrived from Massachusetts to fill out Arnold's regiment. The balance shifted.

Arnold had already decided that Crown Point was the more important of the two posts. It was the ideal location for blocking an invasion from the north and for launching naval operations against an approaching enemy. He established his headquarters there and left Allen at Ticonderoga.

At about the same time, the colony of Connecticut sent north a thousand infantrymen under Colonel Benjamin Hinman, a fifty-six-year-old veteran of the French and Indian War. But Hinman's orders were unclear and his arrival did nothing to establish a chain of command. Meanwhile, Arnold threw himself into the critical work of preparing to meet the enemy.

At every point in his career, Arnold displayed a relentless and focused energy. Now he assigned men to put the two warships in proper shape to fight. He began to collect, clean, and catalogue the cannon at Crown Point in preparation for moving them to Boston. He sent scouts to St. Johns to gather information about enemy activities there. He had men dig cannonballs and sheets of lead out of the ruins of the fort. He assigned carpenters and other craftsmen to repair bateaux and barracks buildings and to construct the carriages needed to move the guns.

He also showed a consistent sensitivity to criticism and slights. In what might have been his earliest such complaint of the war, he wrote to Joseph Warren on May 19, "I have had intimations given me that some persons had determined to apply to you and the Provincial Congress to injure me in your esteem."

On June 5, he again set out with his small Champlain flotilla and sailed northward. He entered the Richelieu River two days later. He was pursuing a habitual urge to gather intelligence. He also felt that extending the war into Canada would help secure the patriots' position in the north. Knowing how few British troops currently defended the province, he thought the time might be ripe to launch an attack on St. Johns. He wanted to see for himself.

He spent several days in the river while scouts surveyed St. Johns. They reported that the three hundred British infantrymen there were busy entrenching the position. Intent on taking the offense, he went back to Crown Point to muster the larger force. As he landed, he was immediately pulled back into the command controversy. He found that a meeting led by Ethan Allen and including James Easton and most of the officers at the base was underway. Since according to military tradition only a command-ing officer could call a council of war, Arnold was furious. He told the men that their discussion amounted to mutiny and that he would not allow them to usurp his authority.

Because most of the rank and file at Crown Point were men recruited for Arnold's regiment, Allen and the others had to back down. Arnold ordered the guard doubled. The next day, Allen and his companions casually headed back to Ticonderoga. Because they had no pass to leave, a sentry sent them to Arnold. James Easton, who had previously raised questions about Arnold's character, complained and tossed insults. Arnold followed his instinct as a sea captain. "I took the liberty of breaking his head," Arnold wrote, "and on his refusing to draw like a gentleman . . . I kicked him very heartily, and ordered him from the point immediately."

Arnold finally took action to reinforce his reputation, sending Eleazer Oswald to Philadelphia with a message to Congress. It was the first that body had heard of Arnold. In the letter, he detailed his activities, which included diplomatic overtures to various Indian groups and regular intelligence gathering in the north.

He suggested that an invasion of Canada would "discourage the enemies of American liberty." He had devised a detailed plan for launching such an invasion. "I am positive 2000 Men might very easily effect it," he wrote. He pointed out that in addition to guarding against invasion, such an operation would cut off the lucrative fur trade and deprive the British of Canadian wheat. He even suggested that it would be cost-effective, since it would be less expensive than rebuilding the lake forts. He wrote that Oswald would give further details.

Although still only a provincial colonel, Arnold offered to lead the Canadian expedition if no one else came forth. He would "answer for the success of it" provided that Congress furnished the men and supplies "without loss of time." Congress would indeed put in place a plan to invade Canada, but it would not be the lightning strike that Arnold recommended, nor would the aggressive colonel be in command.

On June 18, Colonel Hinman came to Crown Point and tried to assert his authority. "But as he produced no regular order for the same," Arnold noted, "I refused giving it up."

Four days later, a committee from the Massachusetts Provincial Congress arrived. The colony was now determined to shed the responsibility and expense of involvement with the New York forts. While offering praise for Arnold, they ordered him to serve under Hinman and to account for his public expenditures since leaving Cambridge.

Because Arnold's authority derived from his commission as a Massachusetts colonel, he could not dispute the order. But neither would he subordinate himself to Hinman nor cooperate with incompetent officers like Allen and Easton. Instead, he resigned his commission, stating that he could no longer hold it "with honor." He prepared to leave Crown Point.

With Arnold's resignation, his regiment was disbanded. Some of his men, feeling cheated out of back pay, staged a short mutiny. Arnold promised to make good what was owed out of his own pocket. Hinman resolved the dispute by enlisting Arnold's men into a new regiment headed by Easton, the Massachusetts tavern keeper. The men, determined to receive their promised pay, had no choice but to go along. The handling of the affair disgusted Arnold, and he declared he had been treated badly by the unappreciative authorities.

As a deeply disappointed Arnold departed Crown Point on June 24, 1775, he noted in the final entry of his memorandum book: "Had a rumor of an engagement at Cambridge between the Regulars and the Provincials in which it is said there is many thousand killed on both sides."

The rumor was true. On June 17, patriots had fought a battle at Bunker Hill on Charlestown peninsula across the bay from

Boston. British authorities were stunned by their casualties, which totaled more than a thousand Britons killed or wounded, including eighty-one officers. The American attempt to gain control of the peninsula failed. Their own casualties were high. Charlestown was burned to the ground. The war had suddenly taken on a grim new seriousness.

Before Arnold left Crown Point, the citizens of the region presented him with a proclamation expressing their gratitude for his "uncommon vigilance, vigor, and spirit." They lauded his "polite manner" and "generosity of soul, which nothing less than real magnanimity and innate virtue could inspire" and hoped he would receive "rewards adequate to your merit."

In early July, Arnold traveled to Albany, where he lodged in the mansion of Philip Schuyler, an aristocrat who had been assigned to oversee the northern army and to supervise Ticonderoga and Crown Point. As the two men conferred about what should be done at the forts, Schuyler recognized Arnold's keen strategic sense and devotion to the cause.

Schuyler had already received a letter from Colonel Hinman, clearly over his head at the forts, admitting, "I find myself unable to steer in this stormy situation," and urging Schuyler to come north and set matters right.

Arnold admired Schuyler. The successful merchant from a venerable Dutch family was eight years older than he was, with the college education that he lacked and the refined manners that he aspired to. Schuyler had served as a supply officer in the British Army during the French and Indian War. He offered to make Arnold his adjutant. Arnold declined. He needed to go home first, then proceed to Boston to settle his accounts and recover the expenses he had incurred during the past three months.

During the time he spent at Albany, Arnold received grievous news from home. His beloved Peggy had died quite suddenly on June 19 at the age of thirty. Arnold's grief was compounded when he learned that Peggy's father, "Papa" Mansfield, who had been a friend and business partner, had died three days after his daughter.

"How soon our time will come we know not," Arnold's mother had written to him when he was at school. He had saved her letters, in which such reminders were frequent.

"Every recollection of past happiness heightens my present grief," he wrote now, "which would be intolerable, were it not buried in the public calamity."

Arnold packed up and prepared to return to New Haven, where his sister, Hannah, had assumed responsibility for his three boys. Along the way, more news of the public calamity reached him. One of the casualties of the bloody battle at Bunker Hill was Joseph Warren. The zealous thirty-four-year-old doctor had insisted on placing himself in the thick of the fighting. A British infantryman had shot him in the face while Warren was covering the retreat of his fellow soldiers.

Arnold had felt an instant bond with Warren when they met. His fate brought home the life-and-death gravity of the cause which they both had embraced with such eagerness. But however shaken, Arnold did not give in to depression or spend much time in mourning. "An idle life under my present circumstances," he wrote to a friend, "would be but a lingering death." After a short stay at New Haven, he set off for Boston once again. He was determined to find another role in the great drama unfolding around him.

4

The Welfare of the Continent

A S THEY STEPPED INTO THE RIVER, THE ICE-COLD CURRENT
tore at their thighs. They steadied their boats along the bank
of the Kennebec and heaved them onto land. Benedict Arnold and
his men were about to climb the Norridgewock Falls, the longest
portage so far. To the forlorn music of wind humming through
stone pines, they unloaded barrels of salt pork, dried peas, and
flour. They hoisted kegs of gunpowder, retrieved muskets, shoul-
dered their burdens, and set out walking along an uneven trail
that stretched more than a mile uphill.

A thousand men, a small army, were forcing their way through
the forests and mountains of Maine. Their plan: to cross the divide into Canada, descend to the St. Lawrence River, and capture
the fortified city of Quebec. The venture was so improbable, so
audacious, that the enemy could barely conceive of the threat.
The men were sure they would take the defenders by surprise. The
people of the vast northern colony would join the Revolution.
The war would end. America would be free.

But now, all was going wrong. Before they reached Norridgewock, they "were often obliged to haul the boats after us through
rock and shoals," noted Pennsylvania rifleman George Morison,

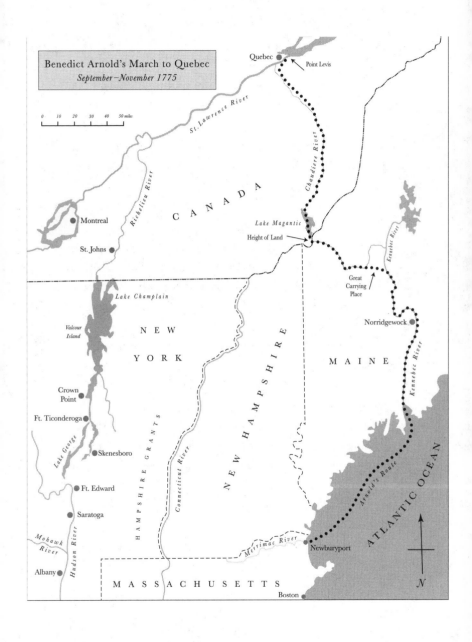

Benedict Arnold's March to Quebec
September–November 1775

0 10 20 30 40 50 miles

Quebec
Point Levis
St. Lawrence River
Chaudiere River
CANADA
Montreal
Richelieu River
St. Johns
Lake Magantic
Height of Land
Kennebec River
Great Carrying Place
Lake Champlain
Norridgewock
Valcour Island
NEW YORK
NEW HAMPSHIRE
MAINE
Kennebec River
Crown Point
Ft. Ticonderoga
Lake George
Skenesboro
HAMPSHIRE GRANTS
Connecticut River
Ft. Edward
Saratoga
Mohawk River
Hudson River
Arnold's Route
ATLANTIC OCEAN
Albany
Merrimac River
Newburyport
MASSACHUSETTS
Boston
N

"frequently up to our middle and over our heads in the water; and some of us with difficulty escaped being drowned."

Although it was still early in the journey, their hastily made boats were "so badly constructed, that whether in or out of them we were wet." Torn by the river rocks, pounded by rapids, the vessels were falling to pieces. Water that seeped in or sloshed over the gunwales had spoiled the salt fish lying in the bottoms of the boats, and had penetrated and ruined whole barrels of biscuits and peas. The men opened casks of salted beef to find the meat green and rancid.

Even with the help of teams of oxen lent by local settlers, they would spend a week forcing the Norridgewock precipice. Then, leaving behind the last dwellings of European-Americans, they would continue up the river through a wilderness of virgin forest.

Late September and they were already feeling the breath of winter. "What we most dreaded," wrote Abner Stocking, a twenty-two-year-old Connecticut private who had fought at Bunker Hill, "was the frost and cold from which we began to suffer considerably."

In the brittle evening air, they heard the honking of great wedges of geese heading south. Nightly frosts had made the hardwood trees explode in orange and yellow. Now the leaves were taking flight in the wind. Now it was the first of October. Now they were finding their wet clothing frozen as thick as panes of glass in the morning—"very disagreeable," a soldier recorded. Now they were entering the limitless woodland that still dominated the continent.

"Now," wrote Private Caleb Haskell, "we are learning to be soldiers."

BENEDICT ARNOLD WAS responsible for their lives. Determined to succeed against the odds, he spent a week at Norridgewock, keeping order, hurrying the army ahead, making light of the difficulties to come, talking confidence to his men. He had thought the entire trip to Canada would take three weeks. They had already used up two of those weeks, and the hardest part of the journey was just beginning.

After his success at Fort Ticonderoga, Arnold was surprised to find that his honor had been questioned. His enemies had maligned him. Congressman Silas Deane, one of Arnold's few friends in politics, wrote, "I think he has deserved much and received little, or less than nothing." Here was his opportunity to vindicate himself.

"Upon your conduct and courage," George Washington had told him, "and that of the officers and soldiers detached on this expedition, not only the success of the present enterprise, and your own honor but the safety and welfare of the whole continent may depend."

The whole continent. After his rude dismissal at Ticonderoga and the sudden death of his wife, Arnold had traveled to Massachusetts to clear his accounts and plunge back into the war of rebellion. All during the sultry month of August, he had negotiated with the Massachusetts Committee of Safety. With the death of his friend Joseph Warren, he had to deal with Benjamin Church, another Boston physician. Church questioned many of his expenditures and dismissed half of them.

Ostensibly a fervent patriot and member of the Sons of Liberty, Church would be uncovered a few months later as a spy who had been funneling the patriots' secrets to British general Thomas Gage. He would be banished from the colonies for his treason.

George Washington, on the other hand, was impressed by Arnold's achievements on Lake Champlain. He ignored Arnold's dispute with the Massachusetts authorities and the gossip spread by Arnold's enemies. He was anxious to meet this dynamic officer and was not disappointed when Arnold walked into his headquarters overflowing with ideas and information. The two men quickly formed a bond. Both were practical businessmen, not intellectuals. Like Arnold, Washington saw the answer to the current crisis in aggressive military action. The commander in chief was on the lookout for an energetic man he could trust.

Although America was careening toward all-out war, Congress continued to dither as the delegates chased the mirage of reconciliation. During July, they passed the so-called Olive Branch Petition, expressing their hope that "the former harmony between [Britain] and these colonies may be restored." King George scoffed at the appeal and in August declared the colonies to be in open rebellion.

In talks with Washington, Arnold emphasized the weakness of the British forces in Canada. Even before the fighting at Lexington, General Gage had ordered Guy Carleton, the governor of that province, to send more than half the troops under his command to Boston to deal with possible rebellion there. This left a skeleton army to defend the vast territory to the north. Arnold pushed for an invasion.

Congressmen were nervous about taking on an expensive operation that would demolish the idea that Americans were only defending themselves against British aggression. But as weeks passed, their view shifted. Taking Canada would reduce the enemy presence in America to the British toehold in Boston. In the event of reconciliation, Canada could serve as a critical bargaining chip.

The conclusion, John Adams noted, was "that it is best to go, if we can be assured that the Canadians will be pleased with it, and join us." At the end of August, the congressional delegates issued orders to General Philip Schuyler to invade Canada via Lake Champlain if he found it "practicable" and if it would not be "disagreeable to the Canadians."

It would take time for Schuyler to form an army and make

his move. In the end, illness would prevent his leading the attack. Washington didn't want to wait. Far better to strike before the British had a chance to prepare. He focused on an intriguing idea that had been discussed in camp and that Arnold now laid before him. Native Americans had on occasion used a forest path through the Maine mountains to navigate the north country. The French knew of it, and British officer John Montresor had drawn a rough map during the French and Indian War. Washington envisioned a classic pincer movement, with one attack coming up Lake Champlain and another through Maine.

The commander in chief knew that organizing and moving an army with all its baggage over rough terrain was immensely difficult. He needed a leader of exceptional resourcefulness and imagination. He put his trust in Arnold and made him a full colonel in the nascent Continental Army. His only qualm, which he warned Arnold about, was Arnold's assertive nature. Washington knew of the disputes that had broken out at Ticonderoga. Once in Canada, he insisted, Arnold must remain strictly subordinate to the chain of command.

TERRAIN AND TIMING both dictated a light, mobile army without field cannon or excess supplies. Once over the mountains, the men would have to procure provisions from the local inhabitants. Surprise was the key to their strategy.

The men of this expeditionary force should be tall, young, and exceptionally fit, preferably experienced woodsmen and men who knew how to handle boats. Bored with military routine, men from the army massed around Boston jumped at the chance for action and glory, whatever the mission. Plenty volunteered.

Arnold quickly selected 676 privates and officers and organized them into ten companies. Washington added three rifle companies. These were special forces, frontiersmen used to living in the open, crack shots with their precision rifled weapons. Some New Englanders saw them as a new race of men, embodying a type of stamina and ingenuity bred in the New World.

One group from Virginia had been organized by Daniel Morgan. Hearing of the violence at Lexington and Concord, Morgan had quickly gathered a company of fighters and marched them toward the action. Along the way, crowds of spectators had gathered to watch the woodsmen pass by. Morgan was an exacting but fair commander. "His manners were of the severest cast," one of his subordinates wrote, "but where he became attached, he was kind and truly affectionate."

Even stopping twice to tar and feather suspected loyalists, they had covered the six hundred miles to Cambridge in a remarkable twenty days. At headquarters, the men, dressed in long linen hunting shirts, leather breeches, and moccasins, attracted the curiosity of the New Englanders. They showed off their marksmanship, fought brawls, and raided local farms for food. Washington, determined to create a disciplined army, was happy to find a suitable mission that would rid them from camp.

The thirty-nine-year-old Morgan, who would later rise to the rank of general, was a large, ironfisted frontier teamster. As a contractor for the British Army during the French and Indian War, he had answered a slight from an officer with a punch in the face. He still wore the scars from the hundred lashes he had received in return. Benedict Arnold would have to find the right combination of resolve and forbearance to impose discipline on Morgan and his unruly men.

Fueled by Arnold's enthusiasm, the operation moved ahead quickly after receiving General Schuyler's approval on September 2. By the middle of the month, the men were in Newburyport, forty miles north of Boston. They paraded proudly through town and stacked their arms in the aisles of the First Presbyterian

Church while they listened to their chaplain, Reverend Samuel Spring, preach on the verse: "If thy spirit go not with us, carry us not up hence."

A makeshift collection of sloops and schooners then carried them a hundred miles up the coast to the mouth of Kennebec River near present-day Bath. When the ships could go no farther upstream, they switched to a fleet of two hundred river cargo vessels, which Arnold had ordered constructed. Boatbuilders had hammered together these rowboats, known as bateaux, in little more than two weeks. The Indians called them "White men's canoes." They were heavier than the natives' birchbark variety, but still portable enough to be carried around obstacles. The soldiers loaded them with provisions and military equipment and rowed a few miles farther north to the staging area near what's now Augusta.

There, Arnold divided the army into four divisions: Captain Morgan's riflemen would act as trailblazers. Lieutenant Colonel Christopher Greene, a Rhode Island millowner, would lead several companies of musketmen. Major Return Jonathan Meigs, the thirty-four-year-old son of a Connecticut hatter, would head up another infantry division. His group would include a company under Captain Henry Dearborn, a young New Hampshire physician, who brought along his pet Newfoundland dog.

Lieutenant Colonel Roger Enos would command the final division, the rear guard. At age forty-six, Enos was the oldest officer in a group of young men. He had plenty of experience, having marched to Canada twice with the British Army during the French and Indian War. His division hauled the army's extra provisions and equipment, taking advantage of the route opened and improved by the men in front. Enos was destined to become the focus of a major controversy before the mission was over.

The divisions started out a day apart so as not to encroach

on each other on their way up the narrow trail. The bottleneck of the Norridgewock Falls was now creating delays as each division had to wait for the one ahead to portage.

BENEDICT ARNOLD UNDERSTOOD a commander's duty to gather intelligence. He left nothing to chance. Before the men left Newburyport, he sent sailors up the coast to make sure no British warships were lurking. He recruited Indians familiar with Maine to serve as guides. As the divisions were preparing to move out, he selected a lieutenant of the Pennsylvania riflemen, Archibald Steele, to lead a scouting mission with eight other riflemen. Steele, who had left behind his bride of three months to fight for the cause, traveled by canoe to trace the route through the trackless wilderness. The ground around them was rugged enough, but the peaks ahead appeared as a saw-toothed barrier. The mountains "made an impression upon us," one of his men recorded, "that was really more chilling than the air which surrounded us."

Their information helped guide the army. Arnold sent out another group, including a surveyor, to further map the path and determine distances. He made repeated attempts to keep abreast of the situation in Quebec—he had contacts there from his days as a merchant. He sent envoys ahead with letters requesting information about the state of British defenses at the city and the attitude of French Canadians toward the Americans.

JUST BEFORE THE army left, a private named James McCormick, young and illiterate, got into a drunken brawl with another soldier and shot him dead. A quick court-martial sentenced McCormick to hang. He broke down when he caught sight of the gallows and begged for his life. Arnold judged him "very simple and ignorant," a man who sober was a "peaceable fellow."

Although Arnold had an aversion to drunkenness dating to his father's alcoholism, he gave the man a reprieve and sent him back to Cambridge with a recommendation to George Washington for clemency.

At the same time, Arnold ordered several soldiers, caught stealing, to receive thirty-three lashes and be dismissed from the army. His mix of firm discipline tempered with compassion won the respect and affection of his men.

To GET TO Canada, the expedition had to veer northwest up a tributary of the Kennebec called the Dead River. Before it joined the Kennebec, the Dead took a northward turn, traced a great loop, then tumbled down a stony staircase. Indigenous people had long ago learned how to cut off this loop. They would break from the Kennebec forty miles north of Norridgewock Falls and carry their canoes twelve miles due west to the banks of the Dead. Three ponds along the way gave respites along this burdensome Great Carrying Place.

While the rear divisions of the army were still struggling up the passage at Norridgewock, the riflemen had reached this stretch and begun to clear a passage for the rest of the men. By October 11, Arnold had caught up with Morgan and Greene at the first of four challenging portages that would lead them across the carry to the Dead River. Morgan's riflemen had performed important work here, widening a single-file path through the woods to about ten feet. Although the men would have to step over the stumps of trees, they could walk two abreast with a bateau carried between them.

Arnold penned a letter to be sent by messenger to George Washington: "We have been obliged to force up against a very rapid stream, where you would have taken the men for amphibious animals, as they were great part of the time under water."

Arnold had expected to be over the mountains and descending toward Quebec by now, but the delays had piled up and the going had proven far more difficult than expected. To cross this first carry, they would have to unload the boats at the bank of the Kennebec. Four men would balance each vessel on poles to carry it three miles to the first pond, gaining eight hundred feet of elevation in the process. They would then return and make several more trips to fetch a half ton of supplies, hauling the barrels in slings. Carry, return, carry, return, carry, return—in this way, the twelve-mile uphill trek turned into a fatiguing seventy miles, half of it carrying heavy burdens.

The blessing of the Great Carry was fish—trout weighing half a pound each teemed in the first pond. Wily anglers among the men brought them in as fast as they could bait their hooks. The fish offered a delicious change from biscuit and salt pork. They were the only bounty that nature offered along the way. Game like moose or grouse were long gone before the noisy thousand-man army arrived.

After reloading the boats and rowing across the narrow first pond, the men carried their burdens over a short stretch to the two-mile-wide second pond. This portage passed through a morass made worse by recent rain. Dead trees and tangles of roots and mud slowed their progress.

Yet Arnold wrote to Washington "the officers, volunteers and privates have in general acted with the greatest spirit and industry." He spent his time carrying loads like any private—he was noted for his strength and stamina. All the while, he talked to the men, encouraging them and scoffing at the exhausting work. One man recorded of the carry: "We were half leg deep in mud, stumbling over fallen logs, one leg sinking deeper in the mire. Then the other, then down goes the boat and the carriers with it. A healthy laugh prevails."

Earlier, George Morison, the Pennsylvania rifleman, who had a philosophical bent, compared the difficulty of the troops' ordeal with the lives of "sons of ease." The soldiers, he wrote, were immune to "spleen and melancholy." The challenges they faced and their attachment to each other helped to "keep up a constant glow of soul, which the indolent and luxurious never feel."

EVEN AS HE continued to exude confidence, Arnold understood that he had to be ready for contingencies. At the first pond, he ordered the men to build a crude shelter. He sent back to agents in the settled region to the south to forward provisions to be stored there "that our retreat may be secured in case of any accident."

"Retreat" was not a term anyone was using yet, but a commander had to be ready. War, even war against the elements, depended on options. Arnold sent word back to Cambridge expressing the hope that additional supplies would be forwarded from headquarters to sustain the troops if they had to turn around.

Before they went farther, he faced another bleak reality of the operation. The cold nights and the continual wet were taking a toll on some of the men, hearty as they were. They were falling ill with fever and dysentery. Arnold ordered a hut constructed to serve as a shelter for the sick. The log-built "Arnold's Hospital" quickly filled with suffering men.

The mile-and-a-half portage that led to the third pond was "extremely bad, being choaked up with roots." But the sight of the still, clean water of the pond, with snow-topped mountains in the distance, inspired Arnold to note, "The prospect is very beautiful & noble." After rowing across the pond, the men faced a three-mile carry to the stream that would take them to the Dead River. This stretch was largely downhill, but the land was rugged. When the men suddenly emerged from the woods, they took in the mile-wide, largely treeless expanse that awaited them. Their hopes rose. A meadow that afforded easy walking was a rare sight in the mountains.

They were quickly disabused of their optimism. This flat grassland—Arnold referred to it as a "savanna"—was in fact a stretch of what the indigenous Cree people called "muskeg." A feature of northern landscapes, it was a peat bog. The bright-green moss that covered its surface concealed a tangle of muck and tree roots into which the men sank to their knees or even waists. What they walked through was not mud but a putrid black accumulation of rotting organic matter.

The roots and deadfall made for treacherous footing. Many fell into the cold, stinking water as they heaved and dragged their loads forward. When they reached the far side, they trudged back through the nightmare terrain for another trip.

This, Arnold calculated, might be the most challenging part of the trip. In his letter to Washington, he said he planned to be in Canada in a week, "the greatest Difficulty being, I hope, already past."

He also wrote to General Schuyler, whom he imagined to be moving swiftly along Lake Champlain and the St. Lawrence River. He hoped "in a fortnight of having the pleasure of meeting you in Quebeck," and to "co-operate with your Army."

THE DEAD RIVER was so corpse-like that the men had a hard time detecting which way it flowed. It meandered through a flat, "truly dismal" landscape, now carrying them toward the high mountains in the northwest, now changing its mind and veering away. "A dreary aspect, a perpetual silence, and universal void, form the face of nature in this part of the world," one of the soldiers recorded in his diary.

The men of each division, as they reached the river, felt enormous relief. This was their reward for the struggle up the steep portages of the Kennebec and the hellish crossing of the Great Carrying Place. Here they could glide over the black, funereal depths with each stroke of oar or paddle. The first day and a half they covered forty-six miles. When they reached sections where the river widened out over pebbled shallows, they had to resort to the setting poles. Their progress slowed, but they were still able to advance at least ten miles a day.

Benedict Arnold entered the Dead River on October 16, leaving only Roger Enos's rear guard to finish the arduous carry. He sped forward in his canoe, made good time, and soon came up with Christopher Greene's division, which had taken the lead while the riflemen were working on the road through the Great Carrying Place.

Greene immediately presented the commander with a new and serious problem. The spoilage and loss of food along the way had hit this group especially hard. Through the carry, the men of all the divisions had kept up their strength with the fish they caught and the two oxen that Arnold had ordered sent forward from the supply unit to be butchered. But yesterday's food cannot satisfy today's hunger.

The day before, dwindling provisions had already induced Arnold to put all the men on half rations, twelve ounces of flour and the same of salt pork. To consume the flour, men added water and formed a simple stiff dough, patted it into cakes, and laid these on hot ashes to cook. The amounts were not enough to satisfy men who spent the day rowing or marching through rough terrain. Greene's men had to subsist on even less—nearly all their pork had been eaten or gone bad.

Arnold sent back for additional provisions from Colonel Enos. Greene's second-in-command, Major Timothy Bigelow, a Worcester, Massachusetts, blacksmith before the war, took a company of soldiers and twelve boats back down the stream to collect the food. Arnold told Greene to hold in place until these men returned.

THE NEXT DAY, Morgan's corps passed Greene's division and again took the lead. The riflemen were on their way to the pass over the mountains known as the Height of Land, where they would work to open a trail for those behind.

Two days later, on October 19, Major Meigs's division passed by Greene's and continued up the Dead. Enos's men had just traversed the Great Carrying Place. That afternoon, the gray sky sagged and let loose a light rain. The men ignored it as they pushed ahead. Arnold observed that the countryside in the Dead River valley was flat, erratically wooded with spruce, cedar, and fir. Here and there, the white bark of a stand of birches stood out. The highland soil was "cold and barren."

On the twentieth, the rain, rather than subside, became "prodigious." Arnold allowed his small party to stay in their tents for part of the day. Meigs's division passed by them, but they too stopped to camp well before dark. Rain continued through the night. By daylight, Arnold could see that the river, normally low in the autumn, had risen three feet. In places, the deeper water made rowing and paddling easier. But it also meant that the men now had to work against an increasingly stiff current.

With the rain still pouring from the leaden sky, Arnold surmounted a series of low falls. He passed Morgan's division, who had made camp along the river. Arnold's group went a mile farther to a spot he judged a better place to spend the night. His men, "very wet and much fatigued," started a large fire and spent hours drying their clothes and themselves. The wind, which had been blowing from the southwest for days, mounted to a fury. Trees convulsed, branches cracked, rain came in torrents—the men were enduring the remnants of a late-season hurricane.

Nevertheless, the weary soldiers wrapped themselves in blankets and plunged into dreams. At four in the morning, they awakened to a nightmare. The river "came rushing at us like a torrent, having rose 8 feet," Arnold wrote. The men grabbed for their baggage, which was already being dragged away by the racing current. They stumbled up a small hill nearby and "passed the remainder of the night in no very agreeable situation."

SORROWS, SHAKESPEARE HAD written, come not as single spies, but in battalions. "This morning presented us a very disagreeable prospect," Arnold wrote in his diary. The scene was surreal. "The country round entirely overflowed, so that the course of the river, being crooked, could not be discovered."

The currents formed whirlpools as they rushed down from the mountain. Branches and toppled trees heaved and jutted from the muddy water. Dr. Isaac Senter, a twenty-three-year-old Rhode Island physician who served as the army's surgeon, wrote that "from a Dead river, it had now become live enough."

The men of the army were stunned by the catastrophe. Yet almost by reflex they began to move forward. Morgan's riflemen passed Arnold's camp. Meigs's men made slow progress against the current. Arnold's party fell in behind them. Greene's division gave up hope of being resupplied and began to paddle up the now raging Dead.

Those who manned the bateaux strained sinews just to keep from being swept backward. They rowed and shoved with poles while the current batted their bows one way, then another. Men reached over the gunwales to cling to the trees and bushes that poked above the water. Inch by inch they pulled the vessels forward. The men who marched parallel to the river had to swing away in miles-long detours to find passable ground.

The days were now noticeably shorter than when they had

started out. "We exerted every nerve to the best advantage possible," Dr. Senter recorded, "so as not to lose a minute of daylight." He also noted that "several of our men were excessively exhausted with the diarrhea."

Throughout the following day, October 23, the river slowly began to recede. The two lead divisions, accompanied by Arnold, worked their way up until they approached the bottom of a frothing waterfall. As a line of boats tried to ease around a narrow point, the river threw out a watery hand to slap the first one broadside to the current. It immediately capsized. In doing so, it collided with the next boat in line, pushing it into the treacherous swirl. One after another, seven boats went over. All the men, all the provisions, all the guns went into the water and sank or were spirited away downstream.

Those who were still struggling behind suddenly saw wrecked boats, clothing, tents, barrels of food streaming toward them. They snared what they could and pulled struggling men to safety. The expedition had lost valuable provisions, arms, and a box containing hard currency.

"Happily," Arnold noted, "no lives were lost although six men were a long time swimming in the water and were with difficulty saved."

The men went ashore, built great fires, and stripped their sopping clothes off to counteract the effects of the icy water. They decided to go no farther that day. They would spend the night at what they called Camp Disaster.

THAT EVENING, ARNOLD called together the officers from Morgan's and Meigs's divisions—the others were too far down the river to attend the war council. Their situation, quite clearly, was grave. The settlements of Maine were far behind them, the inhabited areas of Canada far ahead. They lacked provisions. More and more men were sickening from bad food, exhaustion, and exposure. They had yet to receive intelligence from the north. They knew nothing of the progress of the other patriot army advancing from Lake Champlain or of British strength at Quebec. They weren't sure whether the French inhabitants in Canada would welcome them or turn hostile.

What to do? Arnold let each man have his say. As the fire crackled, the talk went on into the night. Turn back? They had come so far, endured so much. Go on? The way ahead was an unknown, the men weak, their resources nearly depleted.

"Some of our men appeared disheartened," remembered Private Abner Stocking, "but the most of them, with Col. Arnold stood firm and resolute. They were ready to encounter yet greater hardships for the good of their country."

Benedict Arnold debated with himself. The lives of a thousand men depended on his correct decision. He had talked to them, encouraged them, joked with them, praised them. They had gone beyond themselves for him.

This was the moment of truth. To turn back might be the best way to save them. To go forward might be futile, suicidal. Yet going back meant failure. His leadership at Ticonderoga had been questioned and demeaned. He had staked his honor on this expedition. Washington depended on him. The "welfare of the whole continent" depended on him.

"Our commander, Arnold," wrote sixteen-year-old John Joseph Henry, one of the Pennsylvania riflemen, "was of a remarkable character. He was brave, even to temerity, was beloved by the soldiery . . . he possessed great powers of persuasion."

LEADERSHIP IS AN essential ingredient in any military operation. A leader must display a balance between prudence and rashness, a unique combination of good judgment and an ability to convince by words and example. On this blustery night in the wilderness, Benedict Arnold drew on all his intelligence, grit, and vision.

The cause for which the men were enduring this hardship had become a matter not of calculation but of faith. He took on himself the ideals of his men—their faith in the cause became faith in him. He assured them that whatever they did, they would do it for the sake of liberty.

Radiating calm optimism, Arnold laid out his strategy and allowed the men to discuss every aspect of it. First, they would send back those too ill to keep up with the march. Each sick man would carry three days' rations, which would get him to the Great Carrying Place. They could receive provisions from the stores there and continue to the Maine settlements.

Arnold decided that in order to save his soldiers, he would have to leave them. He would put his trust in his officers to keep the column moving and hurry ahead to obtain provisions from the Canadian inhabitants. He would take along a flying column of fifty men under Captain Oliver Hanchett to help ferry food back to the army.

Before they retired to a welcome sleep, the officers took a vote. It was agreed, they would follow Arnold's plan. They would go on.

IN DISTANT CAMBRIDGE, George Washington was coping with difficulties of his own. He had just learned that the British had raided Falmouth—present-day Portland, Maine. Their ships had bombarded the defenseless town with incendiary shot for more than eight hours. As the flames took hold, soldiers stormed ashore to set fire to more buildings. Soon the whole city was "in one flame." This terror strategy—they would burn more than a dozen cities that year—was stark evidence of British sea power and of their determination to put down the rebellion by ruthless force.

At the same time, the enthusiasm of the militiamen whom Washington was trying to form into a national army was already waning. As their original enlistment periods ended, more and more of the men were returning home to look after farms and families. He had written to Congress that "the greater part of the troops are in a state not far from mutiny."

He faced his own lack of supplies, especially of firepower. The shortage of gunpowder at Cambridge was frightening—his defenders could never withstand a sustained British attack. And the Ticonderoga cannon that Arnold had acquired had yet to be moved to Boston from the forts on Lake Champlain.

The light shining through this gloom was the prospect of Arnold's army taking Quebec City. That would be a major blow to British prospects in America. A victory might end the war. It would certainly shift the odds significantly toward the patriot cause. And it would establish Benedict Arnold as one of the most important figures in the history of his country.

As Arnold struggled northward, he tried repeatedly to gain news of the progress of the army proceeding up Lake Champlain and the St. Lawrence River. General Schuyler had waited all summer for tents and other supplies before finally setting his army in motion. They had arrived in Canada in early September, but after ten days, Schuyler fell ill and had to return to Albany. He left General Richard Montgomery to take over.

Montgomery was a former captain in the British Army, a veteran of the French and Indian War. He had sold his commission and emigrated to America three years earlier. He married Janet Livingston, the wealthy heiress of a prominent patriot family. He hoped to settle down to the life of a gentleman farmer in the Hudson Valley, but when the Revolutionary War broke out, he volunteered. He was named a brigadier general under Schuyler, but he now wondered if Schuyler had the "strong nerves" required for campaigning in the field.

As he approached St. Johns, his first objective, Montgomery sent Ethan Allen out to recruit Canadians for a militia company. Without orders, Allen decided to join the former lawyer John Brown in an attempt to capture Montreal by himself. Brown had two hundred men, Allen barely a hundred. When Brown failed to fulfill his part of the scheme, the attack fell apart. The British captured Allen and sent him in irons to England to be hanged. "I have to lament Mr. Allen's imprudence and ambition," Montgomery wrote to Philip Schuyler.

Montgomery, in spite of his sixteen years in the British Army, lacked Benedict Arnold's sense of urgency. Although the enemy fought at St. Johns from hastily constructed trenches and small redoubts, the Americans found them difficult to dislodge. Montgomery argued with his officers and considered his troops as "the sweepings of the York streets." His enthusiasm was limited. "The instant I can with decency slip my neck out of this yoke," he wrote to his wife, "I will return to my family and farm."

BEFORE HE MOVED ahead of the army on October 24, Arnold wrote to Lieutenant Colonel Enos to inform him of the decision reached by the previous night's council of war. He ordered Enos to hand over three days' rations to the sick men who would be returning. Enos should then come forward with "as many of the best men of your division as you can furnish with 15 days' provision." Arnold added that "I make no doubt you will make all possible expedition."

Battered by the hurricane and discouraged to see the sick men from the lead companies heading toward the rear, Greene's men were slow to get underway. Dr. Senter noted that the division was "destitute of any eatable whatever, except a few candles," which the men melted to make a thin soup. Forty-eight of their own men joined those too ill to go on. On October 25, the rest of the command moved only three miles up the Dead River. That night, Roger Enos and five of his officers came into their camp.

Enos suggested they hold their own council of war. It was a repeat of the tactic used by Ethan Allen at Ticonderoga. Rather than follow orders, they would decide for themselves. The officers from the rear guard argued for turning back. They had no reserves of food, they said. Their men were discouraged. The prospect of reaching Quebec was remote. Death awaited them in the midst of this howling wilderness.

Greene pointed out that they had no instructions to retreat— only the commander of the expedition could give such an order. After a heated discussion, Greene and his four officers voted to go on, while Enos's five officers voted to abandon the mission. Vacillating, Enos first voted to continue, then, after consulting with his men, told Greene he had to comply with his own officers.

When Greene pleaded for food to sustain his men, Enos said his officers were refusing to give up any of the provisions, which they felt they needed to get back to the Maine settlements. He had lost control of his men. A distraught Enos finally allowed Greene two barrels of flour.

On October 26, Enos and his entire division, more than four hundred men, followed the sick men toward the rear. Those who went on had to give up the prospect of further provision from the rear guard. The defection "disheartened and discouraged our men very much," Captain Dearborn wrote. He added, "Our men made a general prayer, that Colonel Enos and all his men might die by the way."

5

Above the Common Race of Men

T HE GLOWERING CLOUDS BEGAN TO SPATTER THE MEN WITH rain. By nightfall, it had turned to snow. Arnold's flying column had pushed ahead of the army on October 24, two days before the mutiny of Enos and his officers. They woke in the morning with the ground white and a north wind biting their cheeks and fingers. Six more inches of snow fell before noon. Passing the point where the Dead River petered out, they moved along a chain of ponds interspersed with dense stands of fir and cedar. They repeatedly lost track of the scantily marked trail.

Arnold caught up with Captain Hanchett's band, who had started first. To speed their progress, Arnold and Hanchett left behind most of their boats before climbing the pass. The rocky divide called the Height of Land was now covered with ice and snow, the footing treacherous. At the peak, they entered Canada and began to descend. Nature seemed to make amends by greeting them with a stretch of flat grassland that resembled a park. A few stately elms completed the picture. They called it the Beautiful Meadow—Dr. Senter would refer to it as "delightsome" compared to the malevolent forest and bogs all around.

Arnold and his group took the four remaining boats and one canoe and went down the stream that led to Lake Megantic. Along

the way, they met Lieutenant Steele and his team of scouts, who
had been working to mark the trail. They gave Arnold the welcome news that the French Canadians "rejoiced to hear we are
coming" and that Quebec City, with no redcoats in sight, still
seemed ripe for the taking.

Arnold camped at an abandoned Indian wigwam along the
lake. He and his men had to return to rescue Captain Hanchett's troop, who had become trapped in a swamp as they tried
to march along the stream. Arnold sent back instructions to the
divisions following to keep to the high ground on the east rather
than march beside the waterway.

As yet unaware of Enos's decision to retreat, Arnold sent
messages to the rear division with instructions about moving
forward. He sent a letter to be passed on to General Washington, updating the army's progress. "Our march has been attended
with an amazing deal of fatigue," he reported, "which the officers
and men have borne with cheerfulness."

The following morning, they started out again. Hanchett's men
marched along the lakeshore; Arnold and thirteen others took to
the boats. The party included the intrepid Eleazer Oswald, who
had served as the commander's secretary through the campaign.

Reaching the south end of the lake at ten in the morning, they
entered the Chaudière River. Its name, meaning "boiling caul-
dron," proved apt given its wild rapids and plunging waterfalls.
They had no time to scout the river in advance but had to take
their chances riding the current. The water rushed them along at
ten miles an hour as they dodged rocks and snares.

They had gone nearly fifteen miles when they suddenly encountered a vicious section of white water. Three of the boats
went over, two were smashed by rocks, and a good deal of their
baggage went into the river. Six men plunged into the icy water
but were able to cling to rocks until the others could haul them
ashore.

The accident, Arnold wrote, proved to be a "happy circumstance." After they built a fire to dry out, they continued in the remaining two boats and canoe. They almost immediately approached the top of a waterfall, but were able to haul up onto shore before going over. Had they been sailing down the main channel, they would have plunged to their deaths.

THAT SAME DAY, October 28, the main body of the army, reduced to six hundred men, was struggling over the Height of Land and descending into Canada. Meigs and Greene had told their troops to leave their boats behind. The men were filled "with inexpressible joy" to at last be free of these burdens. They also abandoned most of their camp gear, including cooking pots, tents, and axes. With almost no food to carry, they went on with only their blankets and muskets. They no longer had to endure the tedious back-and-forth movement to bring forward boats and supplies.

Daniel Morgan was the only officer who ordered all his men to carry their boats over the pass. One observer noted that they "had the flesh worn from their shoulders, even to the bone." The troops muttered against the harsh task but complied.

The riflemen and two infantry divisions finally came together at the Beautiful Meadow. It was there that Greene shared the news about Enos's retreat. The others cursed their cowhearted companions. Captain Dearborn was sure that Enos's men had "Carri'd Back more than their part" of the provisions.

What they could not know was that, back in Cambridge, Colonel Enos would be tried for his mutiny. The court-martial would take place at a time when none of his former companions were available to testify. With only his own officers as witnesses, Enos would be acquitted and allowed to return to service.

What they did know was that no reserve of food would be coming. The officers decided to gather the provisions from each unit and distribute them equally to the men. The individual rations proved pitiful—five pints of flour and a few ounces of salt pork per man. Some of the famished soldiers cooked and ate their entire ration at once, preferring a "feast" to a daily pittance.

Lacking the guidance of a commander, the officers began to act more independently. The leaders of two of Meigs's musket companies, New Hampshire doctor Henry Dearborn and Massachusetts tavern keeper William Goodrich, decided to move on right away. They may have left before Arnold's instructions arrived, because they marched along the stream, the same course that had led Captain Hanchett and his men into the swamp.

The others spent the night at the Meadow. As soon as a bitterly cold morning dawned, with nothing to cook for breakfast, Morgan's men, now glad of having hauled their boats over, started out by water to cover the eight miles down the river to Lake Megantic. Most of the others—Greene, Meigs, and some of the riflemen—followed higher ground to the east. With no trails marked, they had to bushwhack through weeds and dense forest.

For the troops led by Dearborn and Goodrich, the day would end with a trip through hell. Their maps showed the river and Lake Megantic, but no other details. They marched directly into the swamp that surrounded the northern end of the lake. Breaking ice with musket butts, they began to wade, hoping to find a way through to the lakeshore. The farther they went, the more confusing the landscape.

Captain Dearborn, who was gripped by a fever, had found a canoe, apparently abandoned by Indians. He and a few men, accompanied by his dog, went ahead to try to find a passage.

After reaching Lake Megantic and orienting himself, Dearborn turned back to look for the men now thoroughly lost in the swamp. With dark descending, he finally found Captain Goodrich, who "was almost perished with the Cold, having Waded Several Miles Backwards, and forwards, Sometimes to his Arm-pits in Water &

Ice." Dearborn took him into the canoe and they managed to re-turn to the lake and reach the bark wigwam. Arnold had left a few men there as guides to the others. The captains feared for their men, but could do nothing more in the dark.

Meanwhile, Goodrich's leaderless men found a low hummock with barely enough room for them all to crowd out of the water. They somehow managed to light a fire—they were indeed "expe-rienced woodsmen"—and spent the night huddled around the glimmer of warmth. An unknown number of them died from exposure before morning.

The larger group, including Greene's division, was not faring much better. With the guide Arnold had sent back, they traced the high ground toward Lake Megantic. But unknown to all of them, two additional lakes, as well as streams and swamps, clus-tered around the corner of the larger lake. They skirted the same swamp that had entrapped Goodrich's men. By the time it grew dark they were lost and had to bed down on the damp ground.

Private Morison of the rifle division, who had earlier extolled the soldiers' "glow of soul," now admitted that "never perhaps was there a more forlorn set of human beings collected together in one place—every one of us shivering from head to foot."

In the morning, the suffering of the army continued. Dear-born and Goodrich returned as soon as it was light and managed to extract their men from the swamp. Their companies hurried on to the wigwam where they joined Morgan's men around a roaring fire. By afternoon, with barely anything to eat, they made their way south by boat and on foot to the outlet of the Chaudière River.

Greene's division continued through the wilderness, seeking a path around the wetlands. Soon they too found themselves wading through another swamp, which bordered an unmapped lake. "Af-ter walking a few hours in the swamp," one private recorded, "we seemed to have lost all sense of feeling in our feet and ankles. As we were constantly slipping, we walked in great fear of breaking our bones or dislocating our joints. But to be disenabled from walking in this situation was sure death."

Coming to a wide stream, they stripped naked and were able to cross carrying their clothes, guns, and ammunition above their heads. They had to break through the ice on the far shore to climb out.

At this point, almost miraculously, they encountered an Indian who spoke English. He guided them around the wetlands and showed them the way back to Lake Megantic. Worn out by the effort but now sure of their bearings, they set up camp for the night.

TWO WOMEN ACCOMPANIED the army as it struggled through the swamps. John Henry, the young rifleman, noted that Mrs. Grier, the wife of a sergeant in his division, was a "large, virtuous and respectable" woman—she was nearly six feet tall. Wading through the swamp, she lifted her skirts above her waist to avoid getting the fabric wet. No one "dared to intimate a disrespectful idea of her," Henry declared. The young soldier was "humbled, yet astonished at the exertions of this good woman."

Jemima Warner had also kept up with the army, as hardy as any of the soldiers. As she struggled along the trail, she realized that her husband had taken ill and fallen behind. She returned up the path "with tears of affection in her eyes" and found him lying near death. She sat with him until, as one soldier put it, he "fell victim to the King of Terrors." Unable to bury him, she covered the body of her beloved with leaves. She picked up his gun and powder horn and walked on through the wilderness.

ON THE FIRST day of November, Dr. Senter noted, the troops were approaching "the zenith of distress." The famished men were learning a lesson that has held through history. A soldier's duty is not only, not even mainly, to fight. More often it is to walk forward when hungry, to perform one's duty while in pain, and to persevere in the face of the most intense hardship. Men ate moss, candles, lip salve, and broth from boiled shoes.

They began to descend the Chaudière Valley on foot, climbing down a broken terrain of humps and gullies. They kept up no pretense of an orderly march. No longer an army, they were "so faint and weak," one private recorded, "we can scarcely walk." Their officers told them that it was now every man for himself.

All had been on half rations for at least a week. Some had not eaten anything for several days. The terrain was inhospitable. Their resources were drained. Their feet were made of lead. To mount a small rise was to climb a mountain. To descend a rocky slope was to risk a dangerous fall. Soldiers reeled as if inebriated. Hunger, exertion, and the enormity of the snow-covered wilderness cast them into a light-headed, dreamlike state of mind. "That sensation of mind called 'the horrors,' seemed to prevail," wrote Private Henry.

One of their worst experiences was the necessity of abandoning fallen comrades. Their shared ordeal had formed extraordinary bonds among the men. Yet, if a comrade fell, the others lacked the strength to carry him farther or even to help him to his feet. In spite of his pleas, they had to pass by and leave him to "the mercy of the woods."

In describing his reaction, rifleman George Morison hinted at a persistent effect endured by soldiers of all times. Long after the ordeal, he could not keep the men's faces out of his thoughts; they "left impressions on our minds which nothing but death can erase." Abner Stocking noted, "My heart was ready to burst and eyes to overflow with tears when I witnessed distress which I could not relieve."

At first, many of Morgan's men did not have to endure this

rugged march down the valley of the Chaudière. They floated along the river in the boats they had lugged over the Height of Land. But they soon came to the wicked rapids that had undone Arnold's flotilla. Seven of their boats overturned. Supplies, treasured rifles, and their few remaining scraps of food were swallowed by the heartless river. The men grabbed for protruding rocks as they were dragged downstream. All were rescued except one. Remarkably, he was the first of the "amphibious" men to die by drowning.

Now they all continued on foot. Henry Dearborn's company took the lead, although Dearborn himself was "still more unwell." He tried to manage his canoe, but the rapids got the better of him and flipped the vessel over. He climbed onto the riverbank. While he sat with his faithful Newfoundland dog trying to re-cover his strength, Captain Goodrich's company came up, the men "almost Starved."

Dearborn doesn't record whether they asked his permission before grabbing his pet and slitting its throat. For the entire trip, the dog had endured the same ordeal as the soldiers. Now, Dr. Senter wrote, the "poor animal was instantly devoured, without leaving any vestige of the sacrifice." The dog's skin, feet, and en-trails were cooked and consumed "with good appetite."

With evening, the darkness of death seemed to descend on the men. Hollowed out by hunger, they camped and built fires. They fell asleep to the relentless sound of rushing water and awoke to another day of famine. Feeling they could not go on, they went on.

That day, the second of November, the landscape seemed to portend a change. The path grew less gnarled, the descent less steep. The marching became easier. The icy winter faded. The weather, one man reported, was "exceeding fine, clear, and as warm as ever I saw at this season in New England."

Then, suddenly, it was over.

"I set out and marched about four miles," Dearborn wrote in

his diary that day, "and met some Frenchmen with 5 oxen & Two Horses going to meet our People." When they told him how close he was to the first Canadian settlement, Dearborn declined the offer of food for himself. The Frenchmen should take the provisions to those behind him. "Knowing how the men were suffering for want," he wrote, "it Causd the Tears to Start from my Eyes."

"This sudden change," one soldier said, "was like a transition from death to life."

AFTER HIS VESSELS had crashed in the Chaudière rapids, Benedict Arnold and his party had risked continuing down the river in the two remaining boats. On October 29, they found themselves beyond the worst of the white water and were able to proceed forty miles. The next day, they went on farther and came to another section of falling water. Two Penobscot Indians helped them with the portage and passed on the welcome news that they were approaching the settlements. That evening they saw the first house since leaving Norridgewock Falls on October 9.

Relations with the French Canadians were a delicate matter. Like many Americans, Arnold had grown up with the idea that the French were the enemy—they had been fighting the British off and on for generations. New Englanders in particular hated Roman Catholics—the Continental Congress had described the religion as one of "impiety, bigotry, persecution, murder." At the same time, the delegates had appealed to Canadians, claiming to be "your unalterable friends." George Washington, who wanted to attract the Canadians to the American cause, had given Arnold explicit instructions "to avoid all disrespect or contempt of the religion of the country and its ceremonies."

If Arnold was unable to win the support of Catholic peasants, his men would likely starve, or would have to resort to plunder, alienating the locals. Fortunately, he convinced the inhabitants of the outer settlements to come to the aid of his distressed men. They did so with the generosity of the poor. They were impressed by the fortitude of the soldiers they called *Les Bostonnais* and intrigued by Arnold's idealistic rhetoric about liberty.

Arnold emphasized that his troops were not there to loot—they would pay for provisions. They considered the Canadians their friends. These people, who knew what hunger was, understood the urgency. They gathered five oxen and five hundred pounds of flour. Led by Arnold's scouts, eight Canadians started up the river and reached the first division on November 2.

Many of the men, a captain noted, "shed tears of joy, in our happy delivery from the grasping hand of death." When the food arrived, Dr. Senter wrote that "echoes of gladness resounded from front to rear!"

By now, the line of men was stretched out for twenty miles. The Frenchmen drove the oxen up the river—they butchered and roasted them at various points along the trail. Men stood by, intoxicated by the prehistoric aroma of broiling meat. Officers warned them not to eat too much, but some could not keep themselves from gorging, with painful results.

Many, once they had eaten some food, accompanied the scouts back up the trail to find and help those still advancing or fallen along the way. Not everyone was saved. Fifty men were unaccounted for, many having fallen victim to the wilderness. A private who retraced the route the following year found the "bleaching bones" of a few comrades.

The revived army continued northward. The men rejoiced in every meal and looked on a night spent inside one of the cabins of the inhabitants as a royal pleasure. Some took longer to recover. Captain Dearborn, now desperately ill, stayed with a local family for three weeks before he was strong enough to continue. Private John Henry was also ailing. Benedict Arnold noticed him while riding past. Henry was surprised that he "knew my name and character, and good-naturedly inquired after my health." The colonel hailed a farmer and asked him to take the young man in and care for him. He gave Henry two silver dollars to pay for provisions. Henry stayed with the French family for a week. He offered his host the money on leaving, but the farmer refused it.

Henry was one of the soldiers instilled from childhood with intolerance for French Catholics. The kindness that he was shown "made a deep and wide breach upon my early prejudices," he wrote, leaving him with a view "unbounded by sect or opinion."

WHILE ARNOLD'S ARMY pushed toward Quebec City, General Montgomery was finally wrapping up his seven-week siege of the British post at St. Johns. The five hundred men inside the dilapidated fort surrendered on November 3. Their commander thanked the Americans for "leaving us in such slight field Works" for so long rather than assaulting the fortifications weeks earlier.

One of the British officers who had endured that siege and who was sent into captivity was a twenty-four-year-old lieutenant named John André, the son of a Swiss merchant who had emigrated to England. A bright, capable officer, he would later return to his compatriots in a prisoner exchange. He was destined to play a critical role in Benedict Arnold's life.

The American army entered a virtually defenseless Montreal on November 13. The fighting season was ticking away, but Montgomery delayed again when his officers protested his lenient treatment of British captives. He briefly resigned before the matter was resolved. It's hard to imagine Benedict Arnold tolerating similar delays.

IN CANADA, ARNOLD'S finesse at winning over the local inhabitants paid off for the army. They received a generous welcome—

the peasants displayed "much tenderness" toward the sick and worn-out soldiers.

The emergence of these ragged, bearded figures from the forest inspired awe in the locals, who knew very well that a journey over the mountains was a grueling and dangerous feat. For their part, Arnold and his men were surprised that the remote settlements often contained as many Indian inhabitants as French, sometimes more. A few days after arriving, Arnold arranged a meeting with the local tribes. As a boy, he had spent time learning skills from Indians around his home in Connecticut. Now, eighty men, carefully painted and decked out in feathers and beadwork, came to converse with him through an interpreter. Arnold said he was glad to meet "so many of my brethren" and described the ways the English king was imposing on the people of New England. He offered pay and gifts to any braves who joined his force. About fifty signed up.

A few days later, still moving ahead of the army, Arnold reached Pointe Lèvis, directly across the St. Lawrence River from Quebec. The fortress city on the opposite heights had been the scene of a consequential battle sixteen years earlier when British general James Wolfe had defeated the forces of Louis-Joseph de Montcalm, effectively ending French rule in North America.

By now, Arnold understood from contacts in the city that the British had received word of his approach. Some of the letters he had sent forward by messenger had been intercepted. In response, authorities had confiscated all the boats and canoes along the south side of the river.

But the defense at Quebec was in poor hands. Canadian governor Guy Carleton, an experienced and capable military man, had hurried up the St. Lawrence to oversee the conflict at St. Johns and Montreal. He left his lieutenant governor, Hector Cramahé, in charge of Quebec City, not imagining an attack from Maine. Cramahé was a politician rather than a soldier. He sent a letter to London authorities describing "500 provincials" threatening the city from across the river. He found their sudden appearance astounding. "Surely, a miracle must have been wrought in their favor. It is an undertaking above the common race of men."

Arnold remained excited by the prospect of victory. The intelligence from the city was that the Frenchmen dragooned into the local militia would be reluctant to fight. The ten-foot-thick walls that surrounded the town were in bad repair. Cramahé was at a loss and had no redcoats to help defend the town.

On November 7, a messenger brought a letter to Arnold from Brigadier General Montgomery announcing that he had taken St. Johns and would soon march on Montreal. Arnold wrote back that "I propose crossing the St. Lawrence as soon as possible." He still intended to conquer the city, he said, but if that proved impossible, he would meet Montgomery's forces as they advanced down the St. Lawrence.

Arnold soon amassed thirty-six canoes missed by the British dragnet. He kept the men busy making scaling ladders, hooks, and spears for the siege. By November 11, the army, now down to about 550 soldiers, half its original strength, gathered on the shore of the St. Lawrence. They were ready to cross the river and attack the fortress city on the heights.

The departure of a number of ships from the harbor on November 12 indicated that merchants, fearful of war, were abandoning the city. Intelligence reports said that the town gates were often left open at night, and that few cannon had been mounted on the walls. Things were looking up. Arnold called a council of war. Although strong northeast winds were against them for now, his officers voted to make the crossing as soon as the weather allowed.

ALLAN MACLEAN WAS a Scotsman who had enlisted in the British Army during the Seven Years' War and later settled in Canada.

When the current trouble began in America, he organized a regiment, the Royal Highland Emigrants. That autumn, they had traveled to Montreal to fight Montgomery. After the fall of St. Johns, Maclean escaped with 170 experienced fighters and came down the St. Lawrence. Shocked to learn of the arrival of Arnold's force, he abandoned his river transports and quick-marched his men along the north bank, arriving at Quebec on November 12.

The fifty-year-old Maclean immediately took over the defense of the city. In addition to his own troops, he enlisted Royal Navy men and other sailors from the ships that remained at anchor. He reorganized the militia force of French inhabitants. He ordered soldiers and citizens to stiffen the fortifications, erect barricades, and repair walls. He counted a total of 1,126 defenders, but the reliability of the bulk of his militia force remained doubtful.

ALTHOUGH HE DID not yet know of Maclean's arrival, Arnold was aware that the sooner he mounted his attack on Quebec, the better his chances. On the evening of November 13, the wind eased and was replaced by bitter cold. He decided to take the army across the river.

The amphibious advance would be delicate. The fleet of three dozen canoes, each of which could transport five men, would have to cross the river three times to convey the soldiers to the north side. They would have to steer clear of two British ships of war that were standing guard and avoid the barges sent out to patrol along the shore. Their objective would be to reach the same cove where General Wolfe had landed his men in 1759.

Arnold and those in the first canoes had to steer quietly through the dark, avoid the enemy, counteract the tidal current, and be ready to fight as soon as they landed. To their surprise, they found the cove undefended. After removing the boats from the far side, the British did not expect an attack.

When 350 of the men were across, the wind suddenly began gusting again. Arnold chose not to risk further trips for now. As at Fort Ticonderoga, he would make the assault with the men he had. The battalion moved up a road to the top of the cliff on which the city stood. They emerged on the Plains of Abraham, named for a local farmer, the site of the earlier battle, which had reshaped control of the continent.

This was the pinnacle of the enormous effort that had begun back in September. It was an achievement that some would compare to the renowned expedition of Carthaginian general Hannibal, who had crossed the Alps in 218 B.C. to defeat the Romans. British general Sir Henry Clinton privately noted the boldness, fortitude, and perseverance of the small rebel army and described the expedition as one that "will ever rank high among military exploits."

NOTHING WOULD STOP them. They raised three huzzahs in the name of liberty—the sound echoed from the stone walls. Arnold wrote out a proclamation directed at Lieutenant Governor Cramahé demanding the "immediate surrender of the town." If the defenders yielded, they would be treated with honor. If the Americans were forced to storm the walls, "you may expect every severity practiced on such occasions."

The document was delivered under a flag of truce. The response was a cannon shot from the top of the massive walls. Colonel Maclean was making it clear he would "defend the town to the last extremity." Arnold could see that the city was better prepared to resist attack than he had expected.

In the distant past, cities had been captured by soldiers swarming over walls. Cannon and gunpowder had long since made such assaults impractical and changed the techniques of attack and defense. The idea that Arnold's small army could capture the city without a single piece of artillery was pure audacity. During the next few days, Arnold surveyed his chances. Winter was coming on with increasing ferocity. The long journey had left each man with barely five rounds of ammunition, if their muskets could still fire at all.

On Sunday morning, November 19, Arnold told his troops "the situation of our army is such that there is no probability of getting into the city till we are reinforced by General Montgomery." To linger on the Plains of Abraham would be dangerous. At three in the morning, he mustered the troops and began the retreat. They marched twenty miles westward in biting cold to a village on the St. Lawrence called Pointe-aux-Trembles.

"Most of the soldiers," wrote Abner Stocking, "were in constant misery during their march, as they were bare footed and the ground frozen and very uneven. We might have been tracked all the way by the blood from our shattered hoofs."

It was the army's first backward movement. If they had arrived only a few days sooner, Benedict Arnold wrote to Washington the next day, "Quebec must inevitably have fallen into our hands." Now, he explained, he had decided to retreat out of compassion for the brave men of his command, "who were in want of everything but stout hearts."

6

The Most Terrible Night

SNOW PRICKED THE FACES OF THE MEN WAITING OUTSIDE THE city. It was past midnight, the early hours of December 31. They were preparing, at last, to capture Quebec. Their eyes lifted to the display overhead.

"The storm was outrageous," a rifleman wrote, "and the cold wind extremely biting." In the midst of this chaos, the black tangle of sky suddenly flashed with streaks of fire that burst into red, yellow, and orange light. One after another, five rockets flew over the walls of Quebec and exploded above the city, briefly turning the wild dance of snow into a celebration.

The walled city had never been successfully assaulted since it was founded by Samuel de Champlain in 1608. It rested at the eastern end of a high bluff along the north side of the river, the Plains of Abraham. Shaped like a blunt spearpoint, the town was honed along its edges by the wide St. Lawrence to the south and the meandering St. Charles River to the north, with sheer cliffs on both sides. To the east, at the tip of the spear, the city was fringed by a narrow rim of land along the water. This ramshackle Lower Town was a commercial area of wharfs, warehouses, shops, and a few residences.

General Richard Montgomery hoped that the tempest would

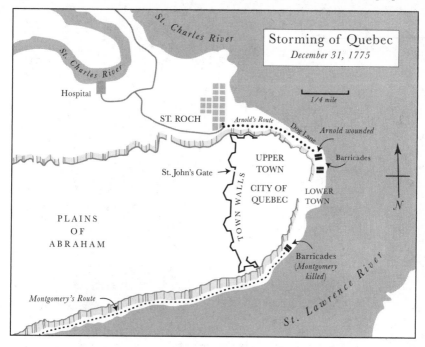

provide cover for his improbable mission. His battle plan relied on
a two-pronged attack. Benedict Arnold, his second-in-command,
would lead a force from the north that would come around the
spearpoint at water level. They would include the five hundred
men of the Kennebec army and an artillery company headed
by Captain John Lamb. Lamb, born in New York City, was the
son of a burglar transported to the New World as a convict. A
successful wine merchant and radical member of the Sons of
Liberty, he had embraced the patriot cause early. A Canadian
newspaper declared, truthfully, that he had "headed mobs, excited sedition, talked treason, abused Loyalists, harangued the
populace, and damned the Toreys."

The first barrage of signal rockets had served to put Arnold's
troops and those of two other units on alert. The men stood
stamping their feet in the northern suburb of St. Roch as they

awaited the signal to move out. On the opposite side of the city, General Montgomery organized three hundred New York infantrymen to descend to Wolfe's Cove, pick their way along the ice-clogged path, and enter the Lower Town from the south, putting the defenders between the jaws of a pincer. The commanders hoped that a feint against the walls of the Upper Town by a third group, who would set a fire near the main St. John's Gate, would create maximum confusion within the city.

The intense blizzard was nature's contribution to the plan. Sights and sounds were obscured by the blinding, screaming snow, the element of surprise enhanced.

WHEN MONTGOMERY FINALLY took Montreal on November 13, Canadian governor and military commander Guy Carleton, dressed as a peasant, escaped down the St. Lawrence to Quebec. The governor's arrival boosted morale there and added new energy to the city's defense.

On December 5, Montgomery himself finally arrived at Quebec leading the 650 New York and Canadian fighters he had brought from Montreal and the 600 remaining Kennebec men, along with a handful of recruits, under Arnold's command. He sent Arnold and an aide toward the city walls under a flag of truce. They were to deliver a letter demanding that Carleton surrender the city. "I am well acquainted with your situation," the American commander wrote to his counterpart. He denigrated Carleton's "motley crew" of defenders, and stated that the Americans had friends among the city's residents. His own troops were "accustomed to success," confident, and inured to danger. He could restrain them only "with difficulty."

This was pure bluster. Some of Carleton's militia troops were of dubious quality, but he now had more than 1,800 men under arms, substantially more than Montgomery's total manpower.

Carleton had ordered workmen to continue repairs to the city's formidable walls and directed carpenters to build sturdy barricades to block entry into the Lower Town.

The ensuing weeks were marked by occasional artillery duels between the two sides. Montgomery had brought some of the Fort Ticonderoga guns and mortars with him, but his cannon were not large enough to breach the stone walls. The enemy could fire at will from the tops of those walls. One cannonball demolished Montgomery's carriage and killed his horses. Another shot decapitated a woman drawing water from a stream. It was Jemima Warner, who had left her dead husband under leaves back in the mountains.

Montgomery had constructed batteries facing the city walls, but because the ground was frozen solid, he ordered his artillerymen to construct breastworks from bundles of sticks filled with snow and whatever dirt they could scrape up. They poured water on the structures to create a mass of ice. With the guns ready to fire, he offered Carleton free passage to England if he handed over the city.

Carleton sneered at the proposal. An artillery duel opened. Patriot fire had no more effect on the city walls, a British officer noted, than "peas would have against a plank." Return shots utterly demolished the ice forts, which one of Arnold's men called "our heap of nonsense."

MONTGOMERY AND CARLETON had both served in the French and Indian War and taken part in a grueling 1762 expedition against Spanish Cuba. The American general admitted that he found it a "hard fate to be obliged to oppose a power I had been ever taught to reverence."

A tall, slender, bald-headed Irishman, Montgomery had the imposing presence of a career soldier—he was, a rifleman observed, "born to command." Seated opposite him in Montgomery's head-quarters, Arnold could study his calm, confident manner. It was the demeanor of the practiced gentleman to which he aspired.

Beneath the surface, they were two very different men. Montgomery, educated and thoughtful, was inward looking. In his private correspondence, he readily admitted his doubts. He had joined the cause "against my inclination and not without some struggle," he wrote to his wife. To Philip Schuyler, he admitted, "I have not the talents or temper for such a command." Premonitions of death plagued him. He was given to philosophical musings. "'Tis a mad world," he told his brother-in-law, "I once thought so, now I know it." He vowed to quit the army as soon as he could do so "with propriety." He wanted "peace of mind."

Benedict Arnold was not a thoughtful man, never entertained doubts, admitted no inner conflict, and cared nothing for a tranquil mind—he lived for action.

But in their discussions, Arnold learned from Montgomery's grasp of strategy and tactics. Montgomery, for his part, appreciated the "active, intelligent, and enterprising" Arnold. He described Arnold's battalion as "an acceding fine one," and praised the American colonel's "style of discipline" as superior to what he generally found in the Continental Army.

During the freezing days of December, the two men parsed their options. Their artillery obviously could not break down the city's massive walls. In all likelihood, the enemy had laid in enough food to last the winter. British reinforcements were likely to arrive in the spring. The enlistments of the bulk of the American troops would expire on January 1. It was clear that the soldiers, like Montgomery himself, wanted to go home.

Only one option appeared open—they would have to storm the town before the year ended. It was the tactic Arnold had planned for when he had his men build scaling ladders. The British forces could not defend every part of the walls. Once inside, the Americans could overwhelm or panic the defenders.

The cannonading and sniper fire the Americans had directed at the town for a month were meant to keep the British guessing. "The object was to amuse the enemy and conceal our real design," musketman Abner Stocking noted. "The intention of General Montgomery was to commence an assault."

AT FOUR O'CLOCK in the morning, Arnold and his men hunched against the barbaric nor'easter. Two more rockets, the signal for the attack to begin, went streaming over Quebec.

The unit ordered to make the diversion fired at the town's western wall. British sentries noticed the flashes from the gun barrels firing from the plain below, but the sound was swept up by the gale. The American soldiers were unable to ignite a fire near the town gate, and the enemy soon caught on that their attack was not a serious one.

OFFICERS CALLED THE town guard, already nervous, to full alert. The entire force of defenders turned out into the cold dark—for days, officers and men had spent the nights fully clothed and with muskets ready.

As if excited by the commotion, the storm burst into even wilder fury. One New England soldier called it "the most Terrible night I ever saw." The howling wind was punctured by the concussions of British cannon, booming from the walls like giant footsteps, a potent answer to American musket fire. American mortars in St. Roch began to heave exploding shells into the town. The bells of all the churches in the city clanged without cease. Drums pounded out urgent signals. Arnold's fighters moved forward into their first real combat.

They began by picking their way along a road that skirted the north side of the heights. The cliffs looming to their right were topped by defensive parapets. A quarter mile east of St. Roch, they emerged from the settled area onto Dog Lane, a narrow trail that ran a quarter mile farther along the mud flat that lined the St. Charles River. It ended where the Lower Town began near the tip of the Quebec spearpoint.

The relentless snow continued to pile up. It turned men to ghosts, slowed their movement, and erased their tracks. "It was impossible to bear up our faces against the imperious storm of wind and snow," one soldier observed. Because the gunpowder in the flashpans of their flintlock rifles and muskets was acutely sensitive to damp, the men covered the weapons with the flaps of their coats in an attempt to keep them dry.

Arnold led the force from the front, accompanied by several dozen picked men. Then came Captain Lamb and his artillery crew heaving a 6-pounder cannon fixed to a sled. Behind him marched the main body of troops. Major Return Meigs's company formed the rear guard. Because of the narrowness of the path, the men had to walk single file and the entire force stretched into a long, thin line.

With its carriage and sled, the cannon was a heavy, awkward burden. The torrents of snow compacted into drifts made it virtually impossible to haul along the narrow path. When the gun became stuck, it held up the units behind. Soon, further efforts were deemed futile. Captain Lamb moved aside to allow Morgan and his men through, then gave up and abandoned the gun altogether.

As they marched along the base of the cliff, the men could hear the clamor from the Upper Town. Now gunshots began to stab through the wind. Men on the ramparts above them were firing muskets. The first of the attackers dropped into the snow, screaming in pain. Then another.

The Canadians hung fireballs over the edge of the walls to light the space below and reveal the approaching men. They aimed their plunging fire. The slippery, crowded trail became a gauntlet. The men forced to stumble forward had no chance of shooting back at their invisible tormenters above.

They groped forward into a warren of "stores, houses, boats, and wharves" erected haphazardly along the edge of the river. "The main body were led wrong," Major Meigs later wrote, "there being no road, the way dark and intricate." They were "harassed at the same time with a constant fire of the enemy from the walls, which killed and wounded numbers of our men."

Arnold and the advance guard reached the entrance to the first road, Sault au Matelot, which cut through the Lower Town. It was lined with shops and houses. But to enter it they had to get past a ten-foot-high wooden barricade. About thirty Canadian militiamen, armed with two small cannon, waited nervously on the far side.

The Americans took cover and allowed more troops to advance. Daniel Morgan soon appeared and told Arnold that their own cannon was out of commission. With no way to breach the barrier, Arnold had to order a direct assault as soon as enough men arrived. He hoped the shock of a charge would confound the defenders. The men huddled in doorways and under the eaves of the buildings along the street, waiting for more troops to gather.

The Canadians were able to get off one shot from their cannon, spraying lethal grapeshot toward the attackers. Luckily, only one American was killed. Men from Morgan's company rushed forward and began to fire through the portholes in the barricade. A few accurate shots from their rifles silenced the enemy's artillery.

The rain of fire from the town walls continued. Captain Jonas Hubbard, a thirty-six-year-old Worcester, Massachusetts, farmer, had written to his wife during the Kennebec march: "I know not if I shall ever see you again . . . But I do not value life or property if I can secure liberty for my children." Hit by a bullet from above, he died in the snow.

Another lead ball fired from the walls ricocheted off the stone cliff before it plunged into Colonel Arnold's leg. Entering below the knee, it lodged in his calf just above his heel. Arnold's boot began to fill with blood. Daniel Morgan noted that his commanding officer was having trouble standing. He summoned the division's chaplain, Reverend Samuel Spring, and a soldier to help Arnold back to the hospital on the far side of St. Roch. Along the way, Arnold "called to the troops in a cheering voice urging us forward," a rifleman remembered.

Arnold and his rescuers had to return under the same dangerous fire aimed at the men advancing. They had not gone even halfway before blood loss and intense pain rendered Arnold no longer able to walk. His companions lifted him and struggled on, anxious to get him to a doctor.

The patriots had set up their hospital in a convent a mile from the scene of the battle. It was already filling up with wounded men shot down along the town wall. By lamplight, Dr. Senter, who had made the trek over the Maine mountains, probed Arnold's lower leg to remove the bullet fragment lodged there. His anatomy studies fresh in his mind, he noted that the bullet had luckily missed the bones of Arnold's lower leg, passed "between the tibia and fibula, and lodged in the gastroeunemia muscle at the rise of the tendon Achillies, whereupon examination I easily discovered and extracted it." After dressing the wound, he and his two medical aides quickly turned to the other injured men.

Colonel Arnold remained bedridden and grimacing against the pain. Soon afterward, Major Matthias Ogden, wounded in the shoulder, entered the hospital with the first report about the attack on the Lower Town. The news was bad—British reinforcements had stopped the men's progress and trapped them between two barricades. A fierce fight was going on but, Dr. Senter noted, "it was his opinion that we should not be successful."

More bad news: A force of Canadian militiamen allied with the British were roaming through the northern suburb. Hearing about the hospital, they had decided to attack the building and take the men there prisoner.

When word of the possible assault reached them, Senter and others begged Arnold to allow himself to be carried into the country beyond. He refused. Instead, he "ordered his pistols loaded, with a sword on his bed, &c., adding that he was determined to kill as many as possible if they came into the room." Muskets and pistols were handed out to the wounded men. "We were now all soldiers," Senter observed.

Lieutenant Isaiah Wool, an assistant in Captain Lamb's artillery company, organized a small force of walking wounded, stragglers, and Canadian volunteers to meet the crisis. He set up two cannon at a turn in the street that approached the convent. When the attackers came around the corner, a blast of grapeshot scattered them. Dr. Senter observed that the twenty-two-year-old Wool "much distinguished himself on this occasion."

AFTER ARNOLD RECEIVED his wound at the barricade, the fight there continued. "Morgan now raised his voice, always terrible in the hour of battle," an early biographer wrote, "and which was heard above the din of arms, ordering his riflemen to the front."

With Morgan in the lead, the Virginia backwoodsmen swarmed over the barricade and took most of the defenders prisoner. Morgan went forward with a French-speaking interpreter and encountered another barrier three hundred yards ahead. It seemed lightly defended. If they broke through, the way would be open to mount the slope into the walled city above.

Morgan tried to hurry his men forward, but enemy resistance at the second barrier was too stiff for the patriot army to overcome without artillery support. Defenders fired their own cannon from over the barricade. The Americans took cover in doorways and buildings. Confronted with a high log wall and heavily outnumbered, "we found it impossible to force it," wrote Lieutenant Colonel Christopher Greene.

The fight filled the street with noise. Men from both sides climbed into the upper floors of the houses and shops to fire over the wall. Captain William Hendricks, leader of one of the Pennsylvania rifle companies, was struck in the left side of his chest and fell, mortally wounded. A fragment of grapeshot smashed into John Lamb's cheek and eye. Left for dead, he lay unconscious and bleeding. A musket ball tore two fingers from the hand of Lieutenant Steele.

Inside the buildings, the fight came down to hand-to-hand combat and bayonet thrusts. The dense, wind-whipped snow continued. The cannon and musket blasts reverberated from the buildings. Men on both sides lacked uniforms, so that discerning friend from foe was difficult. The street turned into a chaotic killing zone.

The tepid light of dawn now began to illuminate the scene through the snowfall. "Betwixt every peal the awful voice of Morgan is heard," a rifleman remembered. "He seems to be all soul; and moves as if he did not touch the earth."

Pockets of musketmen were surrounded and forced to surrender. More and more of the troops, lacking ammunition and hope, gave up. Sometime between nine and ten in the morning, with the wind whitening the day, Morgan was left virtually alone and surrounded. As he saw men throwing down their weapons around him, he "stormed and raged," shedding tears of angry frustration. He finally handed his sword to a French priest rather than surrender to British soldiers. The battle was over.

Morgan and the others were taken to an improvised prison. A British officer wrote home, "You can have no conception of the Kind of men composed their officers. Of those we took, one major was a blacksmith, another a hatter. Of their captains there was a butcher . . . a tanner, a shoemaker, a tavern keeper, etc. Yet they all pretended to be gentlemen."

DETAILS ABOUT THE fate of Richard Montgomery's division did not reach Benedict Arnold for two days. Finally, he heard how the general's force of New York soldiers had struggled along a path clogged with blocks of ice thrown up from the river. They reached two barriers guarding the Lower Town from the south. Unopposed, they chopped their way through one, then the other. About fifty yards in front, a dark house, apparently deserted, crowded the street.

Montgomery led a platoon toward the building while the rest of the men were still squeezing through the barricades. He drew his sword, tossed away the scabbard, and ordered the men to charge the building. Suddenly, bright bursts of flame erupted from the house. The men at the barricade saw the dark landscape suddenly illuminated, the swirling snow frozen in place by the flash. The detonation of a cannon echoed over the river.

Grapeshot tore into Montgomery's head and both thighs, killing him before the sound of the blast reached his ears. Eleven other soldiers lay motionless in the snow, killed outright or mortally wounded.

Thirty nervous Canadians, led by two militia officers, had been waiting in the house, armed with muskets and four small cannon. They had allowed the American invaders to approach the darkened house until they were only yards away before unleashing the fatal barrage.

Command of the American battalion fell to Colonel Donald

Campbell. A supply officer, he was not accustomed to battle-field responsibilities. Shocked by Montgomery's fate, facing an unknown number of cannon and men with muskets, Campbell consulted with the other officers now gathered at the second bar-ricade. Ignoring the fate of the five hundred men in Arnold's detachment who depended on his mission's success, fearful for his own life, he decided to retreat rather than fight.

American captain John MacPherson, one of those whose corpses the snow was already burying, had written a letter to be sent to his father if he was killed during the attack. "Orders are given for a general storm of Quebec this night," he wrote. "I assure you that I experience no reluctance in this cause, to venture a life which I consider is only lent to be used when my country demands it."

STILL INCAPACITATED AND suffering unrelenting pain, Benedict Arnold now took over command of the entire American army at Quebec. On January 2, Major Meigs walked into the hospital. He related details about the assault on Sault au Matelot: The British had killed perhaps four dozen men and taken the rest prisoner, including Captain Lamb, who had lived through his ordeal but lost his left eye. British general Carleton had allowed Meigs, on parole, to fetch the personal belongings of the captured officers. Arnold gave Meigs hard currency from his own purse to pass on to the officers so that they could buy necessities for themselves and their men.

Arnold tried his best to salvage what he could from the sit-uation. The day before, he had sent an express letter to General David Wooster at Montreal, now the highest-ranking officer with the northern army. He had not seen the older man since demand-ing the keys to the New Haven powder magazine on April 22.

Arnold informed Wooster of "the critical situation we are

in" and said he was confident "you will give us all the assistance in your power." He followed with a second letter two days later, detailing his losses: more than 80 men killed, 426 taken prisoner, barely 800 effective troops left. Many of those soldiers, he wrote, were "dejected, and anxious to get home." His tone became more urgent: "For God's sake order as many men down as you can possibly spare." He also told Wooster that "your presence will be absolutely necessary" to take command of the army at Quebec. Arnold was determined to follow Washington's instruction to remain subordinate to superior officers. Because Wooster chose not to come to Quebec, Arnold repeatedly urged Congress to send north "an experienced general" as soon as possible to take over.

Arnold moved from the hospital to the large house that Montgomery had commandeered as his headquarters. He was puzzled that General Carleton had not made any move to finish off the scant force now opposing him, either on the morning that the American attack collapsed or later. Arnold wrote to George Washington that "had the enemy improved their advantage, our affairs must have been entirely ruined."

Sapped of men and ammunition, he ordered the lines strengthened at key points to continue a flimsy siege of the city. He sent out recruiters to induce more Canadians to join them.

A week after the attack, Arnold wrote a letter to his sister, Hannah. He gave a brief account of the debacle. He wrote that his wound had been "exceeding painful" but was beginning to ease. "Providence which has carried me through so many dangers is still my protection," he concluded. "I am in the way of my duty and know no fear."

BEFORE THE NEWS of the disaster in Quebec had reached Congress, the delegates, thrilled by Montgomery's success at St. Johns and Montreal, had promoted him to major general, the highest rank below that of Washington himself. At the same time, they had raised Benedict Arnold, already famous for his miraculous trek over the mountains, to brigadier general.

Regard for Montgomery soared even higher with the jarring news of his death. Congress voted to purchase an elaborate memorial to honor the first general to be martyred in the war.

The American patriots, wading ever deeper into all-out war with Britain, were hungry for heroes. Like Montgomery, Arnold became an exemplar to all good patriots. His startling appearance opposite Quebec in November, along with stories of the hardships he and his men had endured, had quickly filtered back to the United Colonies. Samuel Ward, a Rhode Island delegate to Congress, wrote to his wife that "Arnold's March is considered here as the greatest Action done this War."

One result of the Canadian campaign was an increased agitation for Congress to finally break the colonies' ties with Britain. In February, patriot propagandist Thomas Paine published a tract with the ungainly title *A Dialogue between the Ghost of General Montgomery Just Arrived from the Elysian Fields; and an American Delegate, in a Wood Near Philadelphia.* In it, he reiterated the arguments for independence that he had set forth in his wildly popular screed, *Common Sense,* issued a month earlier. He depicted the revered martyr pleading with his fellow citizens to cast off the chains that shackled them to the mother country.

THE BRUTAL, SNOWBOUND winter dragged on—each day brought the discouraged Americans closer to the time when the St. Lawrence would thaw and reinforcements from Britain would arrive in force.

George Washington sent six regiments north to beef up the Quebec army, but the American effort was facing severe headwinds. Getting men and supplies to Canada in the middle of winter, with lakes and rivers frozen solid, presented enormous difficulties. Smallpox, a painful, disfiguring disease that killed every tenth sufferer, ravaged the army with increasing virulence. By the beginning of March, the additional troops had rebuilt Arnold's army to 2,500 men, but almost a third of them were laid low with smallpox.

As on his arduous march north, Arnold stared into the stern face of nature. January was cold enough to "split a stone." Snowdrifts mounted almost to the tops of the city walls, slowing all movement. Men were struck down by fever, influenza, and frostbite. One sentry's eyelids froze closed as he squinted into the iron wind. Hard currency ran out. Canadians could not be induced to join the struggle.

Arnold's wound gradually healed. By March he could mount a horse and walk some distance, although the movement still tired him. On April 1, David Wooster finally arrived at Quebec to take over. Still leaning on a cane, Arnold gave him a tour of the American lines. Wooster viewed the situation with a lack of interest bordering on contempt, the reaction, perhaps, of a professional soldier to a man he considered a rank amateur at war. The next day, Arnold's horse fell violently onto his injured leg, requiring another ten days of bed rest before he could ride off for his new assignment at Montreal.

A month went by with little improvement at Quebec. On May 1, Major General John Thomas, who had helped force the British out of Boston in March, arrived with another 1,200 troops to continue the hopeless siege. Three days later, the first British warships battered their way through the river ice to relieve Quebec. Town residents celebrated. The American army virtually collapsed. The prospects of Canada joining the rebellion vanished forever.

Part Two

A Fighting General—1776

Royal Savage schooner
(Naval History and Heritage Command)

❧

On the Lake

DURING HIS BOYHOOD, BENEDICT ARNOLD HAD FALLEN IN love with the sea. Leaving from Norwich, he had sailed with his father down the East Coast and all the way to Caribbean trading ports with names like Barbados, Guadeloupe, and Curaçao. There he took in the aroma of steaming pepperpot and curried goat, listened to the lilt of the creole tongue, and witnessed the brutality inflicted on enslaved Africans, who worked under a scalding sun to produce sugar for English tea.

Such journeys filled his summers when he was at school, but ceased as his father's business foundered under debt. After he began to learn the apothecary business as apprentice to the Lathrop brothers, he again had the chance to sail, this time as a supercargo, the person whom the shipper trusted to oversee the handling and sale of his goods.

Daniel Lathrop and his wife, Jerusha, who had lost all three of their boys to childhood illnesses, took a liking to Benedict. He lived with them in their elegant Norwich home, and the couple served as a model of kindness and refinement. Besides putting a great deal of trust in the capable boy, Daniel and his brother helped bankroll him when he established his own apothecary business in New Haven in 1763, at the age of twenty-two.

During the 1760s, Arnold and a partner acquired three ships. While maintaining a shop and warehouse, Arnold sought greater profits; he sailed to ports in the Caribbean, to London, and to Canada. By accompanying his cargos, he was able to take advantage of the most favorable terms in distant markets. He bought out his partner and continued to trade on his own. He sold barrel staves and horses in the West Indies, while buying molasses and rum for import.

Besides helping him amass a sizable, though unstable, fortune, ten years of international trading gave him wide exposure to life at sea and to life in general. The role of sea captain demanded many of the same skills as that of army officer. He had to be able to command the rough men who worked the ships and assert hard but measured discipline to extinguish any notion of mutiny. A captain learned to be decisive and to show no doubt. He had to plan his moves, provision his ships, keep an eye on every detail, and handle contingencies ranging from storms to pirates.

His time at sea left Arnold with a rough and sometimes brutal exterior. He never completely acquired the demeanor typical of a gentleman. Benjamin Rush, a distinguished physician and delegate to Congress, shared quarters with Arnold for three weeks when the former sea captain visited Philadelphia. Although Rush described his companion as "well made and his face handsome," he admitted that Arnold's conversation "was uninteresting and sometimes indelicate. His language was ungrammatical and his pronunciation vulgar." A military officer said that Arnold "did not combine . . . any intellectual qualities with his physical prowess. Instead of engaging an interesting argument, he shouted and pounded the table."

The role of a ship's commander was an isolated one. He had to remain aloof from the half dozen or so men working his ship. He spent long periods without intimate conversation. All decisions and responsibility rested on his shoulders. Arnold had a penchant for such a life, although at times he was touched by loneliness.

He may have sought relief in casual encounters with women. Only hints of his sexual nature have filtered into the historical record—rumors of flirtations during his trips to the Caribbean and of encounters with French women while maintaining the siege in Quebec. He would later admit to partaking of "a tolerable share of the dissipated joys of life, as well as the scenes of sensual gratification incident to a man of nervous constitution." At the same time, he said he preferred "the reciprocity of concern and mutual felicity existing between a lady of sensibility and a fond husband."

His messages to Peggy when he was away at sea suggest that this sentiment was a sincere one. In spite of his aura of self-sufficiency, he wrote to her "with an aching and anxious heart," and was distressed when she failed to respond. In a letter from 1774 he described himself to her as "under the greatest anxiety and suspense . . . not having heard the least syllable from you this last four months. I have wrote you almost every post."

During the fraught years leading to the revolution, seamen had direct contact with the heavy hand of the government. It was on the waterfront that discontent with the British policies that taxed or restricted trade boiled over. Alongshore men formed the mobs that opposed the Stamp Act and other British impositions, and anti-government rioting most often broke out along the wharfs and docks. Arnold soaked up the rough-and-ready ideas of liberty prevalent among the seagoing fraternity and sided with the radicals who sought to push the Revolution forward most vigorously.

IN THE SUMMER of 1776, Arnold's experience as a sailor would prove an enormous asset for the patriot cause. Following the collapse of their effort to take Quebec in the spring of 1776, the army had retreated helter-skelter up the St. Lawrence River, the British at their heels. Arnold, commanding at Montreal, did what he could to stave off defeat. By the middle of June, it became clear the effort was futile.

"The junction of the Canadians with the colonies, an object which brought us into this country is now at an end," Arnold wrote to General John Sullivan, now the ranking officer in Canada. "I am content to be the last man who quits this country, and fall, so that my country rise. But let us not fall together."

On June 18, 1776, Arnold was indeed the last American patriot to depart from the ruins of St. Johns. With redcoats bearing down on him, he stepped into a bateau minutes before the arrival of British soldiers. When Lord Germain, the secretary of state for the colonies, heard of his narrow escape, he wrote to Governor Carleton, "I am sorry you did not get Arnold, for of all the Americans, he is the most enterprising and dangerous."

Arnold now found himself back where his military adventure had begun, at Crown Point on Lake Champlain. Enemy armies were converging on the waterway that ran along the lake and the Hudson River to New York City. The British plan was to split the colonies, isolate rebellious New England, and end the war in a single fighting season. Radical patriots had wanted war—now the English armies were determined to give them war.

ON JULY 7, Arnold joined other officers in a stifling headquarters room at Crown Point. Major General Philip Schuyler, in overall command of the northern army, directed the council of war. On his right hand sat Horatio Gates, the army's field commander. At forty-nine, Gates had served as a staff officer in the British Army for nearly a quarter century. The son of a housemaid, he lacked the status needed to advance far in the military hierarchy. After some years as a major, he sold his commission and immigrated to America in 1769. He was both an ardent supporter of the patriot cause and an officer determined to get ahead in, and perhaps lead, the Continental Army.

Gates had served for nearly a year as George Washington's adjutant, his chief administrative aide in Boston. He had transformed a diverse conglomeration of militia units into a functioning army. What he coveted was an independent field command. When he arrived in upper New York State, he had tried unsuccessfully to supplant General Schuyler.

Opposite him sat the gloomy Brigadier General John Sullivan, a New Hampshire lawyer before the war. The last commander in Canada and a man of uncertain abilities, he was disgruntled about being replaced by Gates. He would soon take his case to Congress in Philadelphia, where his friends would secure his promotion to major general. At the far end of the table, a Prussian adventurer named Baron de Woedtke followed the proceedings. Recruited in Europe by Benjamin Franklin, he had convinced Congress to give him a general's commission based on his presumed military expertise.

The men had only to look out the door to see the army's problems on graphic display. Many of the soldiers who had survived Canada were sick. Smallpox victims were stretched on the ground in all directions, many covered with lesions and fetid sores. Some were blind and delirious, some swarming with maggots. The wounded lacked adequate medical treatment and shelter.

Healthy soldiers were low on weapons, morale, and discipline. They idled around the disorderly camp, trying to recover from a long, desperate retreat. "A horde of Tartars," Woedtke called them. Another observer said they "were not an army but a mob."

A hundred miles to the north, thousands of fresh British troops, mercenaries hired from Germany, and Native American allies were massing just above the Canadian border. As soon as they built a sufficient war fleet to take control of the lake, they would descend on the beaten American army. The Royal Navy would soon deposit another, even larger force at New York City. The strategic goal was to "place the Rebel Army between two Fires" along the Lake Champlain–Hudson River corridor, then attack from both directions.

Benedict Arnold, who held the lowest rank among the officers in the room, was asked to speak first. He presented his ideas clearly and with confidence. He was aggressive by nature, but he understood that the American patriots, in their current shattered condition, could not hope to defeat a larger, better-armed enemy. Their goal had to be delay. They needed time to rebuild their defenses and to breathe life back into their army.

Having faced British general Guy Carleton during the winter and spring, he understood him to be a careful and deliberate strategist. Arnold felt that his caution could be used against him. American boldness could make Carleton hesitate, buying time for the patriots.

He emphasized the importance of terrain. Lacking roads, Carleton's only option was to move by water. It would be easy for the enemy to amass a fleet of transport boats to carry troops and supplies. But without the protection of warships, such vessels would be vulnerable to attack by the armed ships that the Americans already had on the lake, including the sloop Arnold had captured at St. Johns the previous spring.

Arnold felt that if the patriots augmented their fleet, Carleton would be forced into an arms race that could last weeks, perhaps months. The Americans would have time to stiffen the fortifications at Ticonderoga. He predicted that the British would quickly become masters of the lake "unless Every nerve on our part is Strained to exceed them in a Naval Armament." In addition to gunboats and larger row galleys, he recommended building a thirty-six-gun frigate able to fire a broadside from powerful cannon.

Arnold's grasp of the situation was so complete and his plan so persuasive that little further debate was required. The officers adopted his strategy in its entirety except for the frigate—their shipbuilding resources on the lake were too meager to make construction of such a vessel feasible.

Next came the question of the men's roles in the planned campaign. Sullivan had already asked for leave to depart—Schuyler was glad to be rid of him. Woedtke had little to offer and would die of drink and illness a few weeks later. General Gates, who disavowed any knowledge of naval affairs, would take on the task of rebuilding the northern army and preparing defenses at Ticonderoga. Schuyler would assume the enormous logistical problem of buying and sending supplies to support patriot preparations. That left Arnold to build a navy and lead it toward an expected confrontation with the enemy.

Philip Schuyler, like Arnold, was a merchant with his own trading sloops and schooners, one- and two-masted sailboats adept at both coastal sailing and trips to the West Indies. The armed boats he ordered built included the fifty-foot open gunboats known as gondolas, and the larger, seventy-foot row galleys that Arnold had spoken of. The flat-bottomed gunboats were relatively easy to build. The galleys, with their shaped hulls and keels, required the expertise of experienced shipwrights. Both called for specialized rigging and nautical supplies that were hard to come by in the interior of the country.

Skenesborough, the spot on the southern tip of Champlain chosen for the patriot shipyard, was the estate of retired British officer Philip Skene. He had built a sawmill, docks, and warehouses there before being arrested as a Tory. The site could only be reached from the south by a narrow stream or a crooked, mud-clogged road.

Up to this point, Philip Schuyler had left the maritime affairs in the hands of two members of the local Dutch fraternity. Jacobus Wynkoop had assumed the undefined rank of "commodore" of the Lake Champlain fleet. General Gates complained that the fifty-six-year-old merchant captain was "slow" and that he ignored any orders except those that came from his friend Philip Schuyler, who spoke Dutch at home. Overseeing the boatbuilding was Hermanus Schuyler, a onetime sheriff of Albany County and distant cousin of the general. Under his supervision, the construction of armed vessels had been going on for weeks, but the men had finished only one boat.

While Schuyler and Gates both pushed to speed naval construction, Arnold scoured the sawmills along Lake Champlain for needed lumber. Gates urged him to supervise the boatbuilding and to take command of the proposed fleet as soon as it was ready. When he arrived in Skenesborough on July 23, Arnold found only two gondolas partly finished and no work proceeding on the more important row galleys. A few days later, Gates wrote to Congress of the naval effort: "I have committed the whole of that department to [Arnold's] care, convinced he will thereby add to that brilliant reputation he has so deservedly acquired."

For his part, Arnold promised "we shall have a very formidable fleet" in less than three weeks. But to keep the building moving ahead, he told Gates he needed anchors, hawsers, linseed oil, paint brushes, tar brushes, frying pans, speaking trumpets, spyglasses, fishnets, grapeshot, canister shot, and much more. He also noted a "want of seamen or marines" to work the boats.

It was the beginning of a summerlong struggle to build a fleet in a virtual wilderness. Shipwrights in particular were hard to attract to the interior—few wanted to leave the coast, where lucrative jobs were plentiful. Schuyler had to scour New York and New England for the needed supplies, stripping ships that were stranded in Albany and other Hudson River ports by the British blockade at New York City. George Washington emphasized to Congress that it was "of greatest importance to have a sufficient force to prevent the enemy passing the lake."

The work accelerated under Arnold's insistent attention. Fortunately for him, Schuyler was able to send 150 experienced ship carpenters to Skenesborough before the end of July. More were attracted by generous bonuses and travel money promised by Congress.

As the hulls were finished, they were launched at Skenesborough and rowed to Ticonderoga where additional workmen installed masts and the complex web of hemp rigging needed to work the sails. They mounted one-inch swivel guns on the rails and heavier cannon attached to wheeled carriages on deck.

"As soon as all the vessels and gondolas are equipped," Gates wrote to Washington, "General Arnold has offered to go to Crown Point and take the command of them. This is exceedingly pleasing to me, as he has a perfect knowledge in maritime affairs, and is, besides, a most deserving and gallant officer."

The entire northern army bristled with urgency. The men building redoubts and fortifications at Ticonderoga kept looking over their shoulders, not knowing when a fleet of British warships and an army of redcoats would descend on them.

A rare bright moment came on Sunday, July 28. After divine worship at Ticonderoga the troops were assembled to hear the reading of a proclamation from Congress. *When in the Course of human events,* it began. It spoke of *certain unalienable Rights* possessed by all citizens. After a catalog of grievances, it defiantly concluded that the American colonies *are, and of Right ought to be, Free and Independent States.*

"It was remarkably pleasing," an observer wrote, "to see the spirits of the soldiers so raised, after all their calamities; the language of every man's countenance was, Now we are a people; we have a name among the States of this world."

IN THE WEEKS after his arrival at Skenesborough, Arnold was able to give "life and spirit to our dockyard," as Gates put it. Gates told him that he faced a "momentous" assignment. It was vital that he secure "the northern entrance into this side of the continent . . . from further invasion."

First, he needed to take care of a vexing bureaucratic matter. In order to restore military discipline at Ticonderoga, General Gates had ordered any soldier accused of a breach of regulations to face a court-martial. Many of the trials concerned minor offenses—stealing, fighting, failure to attend to duties. Some took up alleged crimes that had occurred during the hasty retreat from Canada and could only now be addressed.

One of these was an accusation against Colonel Moses Hazen, who had briefly commanded in Montreal before General Arnold arrived from Quebec City. Henry Knox, Washington's artillery commander, would later describe Hazen as having as "obstinate a temper as ever afflicted humanity."

As the main British Army came down the St. Lawrence and the Americans' chaotic final retreat began, Arnold had sent supplies to the troops. He had confiscated the clothing, blankets, and utensils from Montreal merchants with the promise of payment later.

Hazen had neglected to secure the cargo and the items were "stolen or plundered." With the containers broken open, it became impossible to determine who was owed compensation. Arnold reprimanded Hazen—Hazen demanded a trial to clear his name.

Thirteen field officers heard the case on July 31. Hazen denied responsibility for the missing supplies, and scanty records yielded no documents to back up Arnold's charge. The court barred the one man who could settle the matter in Arnold's favor from testifying. An enraged Arnold protested the maneuver as "unprecedented and I think unjust." The officers demanded that Arnold apologize to the court.

Instead, he accused members of "indecent reflections on a superior officer." As soon as military expediency allowed, he said he would "by no means withhold from any gentleman of the Court the satisfaction that his honour may require." Dueling was common during the era, and the implications of the statement were deadly serious.

The court acquitted Hazen, implying that Arnold was a liar. Members demanded that the general be arrested for using "profane oaths" and "menacing words" toward them.

General Gates decided that it was they who had gone too far. Although he acknowledged "the warmth of general Arnold's temper," he could not accept the loss of his naval commander. He wrote to General Schuyler that he was "astonished at the calumnies" of the junior officers against Arnold. He dissolved the court-martial, declaring, "The United States must not be deprived of that excellent officer's services at this important moment."

Hazen joined the growing list of Arnold's enemies. Gates told Arnold he would write to Congress that "every report to your prejudice is founded in calumny." Captain James Wilkinson stated that Arnold's enemies had slandered a man who had "fought and bled in a cause which they have only encumbered."

The August 1776 court-martial was an insignificant detail in the scope of the Revolution, but it highlighted Benedict Arnold's sensitivity to slights and his habit of thoughtlessly antagonizing others. The friction resulting from unclear lines of authority or fractious subordinates struck sparks in his nature. Rather than ignore or dismiss the acrimony, he took it to heart. And he would not forget.

ARNOLD UNDERSTOOD THAT time is always a precious commodity in warfare. An urge to get the jump on the enemy kept worrying him. Other officers thought the idea of rushing a small, incomplete squadron of warships toward a clash with the Royal Navy was lunacy. Even Matthias Ogden, who had accompanied Arnold over the Maine mountains, observed that "he says he will pay a visit to St. Johns. I wish he may be as prudent as he is brave."

Under Arnold's direction, the carpenters and shipwrights had so far managed to build and rig six gondolas. They had worked on several of the more powerfully armed row galleys, but had yet to complete any of them. In the heat of mid-August, the swampy region around Skenesborough bred contagion. Workmen fell ill and progress slowed. Arnold himself reported feeling "a little feverish" when, on August 16, he took command of the partial fleet at Crown Point.

During the next week, he had to endure another dispute resulting from tangled lines of command. "Commodore" Jacobus Wynkoop, who had previously commanded the naval effort, ignored General Gates's orders to hand over the fleet to Arnold. Wynkoop's authority was from Philip Schuyler; he would take orders from no one else. He went so far as to order a shot fired over the bow of an American vessel that Arnold had ordered to sail.

Arnold informed Wynkoop that "you surely must be out of your senses to say no orders shall be obeyed but yours." If Wynkoop did not relent instantly, "I shall be under the disagreeable necessity of convincing you of your error by immediately arresting you."

When word of the incident reached General Gates, it ignited

his smoldering antagonism with Schuyler. He ordered Wynkoop arrested and sent him on to Albany, stating his hope that Schuyler would "without a Scruple, forthwith dismiss him the Service." Arnold, the heat of his anger cooling, took a more generous view of his fellow mariner. Wynkoop, he told Schuyler, "now seems . . . sorry for his disobedience of orders." He asked that he simply be allowed to return home without punishment.

LATE IN THE afternoon of August 24, barely seven weeks after the decisive council at Crown Point where Arnold had laid out his war plan, he was ready to sail. The wind was from the south and his vessels were aligned in neat rows. He commanded from the *Royal Savage*, a schooner of war that General Montgomery's invasion force had captured from the British at St. Johns the previous autumn. Beside her was the sloop *Enterprise*, which Arnold himself had seized right after the occupation of Ticonderoga in May. Next came the six new gondolas, with two more small armed sailing vessels bringing up the rear. The soldiers at Crown Point who witnessed the short parade sent up cheers that were returned by the men on the ships. After months of retreat and weeks of waiting, the northern army was on the move again, advancing toward the enemy.

For Arnold, it was an opportunity to savor the pleasure of being on the water. Finally, he was free of the bureaucratic entanglements endemic to the military life. He still had to act under the chain of command, but Gates, an experienced staff officer, had made his orders deliberately ambiguous. On the one hand, he emphasized that "it is a defensive War we are carrying on," and warned Arnold against any "wanton risque, or unnecessary Display of the Power of the Fleet." But should the enemy "attempt to force their way through the pass you are stationed to defend, in that case you will act with such cool, determined valor as will give them reason to repent their temerity."

Gates also suggested that while Arnold not risk the fleet, he should let drop hints that would "induce our own People to conclude it is our real Intention to invade the enemy. . . . It will keep up their Spirits."

As darkness fell that day, Arnold stood on the quarterdeck of the *Royal Savage,* feeling the wind draw the ship toward the unknown. It was a relief to be under sail, whatever danger lay ahead. He may have remembered the letter his sister, Hannah, had sent him a few weeks earlier.

"I am sorry to hear you are going upon the lake," she wrote. "Have been hoping you would quit the service but it seems you have no such intention." Indeed, his intention was the opposite: to risk his life and the lives of his men for the cause they had embraced.

Now all pettiness, all carping and envy, fell away. "Preventing the enemy's invasion of our country," Gates had informed him, "is the ultimate end of the important command with which you are now intrusted."

8

⌘

Stained with Blood

THE DAY AFTER LEAVING CROWN POINT, THE INEXPERIENCED sailors aboard Arnold's partial fleet saw the lake's angry face. A storm roared down on them from the north, the winds mounting hour by hour. With the gale, the water bared its fangs. The boats heaved. The crew members learned a sudden lesson about the dangers of sailing. The fleet went to anchor, but the wind threatened to drag them onto the rocks. Arnold soon ordered a retreat to a sheltered bay for safety. He climbed into his own ship's boat and rowed over to the gunboat *Spitfire*, which was in danger of foundering. He shouted instructions to the captain, then accompanied the other vessels to safety. It was a whole day before the *Spitfire* reappeared, battered but intact.

While they waited for the storm to calm, Arnold invited his officers onto shore for what was described as a "most Genteel feast"—a pig roast and marksmanship contest enhanced by generous rounds of wine, punch, and cider. The men toasted their general, who had guided them through the maelstrom.

The water calmed, the fleet continued under a fair wind. When they reached the Canadian border, Arnold ordered them to continue on into the Richelieu River toward St. Johns, only to fall back the next day. His bluff convinced some of his own crew that their mission would include a new attack on Canada. Rumors of an invasion reached the British, who were startled by the patriots' boldness. Their own thoughts turned to defense— General Carleton ordered gun emplacements to be mounted at the mouth of the river.

Arnold was content to wait in the northern reaches of Lake Champlain. Every day that went by without an enemy attack was another day to build more boats and further reinforce Ticonderoga. But the duty in the north was stressful for both officers and men. The gondolas had only canvas canopies to fend off storms, which became more frequent as autumn approached. Constantly wet, the men had no bunks or hammocks in which to sleep. When off duty, they simply slumped onto the damp deck. Because each fifty-foot boat held a crew of more than forty men, space was limited.

Arnold gave the sailors little time to contemplate their bleak and dangerous situation. He urged the captains to train the men in the basics of seamanship. He sent them on patrols. He told them to observe the terrain, to take soundings, study wind patterns, and learn how to use the maze of islands, coves, and bays to their advantage.

On one occasion, work parties went ashore to gather wood. Suddenly, they were "attacked by a Party of Savages, who pursued them into the Water." A British officer called for them to surrender. Several blasts from the boat's swivel guns gave the men cover to escape, but three had already been killed. The danger of going on land increasingly confined the men to the cramped boats.

Although no British warships appeared on the lake, Native Americans were able to penetrate patriot lines in canoes. Arnold redoubled his patrols and sent armed escorts to accompany supply boats coming up from Ticonderoga. He ordered half of the men from each crew to remain on guard day and night.

INTELLIGENCE GATHERING WAS one of Arnold's obsessions. As soon as he reached the north end of the lake, he dispatched scouts and spies to investigate British activity at St. Johns. One four-man group was under the command of Lieutenant Benjamin Whitcomb, an experienced woodsman. On a scouting mission to Canada in July, Whitcomb had fired on a British general from hiding, killing him. The act was condemned by officers on both sides as murder rather than the type of warfare suited to a gentleman, a sentiment quickly becoming outdated.

Whitcomb returned to tell Arnold that at St. Johns "there is a ship on the stocks . . . designed to mount twenty guns, nine and twelve-pounders." It was the type of large warship that Arnold himself had earlier pushed his own side to build. The scout confirmed that "there was talk of crossing the lake soon."

WHILE ARNOLD AND his men floated on the wilderness lake, a drama was unfolding at the southern end of the water corridor that ran through the heart of the colonies. By March, the young artillery colonel Henry Knox had managed to transport a selection of the Ticonderoga guns overland to Boston, dragging them through the snow on sleds. The weapons, mounted on Dorchester Heights, forced the British to abandon the city—the patriots chalked up their first major victory.

In April, Washington moved the bulk of the Continental Army to New York City, where he expected an enemy attack. At the end of June, the Americans watched forty-five British warships and transports sail into New York Harbor. Then more ships. And more. The enemy landed tens of thousands of soldiers on Staten Island without opposition. By August, more than thirty-two thousand English and German troops under General William Howe were facing the twenty thousand men that Washington had been able to muster.

So slow and uncertain was the flow of information to Arnold's waiting fleet that he could never be certain what was happening in the populous region below. On September 9, word arrived of a significant battle fought on Long Island. Apparently there had been much loss of life on both sides. Only later did Arnold learn that Washington's army had suffered an epic defeat at the end of August, with almost a quarter of their numbers casualties. On September 15, the enemy forced him out of New York City altogether and took possession of the second largest city in America.

Arnold, whose mind ranged toward the broad strategic picture, yearned for "particulars of the affair at New York." If the British in Canada were to hear that General Howe had captured New York City, "they will doubtless attempt a junction with him." Washington's series of disasters in New York and New Jersey that autumn would place the responsibility for seeing that such a junction should not take place entirely on Arnold's shoulders.

HIS MEANS WERE meager. The high command was able to recruit enough capable captains and mates to serve as officers for Arnold's fleet, but "a greater part of those shipped for Seamen," Arnold complained, "know very little of the matter." The men were a "wretched motley crew ... the refuse of every regiment."

They would have to do. Training helped, but the men could hardly be expected to gain the skill of British sailors, who had followed the sea since they were children. Arnold continued to demand "seamen (no land lubbers)." But he would have to shape his strategy to the capabilities of the crews he had.

In addition to men, Arnold lacked supplies. Having sailed north in August, his men had only summer clothes. He needed more gunpowder, for practice as well as for battle. He also asked for caulking irons, spare anchors, blankets, twine, sail needles, tar, and rope. "When you ask for a frigate," Arnold wrote, "they give you a raft. Ask for sailors, they give you tavern waiters. And if you want breeches, they give you a vest."

Gates did his best to provide for the fleet, but he tired of Arnold's continual demands. He was providing what was available, he wrote. "Where it is not to be had you, & the Princes of the Earth must go unfurnish'd."

By far the most important items that Arnold lacked were the row galleys still under construction in Skenesborough. These maneuverable vessels were to be the main armament of the fleet. October was approaching. Where were they?

"I am greatly at a loss," Arnold wrote to Gates, "what could have retarded the galleys so long."

Isolated in the far north, enduring hardships, Arnold was vexed by the stinginess of Congress. Why did American patriots not recognize the important contribution he and his crews were making in the north? "I am surprised by their strange economy or infatuation below," he complained. "Saving and negligence, I am afraid, will ruin us at last."

Isolated beneath the vast northern starscape, he had time to contemplate. He could not understand why others did not share his devotion to the cause. He had been willing to leave behind his business and his family. He was resigned to give his life if needed. Yet his fellow citizens could only stint and chase after their own gain. The yeast of discontent was beginning to work in his soul.

He was particularly incensed by the attacks on his reputation. He fumed in a letter to Gates, "I cannot but think it extremely cruel when I have sacrificed my Ease, Health and great part of my private property in the Cause of my Country to be Caluminated as a Robber and thief, at a Time too when I have it not in my Power to be heard in my own Defence."

Kind words from home were a welcome balm. His sister, Hannah, sent him four waistcoats and three pair of stockings. She wrote, "Little Hal sends a kiss to Pa and says, 'Auntie, tell my Papa he must come home, I want to kiss him.'" Earlier, she had written that Harry wanted Papa to buy him "a little horse and a pair of pistols." The boy was, "as far as courage goes," very like his father.

But not all the news was heartwarming. Hannah reported that his business had practically collapsed. She had been forced to sell most of his assets to pay debts. "If you ever live to return, you will find yourself a broken merchant."

She reverted to the Puritan stoicism they had both learned as children. "To the great Disposer of all events we must commit the issue," she wrote. "We all want to see you, but whether that happiness is again to be repeated to us, God only knows."

By September 23, Arnold and his officers were beginning to imagine that the enemy might not challenge them on the lake that season after all. Continually adjusting his strategy to the conditions, Arnold decided to move the fleet another twenty miles south to the bay behind Valcour Island. The rocky, two-mile-long fragment of land lay barely a mile from the New York shore. It would provide shelter in case of severe storms as well as concealment from the enemy. The move brought him closer to the forts in case he had to retreat farther.

He told Gates that the island had "an exceeding fine, secure harbor ... the fleet will be secure and we can discover the enemy if they attempt to pass us." He later explained that in the bay, "few vessels can attack us at the same time & those will be exposed to the fire of the whole fleet." Gates, who was content to allow Arnold flexibility, approved the new position and wrote that he was sure "zeal for the public Service will not suffer You to return One Moment sooner than in prudence & Good Conduct you Ought to."

On the last day of September, the men were gratified to see the first of the row galleys coming to join them. The *Trumbull* was certainly welcome, but Arnold complained to Gates that she was "not half finished or rigged; her cannon are much too small."

After another week of cold rain and angry skies, two more galleys arrived. The *Washington* carried David Waterbury, an experienced Connecticut ship's captain who was to serve as Arnold's second-in-command. Her sister galley, the *Congress,* was equipped with two 18-pounders, the most powerful cannon of all those on the vessels, and was more maneuverable than the *Royal Savage.* Arnold made her his flagship.

The galleys brought at least some of the supplies needed, including warmer clothes for the crews and a welcome keg of rum for each of the boats. Time continued to tick away.

WHEN ARNOLD WAS thirteen and still studying Latin with a Yale scholar, his tutor wrote to his mother describing a boy "full of pranks and plays." He noted an incident in which a local barn had caught fire. Onlookers were horrified to see a boy emerge from the smoke and walk the length of the burning structure's roof beam. It was young Benedict, out for a thrill and eager to impress.

More than impress. There was something about the precarious gap between life and death that attracted him. It was on that knife-edge that he felt most fully alive. No wonder he excelled at war. A battle was for him a kind of homecoming, a place where he found himself poised on the roof beam of existence.

On the morning of October 11, an American crewman wrote, "We had alarm that the Regular fleet was Coming on us." Men on the scout boats that Arnold always kept out hurried into Valcour Bay to report sails on the northern horizon. A fleet was approaching. It included a full-blown frigate, a three-masted, square-rigged warship named *Inflexible*. A single broadside from that ship's line of 12-pounder cannon would nearly match the firepower of the entire American fleet. Beside her sailed a huge artillery barge, capable of fighting ships on the water or bombarding forts on land. Two schooners of war flanked these ships. They were followed by more than twenty gunboats, some with substantial 24-pounder cannon. Then smaller warships, armed longboats, and a swarm of canoes paddled by Indian allies.

Arnold called for the captains of all his boats to gather in the cramped cabin of the *Congress*. Two possibilities: stay and fight or retreat toward the forts. If they stayed, the enemy's superior firepower might destroy the fleet. If they ran, the faster British ships might chase them down. If they stayed, they might hold off the enemy and eke out more days of delay. If they ran, they might make it to Ticonderoga where they could support the fort from the water.

David Waterbury, an experienced seaman eighteen years older than Arnold, argued that they should retreat. The restricted bay was a death trap—the shoal-clogged north end blocked movement in that direction. The wind could easily swing around from the south and favor the British. "I gave it as my opinion," Waterbury later said, "that the fleet ought immediately to come to sail and fight them on a retreat."

No. Arnold knew that his inexperienced crews would be no match for Royal Navy men in a battle of maneuver on the open water. Only by fighting from a fixed position would they have a chance. Retreat engendered fear. Fear was contagious. If it touched the green troops at Ticonderoga, it could spread like a

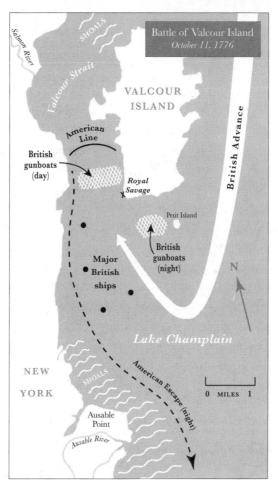

fever. They had to make a stand. They would make it at Valcour Island.

As in the council of war during the worst of the march to Quebec, Arnold showed complete confidence. He praised his captains' abilities and assured them they could prevail. The enemy were far from invincible. "Carleton the Haughty," as Arnold called him, had not even sent out scout boats. The arrogance of the enemy would be their downfall.

Staring into each man's eyes, putting assurance into each word, he snuffed out doubt and hesitation. He induced the men to share his optimism. If they were to die, they would die. But that day they would fight for a cause. And they would win.

The British fleet hurried south along the lake, paced by a brisk north wind. Arnold had counted on that. He could practically read General Carleton's mind. The British commander would assume that the Americans, no longer visible on the northern lake, had already retreated toward the forts. He would not waste time searching every cove and inlet.

From intelligence reports, Arnold knew that Carleton had been waiting to complete a ship large enough to give him assurance of victory. His men had spent an extra month finishing *Inflexible*. Now the mighty frigate passed Valcour Island and rushed southward. Suddenly, Carleton and his naval officers were startled by the boom of a cannon. Heads swiveled—the sound had come from behind them.

"Come about!" British sailors flew into action. Lines were heaved, spars creaked, sails flapped. The ships slowed, skidded sideways as their rudders tried to push them into the wind. But the laborious task of tacking required space—even the best sailors in the world could not maneuver large ships into a small bay against the wind.

The American schooner *Royal Savage*, which had ventured out to fire at the enemy, had the same problem as the enemy ships. As she tried to tack, a gust swept her onto a rock ledge off the southwest corner of the island. British gunboats fired, her captain ordered his men to swim to shore. One of the most effective of the American warships was lost in the opening minutes of the battle.

The British gunboats, rowboats similar to the American gondolas, were the only enemy vessels that could easily maneuver into the narrow bay. There they encountered an arc of American warships bristling with cannon and stretching from the western shore to the island. The British boats, each with a single large gun in its bow, formed a line about three-quarters of a mile south of the Americans. Both sides began to pound each other with cannon fire. The frustrated officers of the larger British ships could not get near enough to be effective—they were forced to remain spectators outside the bay's mouth.

The patriot crews, after nearly six weeks of increasingly tense waiting, finally plunged into the death-drenched struggle of combat. The firing of a single cannon blasted a sound that was felt as much as heard, that echoed from mountains. The guns' thunder numbed senses and left ears ringing. The crashes came not as single notes but in monstrous chords, giant arpeggios of explosions, a concussive roar that suffocated thought. The sharp crack of musket fire punched at the men from shore—Indians and British infantrymen had occupied both the mainland and the island. Shouts, curses, warnings, screams of pain added to the din. Iron balls flew past at supersonic speeds, each tearing the air with a breathtaking banshee whine.

"During the affair," remembered Captain Georg Pausch, a German artillery expert on one of the enemy gunboats, "it could have been a bit after one o'clock, the naval battle became very serious." It was a veteran soldier's way of saying that the Valcour channel had turned into a scene of intense violence.

During the age of sail, war on water was chaotic, dynamic, and extraordinarily brutal. Cannonballs could penetrate oak planks. Crew members had nowhere to hide or take cover and could not run away. A seventeen-year-old Connecticut marine had his face splattered with a comrade's "flesh and brains" when a cannonball took the man's head off.

The Puritan sect, in which Benedict Arnold had been raised, put the contemplation of death at the center of human spiritual existence. "A prudent man," the clergyman Cotton Mather wrote, "will die daily."

While Arnold showed few signs of deep religious conviction, he saved the letters his mother had sent him when he was a boy. Her admonitions that "we have a very uncertain stay in this world" and that he should always be ready to "step off the banks of time" struck a chord that reverberated into adulthood.

The crux of war is the ability to act effectively in the face of death. The cannonballs that flew around Arnold's head, that arbitrarily killed crewmen beside him, were the concrete reminders of mortality. Arnold's ability to face the possibility of extinction without flinching and to navigate danger with cool equanimity were qualities that made him an indispensable leader in battle.

To ARNOLD'S AMAZEMENT, and because of his inspiring example, the motley crews, the men he had scorned as the "refuse of every regiment," held their own. They did their duty.

"Our decks were stain'd with blood," wrote Isaiah Canfield, a soldier drafted for lake duty on the galley *Trumbull.* Jahiel Stewart, a crewman on the American hospital ship *Enterprise,* remembered, "The Doctors cut off great many legs and arms and See Seven men threw overboard that died with their wounds while I was aboard."

The fight went on and on. Arnold's tactics were working. The Americans were able to hold off the enemy gunboats. The crews cheered when they scored a hit that sank one of them. The only British sailing ship that got into the battle, a schooner named *Carleton* after their commander, received such a barrage of American shot that she was disabled and had to be towed back from the line.

"The Enemy Fleet attacked ours with Great fury," a fourteen-year-old American sailor recorded, "and we Returned the fire with as Great Sperit and Vigar and the most Desparate canannading."

Arnold was in his element. A man who served under him

declared that "he was our fighting general, and a bloody fellow he was. . . . It was 'Come on, boys'—'twasn't 'Go, boys.'" At times Arnold leaped into a boat to row to other vessels to relay instructions or to encourage and shout praise to the hardworking crews.

Arnold would later note that he had been "obliged . . . to point most of the guns on board the *Congress*, which I believe did good execution." It was a duty that a commander would normally have left to a competent gunner, but Arnold's men were unpracticed in the fine art of aiming a cannon on the deck of a plunging boat. The blasts left Arnold's uniform spattered with powder, his face a dark mask pierced by the whites of eager, bloodshot eyes. The echoes from every explosion were "tremendous," Arnold remembered.

Captain Pausch later admitted that "the rebels directed their cannon none too badly"—high praise for amateur soldiers.

THE EXHAUSTED AUTUMN sky, after watching seven hours of fighting, gave up its light. Dark seeped from the forests to cover the water. British sailors managed to work *Inflexible* partway into the bay to fire from a distance. "Five broadsides silenced their whole line," a British officer noted. It was really nightfall that brought the long ordeal to an end. All the guns fell quiet. Stars blinked to life in the firmament.

In a final stroke, General Carleton ordered the *Royal Savage*, the grounded American schooner, to be set on fire so that rebels could not retake her during the night. The flames of the burning vessel would cast a wavering light over the black water for hours.

Arnold called another council of war. The boat captains gathered in his cramped cabin where they had met that morning. Now lantern light showed the table stained with the blood of men who had been treated there for their wounds. The officers stared at each other—their faces had aged ten years in a day.

Benedict Arnold had been right—they had managed to stand up to the ships of the Royal Navy and fight them to a draw. David Waterbury had also been right—they were now trapped inside Valcour Bay. They had expended three-quarters of their ammunition. All their vessels had been damaged, some were taking on water, the gunboat *Philadelphia* was sinking as they spoke. At dawn, if the wind veered, the major enemy ships could roll up the American battle line. The choice seemed between obliteration and striking their colors in surrender.

Arnold revealed another option.

"To our utter astonishment," a British naval officer reported at first light, "under the cover of the night Mr. Arnold sailed thro' a part of our fleet."

Unfamiliar with the waters, the British had deployed their ships cautiously back from the New York shore. They didn't want to risk going aground in the darkness.

The American escape was the stuff of fairy tales. Arnold ordered the captains to arrange their boats in a line, each guided by a chalk mark on the stern of the one ahead. With muffled oars, in absolute silence, the men rowed along the shallows. Their weeks of taking soundings and studying the terrain paid off. They managed to slip south past the entire opposing fleet. As they slid through the water, they could hear talk, laughter, and the banging of hammers from the enemy vessels. By morning they were miles down the lake, rowing for all they were worth.

So began a race south, the Americans with a head start, the British on faster ships. The patriot sailors, having fought all day on October 11 and rowed all night, pushed forward through another day and night, rowing into a storm that sent sleet stinging their faces. By the morning of October 13, the enemy were nearly upon them. David Waterbury had to surrender his heavily damaged row galley along with more than a hundred men.

A few of the damaged American vessels had sunk along the

way, a few were able to escape to Ticonderoga. Arnold's *Congress* and four remaining gondolas took a stand not far north of Crown Point. Arnold dueled with *Inflexible* and the other British sailing ships for two and a half hours. When further resistance became futile, he would not allow his vessels' flags to be lowered in surrender. He instead ordered his captains to sail into Ferris Bay, a small cove on the eastern side of the lake. They ran the boats aground, set them on fire so that they could not be used by the enemy, and waded to shore.

The explosion of the remaining gunpowder on the patriot boats marked the end of the fight. Arnold organized the two hundred survivors. The men improvised stretchers from sail canvas to carry the wounded and began a march southward. They reached the headland opposite Crown Point late that night and joined their comrades. Arnold ordered the men to abandon Crown Point and burn the buildings there. He continued on to Ticonderoga, arriving at four in the morning "exceedingly fatigued and unwell, having been without sleep or refreshment for near three days."

Ferris Bay, on the east shore of Lake Champlain, was later renamed Arnold Bay. It remains one of the few places in the United States named in his honor.

THE MENACE REMAINED. The Americans consolidated their defenses at Ticonderoga. General Gates put Arnold in charge of the main north-facing redoubts. He expected an attack to come as soon as General Carleton was able to deploy his army—the British commander had begun moving his infantrymen to Crown Point as soon as he arrived.

Gates issued orders that the men of the regiments be "well acquainted with their alarm posts." He expected the "the enemy's attack will most probably be rash & sudden." The British would try to panic the inexperienced troops at Ticonderoga, many of them hastily recruited militiamen. The defenders stood at the ramparts, muskets in hand, day after day. Nothing happened.

The Americans were eager for the arrival of "General Winter," who would freeze the lake solid and make further military operations impractical. On October 27, the British brought several ships forward and seemed to study the fort's defenses while Gates's men stood on high alert. The enemy departed without making an aggressive move. Finally, on Sunday, November 3, three weeks after the battle at Valcour, a scout came in and reported that the British Army had left Crown Point.

Now the shape of the long campaign that had begun in July came into focus. Benedict Arnold had seen that, by moving swiftly, the patriots might bring about the one thing that could save them—delay. His decisions to build a fleet, to confront the enemy at the north end of the lake, and to fight before retreating had all served that purpose. Time had defeated Guy Carleton, even though he had prevailed in the contest of armed power.

Even before his retreat, Carleton had told Lord Germain, secretary of state for the colonies, that "the season is so far advanced that I cannot yet pretend to Your Lordship whether anything further can be done this year." He was not about to be stranded 115 miles from St. Johns, with no roads by which to send food and ammunition. Indeed, ice would encroach on the lake before the end of November and Gates would report to Congress that all was secure in the north "until the beginning of May."

The fight at Valcour had demonstrated to the enemy commanders that American patriots were sincere in their rebellion and fanatical in their will to fight. Arnold had put on a show for Carleton's benefit. He had sacrificed most of his war vessels and the lives of more than sixty men. But meticulous preparation, careful strategy, and clairvoyant improvisation had prevailed.

Some American officers criticized him for allowing the fleet to be destroyed. David Waterbury, who felt he had been abandoned during the final hours of the battle, questioned Arnold's tactics. Richard Henry Lee, a Virginia congressional delegate, accused Arnold of being too "fiery, hot, and impetuous" during the campaign.

But those who understood the situation praised his performance. He had "conducted himself like a hero," noted Benjamin Rush. Arnold, he said, had "lost all save honor." Gates was thankful that "it has pleased Providence to preserve General Arnold. Few men ever met with so many hairbreadth escapes in so short a space of time." Even the British credited Arnold for the "defense he made against a superior enemy." Arnold had acted "with remarkable coolness," an officer wrote. "He is certainly a brave man."

ARNOLD'S ACHIEVEMENT SHONE even brighter in relation to the disaster that was unfolding simultaneously around New York City. After the British captured the town in September, George Washington's army continued to retreat. They crossed New Jersey and, in early December, moved into Pennsylvania on the far side of the Delaware River. The Continental Army shrank to barely three thousand "animated scarecrows" whose enlistments would expire in weeks. The situation left Washington "trembling for the fate of America."

Washington called on Schuyler to send as many troops as he could spare to join the army along the Delaware. Generals Gates and Arnold accompanied six hundred veterans who were no longer needed at Ticonderoga down the Hudson River and on a roundabout march to the south. They reached Bethlehem, Pennsylvania, on December 15. With fifty miles still to cover, Gates allowed the men a few days' rest.

Benedict Arnold rode ahead to Washington's camp, where he

stayed three days. It was the first time the two men had been to-gether since Washington sent Arnold over the Maine mountains the previous September. Washington still believed in the "justice of our Cause" and was hopeful that the nation's "prospects will brighten." But he had confided to his brother, and probably told Arnold as well, "I think the game is pretty near up."

Gates had informed Washington that Arnold was anxious "after his very long absence, to see his family and settle his public accounts." But duty called. A British force, nearly seven thousand infantrymen, had just landed in Newport, Rhode Island. The commander in chief wanted Arnold to go there and lead troops to defend New England.

Soon after Arnold left, Washington called a council of war to discuss a secret plan for a counterstroke. On Christmas night, he risked his entire army to cross the Delaware River and attack the Hessian troops in New Jersey. In fierce fighting at Trenton and Princeton, Washington prevailed, reviving patriot hopes and allowing the struggle for independence to go on.

Among the troops who crossed the Delaware that night were veterans who had fought under Benedict Arnold at Valcour Island.

Part Three

In Hell Before Night—1777

Benedict Arnold wounded at Saratoga

(The Miriam and Ira D. Wallach Division of Art, Prints and Photographs:
Print Collection, The New York Public Library)

≈

Dearer Than Life

O N MARCH 10, 1777, BENEDICT ARNOLD OPENED A LETTER that changed the trajectory of his life. George Washington was writing him about the promotion that Arnold felt due to him for his twenty months of nonstop effort on behalf of his country.

In January, when Arnold had stopped at New Haven to visit his family on his way to Rhode Island, he felt the full light of acclaim shining on him. Townspeople in villages along his route turned out to cheer, bands played, cannon boomed in salute, and a large crowd, including his sister, Hannah, and his three boys, along with members of his company of Foot Guards and town officials, had gathered on the New Haven Green to welcome him home. The conquering hero. Visitors poured into his big house to express their pride and affection.

Having been completely absorbed in military matters since his departure for Canada the previous September, Arnold was dazzled by the accolades. Ordinary folk celebrated his march over the Maine mountains, his valiant effort at Quebec, and the audacious stand he had taken on Lake Champlain. The stories of his achievements had inspired the patriotic populace.

During the few days he spent at home, Arnold examined his

damaged business prospects. The British blockade that accompanied the war had upended trade. Now the opportunity at sea was in privateering vessels sent out to raid British commercial shipping. He had already commissioned one such ship to hunt for prizes. He invested in several similar opportunities. But without his own hand on the tiller, his affairs were not prospering. Debts were mounting.

Arnold could not stay home long. In a matter of days he was headed toward his assignment in Providence. British soldiers and seamen under Sir Henry Clinton had taken over one of America's major ports. Washington feared that the incursion at Newport might be a prelude to an invasion of New England, which he had left undefended after he shifted the bulk of his army to New York. The assignment held a special meaning for Arnold, who remembered with pride his ancestor and namesake who had served as Rhode Island's governor.

Officially, command at Providence now rested with Connecticut officer Joseph Spencer, a former judge and militia leader. At sixty-one, a lawyer by profession, Spencer lacked the vigor the situation called for. Nevertheless, Congress had chosen to name him a Continental Army major general. Washington sensed that no one could rally militia better than the hero of Canada and of Lake Champlain. He ordered Spencer to "cooperate" with Arnold, in effect setting up a joint command.

It became clear that the main British objective in taking Newport had been to secure winter anchorage for their fleet, whose duty was to tighten the coastal blockade and suppress privateers. The patriot force in Providence was enough to discourage an enemy incursion, but lacked the strength to drive out the redcoats. The two sides settled into a waiting game.

In February, Spencer asked Arnold to go to Boston and try to hunt up enough militia battalions to begin offensive operations. On the way, General Arnold encountered Colonel John

Lamb, whom he had last seen on a snowy night under the walls of Quebec. Arnold had made a special effort to assure that those captured in the battle were freed in exchange for enemy soldiers. Although he had lost his left eye to grapeshot, Lamb had recovered from his injuries in Canada and returned to active duty following his exchange. He had organized a Continental artillery regiment with Arnold's old friend Eleazer Oswald as lieutenant colonel. The formidable Daniel Morgan, Arnold learned, was back in Virginia raising his own regiment of riflemen.

Lamb greeted Arnold warmly and explained his frustration at failing to acquire funds promised by Congress to attract recruits for his unit. Arnold immediately wrote him a draft for a thousand pounds on his own account as a loan to get the venture moving.

During his stay in Boston, Arnold made little progress in attracting additional troops for Rhode Island. The enthusiasm of the war's early days had faded among many of the citizens. With the city cleared of redcoats, men who now understood the sacrifices entailed in army duty were reluctant to enlist. Massachusetts authorities were hard pressed to muster enough men even to protect Boston.

Inspecting the waterfront, Arnold's thoughts turned again to the sea. "I should be fond of being in the navy," he wrote to Horatio Gates, "which to our disgrace is now rotting in port, when, if properly stationed, might greatly distress if not entirely ruin the enemy's army by taking their provisions ships."

As a celebrated general, Arnold was the talk of all the colonies. He could hardly keep up with the invitations to dinners and galas—every hostess in Boston wanted him at her table. He asked Paul Revere to help him acquire gold braid, a sword knot, epaulets, and "one dozen silk hose" to spiff up his dress uniform. Perhaps he was anticipating a promotion, or he may have wanted the finery in order to impress the ladies.

During his stay, the thirty-six-year-old widower managed to fall in love. Betsy DeBlois was only sixteen, the daughter of a loyalist merchant. She had remained in Boston with her mother after her father fled with the departing British Army. Arnold found her "heavenly." Undeterred by the age difference, he plunged into an avid courtship. Not wasting time, he sent her an entire trunk load of luxurious silk gowns and a flashy ring as an inducement. The gifts, which smacked more of bribery than love, seemed the act of a man with little feel for the nuances of romance. In the music of human relationships, Arnold often had trouble finding the right key.

He asked Lucy Flucker Knox, the wife of Henry Knox, to intercede for him. Lucy's loyalist family had also left the city. Until he received Betsy's answer to his suit, he wrote, he would be "under the most anxious suspense," bouncing between "glowing hopes, and chilling fears."

BY MARCH, ARNOLD was back in Providence, keeping an eye on an apparently docile enemy thirty miles down Narragansett Bay. Then Washington's letter arrived. The commander in chief began by discussing his strategic concerns about Rhode Island. He advised his aggressive subordinate not to launch an attack on the enemy "unless your Strength and Circumstances be such, that you can reasonably promise yourself a *moral certainty* of succeeding."

Only in the third paragraph did he mention, "We have lately had several promotions to the rank of major general." Given his record of service and the fact that he was the most senior of all the Continental Army's brigadier generals, Arnold assumed that the coveted rank of major general would be his. It would be a culmination of his meteoric rise through the ranks and a fit reward for his efforts during the nearly two years he had been at war.

Congress had promoted five men to major general. Arnold

was not one of them. The delegates in Philadelphia so insisted on their prerogatives that they had not consulted with Washington about the promotions—they had not even informed him. So far, the commander in chief only heard of the appointments from muddled accounts in newspapers. He wrote to Arnold that he was "at a loss whether you have had a preceding appointment, as the newspapers announce, or whether you have been omitted through some mistake."

In establishing the Continental Army, Congress had reserved for itself the authority to issue officers' commissions. From the beginning, the appointment of men to important posts, especially that of major general, had generated controversies. Too often, politics rather than military merit determined who was chosen. Men with previous military experience, with high rank in state militias, or with superior accomplishments felt slighted.

When an officer saw men of lower rank promoted over his head, he generally responded to the perceived stain on his honor by resigning. Nathanael Greene, raised early to major general, now told John Adams, "I fear your late Promotions will give great disgust to many." He cautioned Adams to strictly follow seniority. Henry Knox was of the opinion that a failure to promote Benedict Arnold "most infallibly pushes him out of the service."

Alarmed, Washington immediately wrote to his Virginia friend, the congressional delegate Richard Henry Lee, asking whether the failure to promote Arnold was "owing to accident or design."

"Surely," Washington pointed out, "a more active, a more spirited, and sensible officer, fills no department in your army." But the omission of Arnold's name from the list of major generals "has given me uneasiness." Washington assumed that Arnold would not remain in the army "under such a slight."

The slight was no accident. On February 19, Congress had promoted to major general four Continental officers of lower seniority than Arnold. Since length of service was an integral part of rank in the army, the delegates were giving "younger" subordinates the right to command their former superior. Another man, Benjamin Lincoln, received the rank without any previous service in the Continental Army—he had only been a general of state militia. None of the promoted men had anything like Arnold's record of accomplishment. They included Thomas Mifflin, a lackluster quartermaster general, and Adam Stephen, who would soon be cashiered for being drunk during a battle.

Arnold wrote back to Washington the day after receiving his letter. Of Congress, he said, "their promoting Junior Officers to the Rank of Major Generals, I view as a very Civil way of requesting my resignation, as unqualified for the Office I hold." The insult stung him to the quick. "When I entered the Service of my Country, my Character was unimpeach'd, I have sacrificed my Interest, ease, & happiness in her Cause." To do anything but resign would permanently stain his honor.

Like every man who aspired to be a gentleman, Arnold was touchy about any denigration of his character. But he was as reluctant to depart from the army, to step away from the ongoing war, as Washington was to lose him. Turning around the meaning of the word "resign," he promised not to act hastily. "Every personal injury shall be buried in my zeal for the safety and happiness of my country, in whose cause I have repeatedly fought and bled and am ready at all times to resign my life."

In a letter to Horatio Gates, Arnold was more forthright. Congress was using him for their "sport or pastime." If they continued down this road, "no gentleman who had any regard for his reputation will risk it with a body of men who seem to be governed by *whim and caprice.*" He was determined to resign from the army, he told Gates. He would not think of again drawing his sword in the cause "until my reputation, which is dearer than life, is cleared up."

In early April, he heard back from Washington, who offered a feeble explanation of the intentions of congressional delegates. They had adopted a new system for promotions, he wrote, in which seniority and merit would be weighed against a third factor: the number of troops mustered by the candidate's home state. Since Connecticut already had two major generals in Joseph Spencer and Israel Putnam, there was no room on the list for Benedict Arnold. "I confess this is a strange mode of reasoning," Washington wrote, but "it may serve to show you, that the promotion which was due to your seniority, was not overlooked for want of merit in you."

However, he continued, the fact that Arnold had been deliberately passed over "does not now admit of a doubt, and is of so delicate a nature, that I will not even undertake to advise, your own feelings must be your guide." Arnold had asked Washington for a court of inquiry to clear his name. The commander in chief told him that "as no particular charge is alleged against you," there was no basis for such an inquiry.

Arnold's sole recourse was to resign his commission. Resignation by an officer who felt he had been slighted was considered honorable and was not uncommon.

IN THE MIDDLE of April, with the situation in Rhode Island stagnant, Arnold returned on leave to his family in New Haven. He planned to make a journey to Philadelphia to argue his case with Congress.

While he was spending time with his sister and sons, news reached him from young Betsy DeBlois. It turned out she was in love with another, younger man—he was, as Arnold had been, an apothecary apprentice. She rejected Arnold's attentions. As Lucy Knox put it in a letter to her husband, "Miss De Blois has positively refused to listen to the genl, which with his other mortification will come very hard upon him."

He now found himself turned down simultaneously by a capricious teenage girl and a fickle Congress. Although Arnold was a natural optimist, the accumulated mortification induced by Congress's failure to recognize his achievement pushed him toward full-blown depression.

For a man so little given to gloomy rumination and so heartened by military action, the news that arrived on April 26, 1777, must have been strangely welcome. It indicated that the war had taken a new and alarming turn. The British had landed a substantial force of armed loyalists and regulars at Norwalk, a village thirty miles west of New Haven. The enemy had struck at his home state.

Arnold's mind lit up with excitement. Duty called. In spite of his vow not to serve, he girded on his sword and galloped toward the scene of the action.

10

✦

Devilish Fighting Fellow

WE ARE ALARMED BY 24 SHIPS OFF COMPO POINT . . . 200 OR 300 are actually landed at Compo Hill. Pray Sir, afford us your Presence & Assistance without Delay. The folded piece of paper had been placed in David Wooster's hands at New Haven on the evening of Friday, April 25, 1777. After sealing his urgent request, General Gold Silliman, militia commander in western Connecticut, had scratched on the back: *Another messenger comes from Compo & says that 1000 men are landed & that the boats are constantly coming & going.*

The message dismayed Wooster, who feared the landing might be a prelude to a British invasion of his entire state. The sixty-six-year-old officer, who two years earlier had briefly denied Benedict Arnold the keys to the New Haven powder house, was now commander of all of Connecticut's militia forces. Knowing that his illustrious neighbor was in the city on leave, he sent a message to Arnold's Water Street home.

He and Arnold set out at dawn on Saturday to hurry down the coastal road to the site of the invasion. They took with them a contingent of the city's militiamen that they had been able to muster on short notice.

While they proceeded along the muddy lane through a light rain, they had a chance to talk. Although at odds more than once during the war, they had been compatriots during the earlier time of agitation, and they could bond over their shared disgust with Congress.

There was plenty of blame to go around for the debacle in Canada, but a group of commissioners sent north in the spring of 1776 had declared to Congress: "General Wooster is in our opinion unfit, totally unfit, to Command your Army & conduct the war." Ineffective in supporting the siege at Quebec, Wooster had also imposed anti-Catholic laws, closed churches, and levied onerous taxes—actions sure to alienate the inhabitants.

The old soldier would not concede his mistakes. When denied promotion, he felt that honor required him to give over his Continental commission. His consolation was the command of his home-state militia. Arnold told Wooster that he too was fed up with fickle politicians. Like his companion, he planned to resign if he did not receive satisfaction in Philadelphia.

When they reached the coastal village of Fairfield late Saturday morning, the generals learned that the enemy's target was the Continental Army supply depot in Danbury, twenty-five miles inland. General Silliman, with a few hundred militiamen, was on the trail of nearly two thousand redcoats. Wooster and Arnold headed north. They shouted to every man they saw to take up a musket or fowling piece and join the fight. The war had come home to Connecticut.

As THE WAR entered its third year of fighting in 1777, British general William Howe, ensconced in his New York City headquarters, contemplated a number of options. He could reinforce General Clinton's regiments in Newport and hit New England. He could try to break through patriot defenses in the Hudson River Highlands north of Peekskill, New York. Or he could march his troops toward the American capital at Philadelphia.

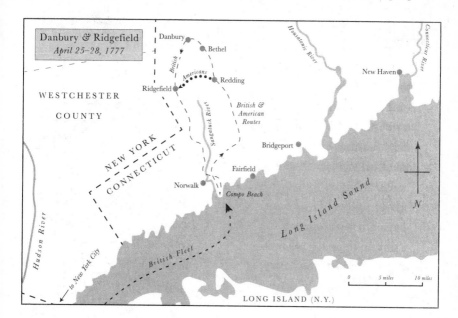

Any of these strategic moves might force George Washington into the decisive battle. Howe was sure his troops would prevail.

His prospects were brightened by the operation then being prepared in Canada. The aggressive General John Burgoyne, who had taken over command of the invasion army from Guy Carleton, was determined to crash through American defenses to reach Albany.

To meet these threats, General Washington had stationed his army at Morristown, twenty-seven miles west of New York City in central New Jersey. From there, he could send troops north to the Highlands or fall back to protect Philadelphia. He also stationed a force at Peekskill to protect the main Hudson crossing. He had called on citizen-soldiers to help defend that crucial post.

One of the militia regiments that marched to Peekskill was from Danbury. In January, General Wooster had complained to Connecticut governor Jonathan Trumbull that sending militia out of the state would "leave all the western part of Connecticut to the ravage and rapine of worse than a savage enemy." Now his prediction had come true.

The terrain grew increasingly rugged as the men proceeded north toward Danbury. The cold rain carried the lingering chill of winter, the roads were little more than sloppy winding trails. Yet as the two generals advanced, more and more volunteers, singly and in small groups, joined them.

One of the questions of 1777 was: Had the patriots' fervor for revolution played out? Recruiting for the Continental Army was yielding fewer soldiers than needed, and the 1775 enthusiasm known as the *rage militaire* was only a memory. Patriots were still eager for independence, but they had farms to tend, businesses to run. John Adams scorned the "stupid, cowardly, Toryfied country people" who refused to serve.

Western Connecticut was home to both Tories and Whigs. British authorities had faith in the idea that Americans, for the most part, rejected insurrection. Loyalists, they thought, with enough encouragement, would emerge as a majority. The king's supporters were rumored to be particularly plentiful in Connecticut.

LATE ON SATURDAY, April 26, under a sodden sky, Arnold and Wooster, with their troop of volunteers, finally caught up with General Silliman in Redding, ten miles south of Danbury. Commanding five hundred men, his force was outnumbered four to one. With rain pouring down and darkness descending, the advance could proceed no farther.

Silliman briefed Wooster and Arnold on the situation. The British had swooped in on Compo Beach, a sandy stretch at the mouth of the Saugatuck River on Long Island Sound in the town of Norwalk. Landing from two dozen ships, they spent hours shuttling men and equipment ashore under the protection of the ships' guns.

William Tryon, an army veteran now serving as royal governor of New York, commanded fifteen hundred redcoats drawn from Howe's most experienced regiments. Three hundred loyalists of the Prince of Wales' American Regiment, decked out in green coats, marched at the head of the detachment. Ten mounted dragoons accompanied them, their plumed helmets adorned with skull-and-crossbones emblems. The six brass field guns Tryon brought along were meant to terrify any rebels they encountered.

At eleven the night before, the British invaders had headed north from Norwalk. After camping along the route, they continued on Saturday morning to Bethel, just outside Danbury. They deployed into a line of battle. Most of the town's 2,500 residents had already departed, loading their belongings into all the available wagons. Only fifty Continental recruits under the command of Jedediah Huntington and about a hundred Connecticut militiamen remained. Outnumbered, Huntington chose to retreat into the hills north of town.

Arnold knew Huntington well. He had been a neighbor when both were growing up in the western Connecticut town of Norwich—they may have played together as boys. Jedediah's father, Jabez, was one of the most successful merchants in Connecticut and someone whom the Arnolds would have emulated. But while Arnold's father's business was declining in the 1750s, Jedediah's family remained prosperous—he graduated from Harvard and joined his father's trading establishment. When the Revolution broke out, both men embraced the patriot cause.

In the spring of 1777, Huntington was leading a hundred Continental recruits westward. At the urgent request of Washington, he had sent half his force rushing ahead toward Peekskill the day before the threat to the Connecticut supply depot emerged.

At first, the British encountered no resistance when they

marched through Danbury's deserted streets on Saturday afternoon. Then shots rang out from a house belonging to Captain Ezra Starr. Three men were inside, one an African American who was being held in slavery. He had been hired out to work for Captain Starr and "being a very zealous friend to the American cause," had taken a shot at the invaders. It cost him his life. All three men were shot dead. Enemy soldiers burned their bodies along with the house.

THE ABSENCE OF wagons in the town meant that the British could not confiscate the supplies in Danbury but had to destroy them. By their own calculations, they set fire to four thousand barrels of salted beef and pork. Joseph Plumb Martin, a Continental recruit from Connecticut, arrived in the town a few days later and reported that "the streets, in many places, were literally flooded by the fat" that ran out of the barrels as they burned. More than a thousand much-needed tents were destroyed, as were five thousand pairs of shoes. Smoke clogged the town as the troops put the torch to shops and storage buildings. The homes of well-known patriots were also targeted.

On Sunday morning, after a day and night of destruction, scouts brought Tryon a warning that the countrypeople were rising. He decided to take a different route on his return. His troops marched westward to avoid Bethel and Redding. Tryon planned to circle south through Ridgefield, a village a mile from the New York border.

Men had joined the patriot force from all over the region. Colonel Henry Ludington, a militia leader in Patterson, New York, had sent his sixteen-year-old daughter, Sybil, to alert the countryside the night before. She had ridden forty miles in the rain to urge her father's troops to congregate at the family farm. Although the story of her heroics did not appear in print until much later, Sybil has gone down in history as the female Paul Revere.

At Redding, the American generals decided to divide their battalion. Wooster would take two hundred men and fall in behind the retreating British to harass their rear guard. The remaining five hundred fighters, under Silliman and Arnold, would cut straight westward to try to head off the British at Ridgefield.

The enemy soldiers had marched Friday night and Saturday morning before spending all of Saturday night heaving barrels and boxes of provisions onto fires. Now, tired and apprehensive, they began their retreat. Knowing that the rebels were preparing armed resistance and that miles of hard marching separated them from the security of the ships, they cast wary eyes on the furrowed landscape.

The two forces marched toward their violent rendezvous. The British slogged southward in a long, drawn-out procession. Livestock confiscated from Danbury farmers slowed their pace. The mud-clotted road to Ridgefield made moving the cannon especially arduous. At one point, they stopped to burn a gristmill and to destroy a hundred barrels of flour.

The patriots, less encumbered, hurried forward behind Arnold and Silliman. Over their heads, Sunday morning sunshine glimmered through trees just beginning to set spring leaves. Many of the men knew little of war except for hometown drills. Now they were about to face the real thing.

DAVID WOOSTER LOOKED out for his Connecticut boys. That morning, he tried to quickly impose some order on his troops, who came from different militia regiments and included farmers who had turned out without any training at all. His main advantage was a detailed knowledge of this uneven, wooded terrain.

His small battalion caught up with the rear elements of the

British regiments about three miles north of Ridgefield. The tired companies at the end of the straggling enemy line had paused to eat a quick breakfast. This gave Wooster the chance to swoop down on them from the woods. Favored by surprise, the Americans swarmed onto the road, killed a few enemy soldiers, grabbed a dozen prisoners, and scurried back into the forest.

When General Tryon at the front of the line heard of this hit-and-run raid, he halted the brigade and ordered three of the command's six cannon to be hauled back to protect the rear. After the delay, the march continued.

Wooster shadowed the British caravan for another mile before again ordering an attack. The enemy immediately unlimbered their guns and let loose an explosive spray of canister shot. Unused to facing artillery fire, the patriots flinched. Wooster pranced his horse forward, shouting, "Come on, my boys, never mind such random shots! Follow me!"

As he charged, a ball from another blast struck the general in the groin and lodged in his spine, knocking him from his horse. The injury left him paralyzed. His men carried him away from the scene of the violence. The rest of the militia, shocked by the loss of their venerable commander and unsure of what to do next, fell into a hasty retreat. Captain Stephen Bradley, Wooster's aide-de-camp, pulled together as many of the soldiers as he could and detoured southward to join the main force preparing to meet the enemy in Ridgefield. Men carried Wooster back to Danbury. He died five days later.

WOOSTER'S ATTACKS GAVE Benedict Arnold time, as one witness reported, to make "the best disposition of his little army on an advantageous situation." When he arrived in Ridgefield, a village of 1,700 souls, he picked a narrow stretch of road on a low rise and set the men to building a barricade of wagons, logs, and heaped dirt and stone.

The town's patriots had organized the First Militia Company of Ridgefield only days earlier. The men hardly expected that they would so soon be thrown into a battle, much less that they would be commanded by one of America's most famous generals.

Arnold massed two hundred defenders on the road immediately behind the barricade. He ordered the remaining three hundred to deploy on either side of the road to defend against flank attacks. The nervous militiamen gripped their muskets with sweating palms. A bright spring breeze hummed in their ears.

Their first hint of the enemy's presence was the distant staccato of musket fire—Wooster's men engaging the enemy. Later, another burst, closer and backed by the ominous boom of cannon. Then silence. The nerves of the men at the barricade stretched to the breaking point. Soon, a faint whisper wafted on the breeze—the unmistakable rhythm of enemy drums. They came ever closer, grew ever louder. Now the waiting men could pick out the high whistling of the fifes. The pounding pattern kept repeating. Over and over. Closer and closer. Louder and louder.

Out along the road, as in a dream, country children gathered to watch the extraordinary, dangerous spectacle. They had never in their short lives seen so many men in one place. The soldiers' muskets flashed bright with sunlight. The colorful flags scolded *tut-tut-tut* in the wind. The polished brass cannon barrels shone like gold.

They noticed flanking skirmishers passing behind them, cutting through brush and orchard. Boys barely older than themselves pounded big drums. Men rode horseback in jolly red coats—piratical skulls grinned from their foreheads.

When he caught sight of the rebel deployment, Tryon ordered his troops to break out of their column and form a battle line. It took time for the six hundred men, backed by the authoritative guns, to form in front of the barricade. Two hundred would move laterally to mount the rocky ridge on the west side. Another battalion would descend into the lowland behind the house on the east.

The drums beat and beat. *Ta ta, ta ta, ta ta TUM. Ta ta TUM, ta ta TUM.*

Three o'clock. The defenders watched the precise maneuvers of the redcoats. Officers on horseback, their uniforms trimmed in glinting gold braid, shouted peremptory orders to their men. The resplendent, high-booted dragoons drew their sabers. The clank of muskets and bayonets rattled the air. The horses whinnied their protests.

The artillerymen unlimbered the cannon, wheeled them into position. The men behind the barricade focused on the round eyes of the guns' muzzles, the small black pupils staring at them impassively.

Arnold trotted his horse back and forth behind the breastworks, reassuring the men, tightening the line, barking at those who showed signs of wavering.

Time stopped. The air held its breath.

Finally, suddenly, came the knee-weakening explosions. Great balloons of smoke blossomed from the barrels. Grapeshot instantly clattered along the barricade. The concussions echoed from nearby hills. Men fell bleeding. Others bared their teeth at the naked reality around them.

An angry chorus of *Huzzah! Huzzah!* rang out from the mass of advancing troops. Commands were barked to ringing ears on both sides. A volley of musket fire. Screams. A return volley from the patriots. The frenzied scramble to reload. The British were in the open, the Americans protected. The barricade held. The redcoats advanced. Another patriot volley made them hesitate.

Men who yesterday were busy with spring plowing or with

sorting seed potatoes looked to their leader. Benedict Arnold shouted orders, steadied them with his fearless calm. Conspicuous in his blue general's uniform, he shouted encouragement, directed fire, waved defiance at the enemy.

The fight at the barricade didn't last long. General Tryon quickly saw that the defenders hunkered behind the fortification would make a frontal assault costly for his men. The British flank companies were already circling around on both sides. They began to break into the patriots' rear. When a squadron of redcoats emerged on the ledge to the left, the American line on the roadway began to come apart. Men turned, shuffled rearward. A few ran for their lives. Arnold hastily organized a retreat down Main Street.

Among those aiding him was Lieutenant Colonel Abraham Gold, a leader of the Fairfield militia. British infantrymen took aim and shot the forty-four-year-old father of seven off his horse. Gold fell dead to the ground, his sword, according to one account, stained with British blood.

Arnold remained at the breastwork until a platoon of redcoats surged forward and fired a volley from thirty feet away. His horse went down and began to kick wildly as it choked out its life. Pinned underneath, Arnold struggled to free himself. An enemy soldier advanced on him with a fixed bayonet.

The dramatists of history have supplied details for the scene that played itself out in the next seconds. A green-coated Tory by the name of Coon was said to be the man who approached Arnold at blade point. "Surrender!" he screamed. "You are my prisoner!" The prospect of taking a valuable captive sparkled in his mind. It was his last thought. In a single movement, Arnold slipped his foot from his stirrup, drew a pistol, answered, "Not yet," and shot the man dead.

The general took the time to remove the saddle from the dying horse and escaped into the brush and swamp just down the road. Bystanders who later examined his mount found nine bullet holes in the animal's hide. It was another of the "hairbreadth escapes" that General Gates had attributed to Arnold the previous autumn.

OVERWHELMED BY NUMBERS and the maneuvers of the enemy, the patriot defenders pulled back. Arnold's leadership kept the retreat from turning into a rout. He mounted a running fight down Main Street. Individual soldiers fired from houses, barns, and patches of woods. British cannon blasted three iron balls at a tavern owned by Timothy Keeler, which had served as a meeting place for patriots. One shot buried itself in an eight-by-eight-inch oak corner post—it remains there to this day.

Several of the British regiments fighting at Ridgefield had endured the disastrous expedition to Lexington and Concord two years earlier. The men vividly remembered the hectic, terrifying return march down a road lined with armed and angry farmers. Their current mission still had seventeen miles to go, the exact distance from Concord to Boston.

The patriots continued to retreat. Tryon decided to go no farther that day. The redcoats butchered and roasted some confiscated cows and stationed a strong ring of sentries before getting a few hours of sleep. Arnold spread the word for his troops to fall back on the Saugatuck River. The enemy would have to cross it in order to reach their ships. He was not done with them yet.

ACCOMPANIED BY LOCAL militiamen who knew the territory, Benedict Arnold spent the night in a village-by-village, farm-by-farm effort to recruit men with guns. For the countrypeople, a sudden visit from the hero of the march to Quebec was a startling surprise. He convinced men who might otherwise have been reluctant to take a stand.

Patriot lethargy and indifference vanished. Farmers and townspeople picked up muskets. Men in small bands set out in the dark and headed toward the rendezvous. By morning, more militia companies had arrived from New Haven. Colonel Jedediah Huntington joined Arnold at the bridge with the five hundred fresh men who had converged on Danbury. Colonel Henry Ludington arrived with the troops his daughter had helped to rouse.

As they passed over high hills in the early light, British soldiers could see the ships awaiting them along the far side of the Saugatuck. All they had to do was to cross the river, march a mile to Compo Beach, and board the waiting transports.

Benedict Arnold now commanded more than a thousand soldiers near the bridge. He was delighted to see his old friend Eleazer Oswald arrive on the scene with three 6-pounder cannon. The 2nd Continental Artillery Regiment was the unit that Arnold had helped finance earlier that spring. Just as pleasing was the sight of the stalwart, one-eyed Colonel John Lamb, the unit's commander. At the alarm, he had ridden sixty miles from his home north of New Haven.

General Tryon continued toward the coast at a deliberate pace so as not to completely exhaust his troops. They paused in Wilton, south of Ridgefield, to take some notorious rebels prisoner and loot their houses. Loyalists informed Tryon of the hostile force waiting at the bridge. They also told him of a ford farther upstream that would allow him to take his army down the east side of the Saugatuck.

He decided to send two dependable regiments of British infantrymen toward the bridge to engage Arnold's forces. The rest of the men would wade across the river and hurry south. Once they reached Compo Hill, a rise of land just north of the beach, the redcoats could set up a defensible position from which they could descend to the water, gain the protection of the ships' guns, and make good their escape.

The action opened at midday. Colonel Hugh Hughes, deputy quartermaster of the Continental Army, had, like Arnold, been home on furlough when the raid began. He volunteered his service and stayed near Arnold during the final fight. He wrote that "as soon as they were within reach of a six-pounder, [Arnold] ordered a shot to be thrown among them which halted the whole first division."

Four hundred redcoats continued to approach the Americans and pressed the defenders hard. The rest of Tryon's men splashed across the river and hurried to gain a safe position. Some broke into a jog. A few were so fatigued they fell in their tracks.

Colonel Hughes described Arnold rallying his men and noted that the general "expos'd himself, almost to a Fault, and had not the Carriage of one of the Pieces given way, and the other two expended their ammunition, we should have gain'd some Laurels."

As the fighting raged, Arnold observed that the enemy had already gained the far side of the river and were moving toward Compo Hill. He stamped his horse onto the bridge and ordered an attack. Dug in at their position, the inexperienced patriot militiamen were loath to rush out and meet the redcoats in the open field.

"Mr. Arnold endeavored to pass the Bridge," a British officer noted, "but was not followed by his men."

The fluid situation quickly shifted. The British infantrymen passed the bridge and moved up Compo Hill. The patriots rallied. The fight spread to the far side of the river, where the British set up a defensive perimeter around the hill. Established on high ground behind a stone wall, and with four of their cannon glowering over their northern flank, they were in a favorable position to fight off the rebel attack.

Colonel Lamb left the operation of the patriot guns to Oswald and gathered a force of two hundred volunteers. He organized an attack on the British guns. It was the patriots' final chance to bag the enemy before they made it to their ships.

Lamb turned to exhort his men. As he straddled the wall, a piece of grapeshot struck him in the back and passed at an angle through his left side, narrowly missing his spine. He slumped to the ground. His troops, who had followed him eagerly toward the booming guns, fell into confusion. The attack lost momentum—they quickly retreated.

Lamb lay stunned for a moment. As he regained his senses, he climbed to his feet and stumbled downhill under a hail of musket fire. The forty-two-year-old colonel would survive this second severe wound and serve for the rest of the war.

Nearby, Benedict Arnold was also trying to organize an attack on the British lines. "Here again," Colonel Hughes wrote, "the General exhibited the greatest Marks of Bravery, Coolness and Fortitude. He rode up to our Front Line, in the full Force of the Enemy's Fire."

Many of the enemy soldiers were as low on ammunition as the Americans. At this point, British officers ordered a bayonet charge. The avalanche of screaming redcoats wielding "cold steel" unnerved the American militiamen and set off a general retreat. The patriots would not challenge the enemy again that day.

Tumbling into the boats that swarmed the beach, the men of the beleaguered British brigade completed their escape without further incident. During the battle, a bullet passed through Arnold's collar and a second horse was shot from under him by a ball through the neck. Once again, his luck held and he emerged unscathed.

General Tryon felt that "having completely destroyed two principal magazines belonging to the rebels at Danbury and

Ridgefield," he had led a successful mission. The raid did deprive the Continental Army of precious supplies—soldiers would march barefoot in snow the next winter for want of shoes. But it was questionable whether the material accomplishment was worth the two hundred casualties that the British incurred, significantly more than the Americans. The operation gave the lie to the notion that loyalist sentiment was latent throughout America. Instead of energizing the Tories of Connecticut, the raid infuriated the patriots who saw their own or neighbors' houses burned and looted.

After the fight, a French diplomat expressed the view that it seemed easy for the enemy, who dominated the sea, to launch coastal raids on patriot strongpoints. George Washington disagreed. He said that rather than show the patriots' vulnerability, the battle demonstrated "the spirit of opposition prevailing among the people." His artillery chief, General Knox, noted that the short campaign gave "pleasing proof that the yeomanry of America have not lost the Lexington spirit."

WRITING AFTERWARD, ARNOLD lamented the death of General Wooster and noted that "many of the officers and men behaved well." Although he played down his own contribution, it was clear to all that his leadership had made the difference. The weekend action would alter the course of his career.

His "intrepidity" and coolness under fire, his battlefield improvisation, and his ability to steady his men in the most stressful circumstances made him an invaluable resource against the king's armed forces. A British officer declared of Arnold that "tho ignorant of a Military Education & of all Military Science, yet by great resolution and a mind full of enterprise, he became a most excellent Partisan." Nathanael Greene wrote to John Adams, noting that "the enemy gives General Arnold the character of a devilish fighting fellow."

The Danbury raid kicked off the 1777 fighting season. It would later be overshadowed by more momentous events, but at the time the battle struck all as an important opening gambit. Arnold's heroics changed the hearts of congressional delegates, and the gentlemen in Philadelphia at last promoted him to major general.

Hearing the news, Washington wrote, "General Arnold's promotion gives me much pleasure; he has certainly discovered, in every instance where he has had an opportunity, much bravery, activity and enterprize."

A week earlier, Arnold had been depressed and on the verge of resigning his commission. It turned out he had not needed to argue his case—his actions had spoken for him. His faith in the cause had been renewed.

Except for one thing—Congress had ignored his seniority and left the five men previously promoted to major general ahead of him on the ladder of command. Even as they rewarded him, the delegates were sending a message: They were in charge. Arnold would be required to accept orders from men junior to him, men like Arthur St. Clair and Benjamin Lincoln.

"But what will be done about his Rank?" Washington asked. "He will not act, most probably, under those he commanded but a few weeks ago." The air had not been cleared after all. Benedict Arnold was still far from satisfied.

II

✑

A Faithful Soldier

J OHN ADAMS WAS THE BUSIEST MAN IN PHILADELPHIA DURING
the spring of 1777. As president of Congress's Board of War
and Ordnance, he oversaw every detail of the patriots' military
effort, from buying bullets to naming Continental officers. He sat
on twenty-five other committees and participated in the debates
of the full Congress. His duties kept him at his desk eighteen
hours a day, sometimes well past midnight.

But although he was the nation's de facto secretary of war,
Adams was no soldier. He would later claim that he had read
more books on military subjects than any officer, but his understanding of war was entirely abstract. Like many congressional
delegates, he had followed the law and made his living dealing
with writs, wills, tenures, and deeds. When he was twenty-one, he
had watched British redcoats march off to war against the French,
but he chose not to join the local militia, the first in his family
line to avoid that routine service.

Nor had he ever witnessed a battle. The gruesome aftermath
of the slaughter at Lexington and Concord so rattled his "tremulous" nerves that his distress prevented him from traveling to
Philadelphia with the other Massachusetts delegates to take up
his duties in Congress.

Adams knew that he lacked the fortitude to be a warrior. Disappointment over missing out on the military life haunted him. "I longed more ardently to be a Soldier than I ever did to be a Lawyer," he claimed. He told himself that, at the age of forty-two, "I am too old, and too much worn" to serve. Washington was forty-five, Israel Putnam fifty-nine, and David Wooster, recently killed in action, had been fighting at the age of sixty-six.

Knowing little of the actual conditions under which soldiers lived and fought, Adams could not grasp how a military officer thought or operated. Yet he and his fellow delegates would supervise the war, forever peering over commanders' shoulders. Most crucially, Congress would help decide what it meant to be a soldier, and particularly an officer, in the army of a republic. The result, as Benedict Arnold was about to find out, was dangerous confusion.

On May 12, two weeks after the attack on Danbury, Arnold arrived in Morristown, New Jersey, to rejoin the army following his leave. As Washington had suspected, the failure of Congress to restore Arnold's seniority remained a bone stuck in his subordinate's craw. Now he presented his commander with a new grievance: John Brown, the Yale-educated lawyer and longtime Arnold nemesis, had recently published a handbill listing thirteen "crimes" committed by Arnold.

Brown had been peddling these accusations for some time. When he approached Philip Schuyler about the matter, the northern commander considered bringing charges against Brown himself for "violent and ill-founded Complaints." Schuyler passed the matter on to General Gates, who expressed his contempt for Brown by noting that "a man of honour in an exalted station" would "ever excite envy in the mean and undeserving."

The charges stretched back to the original friction at Ticonderoga and included Arnold's alleged libel against Brown. Arnold,

Brown claimed, had failed to quell the smallpox epidemic in Quebec and mishandled the fleet on Lake Champlain. In lawyerly language, Brown falsely asserted that Arnold had "put to death by fire and sword" all the inhabitants of villages in Canada and had "made a treasonable attempt to make his escape ... to the enemy" while serving at Ticonderoga in 1775. Brown was "ready to verify" all the accusations.

In the handbill, Brown declared of Arnold: "Money is this man's God, and to get enough of it he would sacrifice his country." Later, the course of Arnold's life gave the warning an aura of prophecy, but the claim was simply another of Brown's smears, its truth belied by the financial sacrifices that Arnold had already endured for the cause.

Arnold insisted to Washington that his name be cleared. He threatened to give Brown satisfaction, "more than he chooses," implying a trip to the dueling ground. He wanted Congress to act on this slander and on his just claim for rank in accord with his seniority. Because he faced no immediate military emergencies, Washington allowed Arnold to go on to Philadelphia to plead his case. He handed him a letter of recommendation to the delegates.

"It is universally known," Washington wrote, that Arnold had "always distinguished himself, as a judicious, brave officer, of great activity, enterprise, and perseverance."

WHILE THE CONTINENTAL Congress at times comprised as many as fifty-six delegates, only twenty showed up when the body reconvened in March 1777. With members continually coming and going, rarely did the head count surpass two dozen attendees.

Arnold found himself a celebrity in Philadelphia as he had been in Boston. Delegates were well aware of his achievements at Ticonderoga, Valcour Island, and now Ridgefield. John Adams praised "his vigilance, activity, and bravery in the late affair at Connecticut." He wrote his wife that Arnold's achievement was "sufficient to make his fortune for life," and mused that congressional delegates might strike a medal in Arnold's honor for his heroism during the raid—they never did.

Perhaps on Washington's advice, Arnold was determined to approach the matter of his rank and reputation with as much tact as he could muster. He drafted a letter to the delegates concerning Brown's slanders. Having made "every sacrifice of fortune, ease and domestic happiness to serve my country," he found himself impeached "of a catalogue of crimes, which, if true, ought to subject me to disgrace, infamy." He politely asked Congress to suggest a way by which the matter could be examined "and justice done to the innocent and injured," meaning himself.

The delegates turned the matter over to the Board of War. In the meantime, they voted to award Arnold a new horse and saddle to compensate him for his "gallant conduct" at Ridgefield. For a man who, in the course of his business, bought and sold horses by the score, the gesture must have seemed paltry.

WHILE HE WAS in Philadelphia, Arnold renewed his acquaintance with Philip Schuyler. Besides representing New York as a congressional delegate, Schuyler had traveled down in early April to be on hand for the examination of his handling of the 1776 campaign.

Like Arnold, Schuyler had his share of enemies and detractors. New Englanders in particular considered him a snobbish aristocrat and reluctant supporter of independence. They preferred the more radical Horatio Gates to lead the northern army. Gates took over the role while Schuyler was in Philadelphia. The verdict of the inquiry would determine whether or not Schuyler would return to command.

Rather than follow orders to remain at Fort Ticonderoga, Gates had moved his headquarters to Albany. He left General Arthur St. Clair to command the forces on Lake Champlain. The patriots knew that at any moment they could be confronted by the invasion that British general John Burgoyne was preparing in Canada. The appointment of St. Clair, a Pennsylvania politician before the war, annoyed Arnold, who had helped take and defend the fort. He was especially angered because St. Clair was one of the officers promoted over him in February.

Schuyler soon received good news: His lobbying skill induced five states to support him, while four voted against. Vindicated, he prepared to return to Albany and resume leadership of the northern army. Now it was Horatio Gates who faced a dilemma. The independent field command that he coveted had again slipped from his grasp. He could either subordinate himself as Schuyler's assistant or resume his former staff position as adjutant to General Washington.

John Adams convened the five-man Board of War on May 21, 1777, to take up Arnold's complaint. They met in rented rooms two blocks up Market Street from the Pennsylvania statehouse, where Congress held its full sessions. Arnold made a convincing case for himself against the charge that he had mishandled public money during the Canadian invasion. He told the members he had begged Congress for a paymaster to oversee accounts, but they had never appointed one. He had passed on the bulk of the allocated money to divisional commanders—many of whom ended up imprisoned in Quebec. An important portion of his own records had been aboard the *Royal Savage* schooner of war when she was burned by the British at Valcour Island. Rather than pocket public funds, he said, he had advanced his own money and credit to meet needed expenses.

Arnold had the backing of Charles Carroll of Maryland, who had gone to Canada with Benjamin Franklin in 1775 as part of a commission to survey the situation there. Carroll had seen firsthand the chaos that made keeping strict accounts impossible, especially as the American venture collapsed into a frantic retreat.

Richard Henry Lee, a delegate from Virginia, was not always an Arnold supporter, but the day before the hearing he wrote to Thomas Jefferson suggesting that the effort to "assassinate the Characters of the friends of America" was part of a disinformation campaign by loyalists or British agents. He mentioned "an audacious attempt of this kind against the brave General Arnold."

The Board quickly decided that the evidence had "given entire satisfaction to this Board concerning the general's character and conduct, so cruelly and groundlessly aspersed." The verdict was satisfying to Arnold—all of Brown's charges had again been repudiated. But once again, the question of restoring his seniority went unmentioned.

ARNOLD REMINDED THE delegates that they had "deprived of his rank in the army a person who since the commencement of the present war, has strenuously endeavored to act the part of a faithful soldier." To the harried representatives, he was just another disgruntled general.

From the beginning of the war, Congress had tried to hammer out a rational way of choosing officers. Radical patriots asserted that in a republic the men of a company or regiment should elect their own leaders. The idea seemed to work in the militia—it gave Arnold his initial rank as captain of the New Haven Foot Guard. But the drawbacks were obvious: Men might elect congenial rather than competent officers, and those officers might avoid imposing the harsh discipline required by war to gain favor.

During the first two years of the war, the system for naming and promoting officers was haphazard and arbitrary. Debating the need for reform in February 1777, Congress juggled three approaches. Promoting officers according to the line of seniority was a clear, sensible method, but it gave delegates little ability to reward achievement. A strict merit system would have pleased radical delegates, but it introduced arbitrary factors sure to create controversy. Determining rank according to how many troops a man's home state contributed appealed to the politicians because it established a regional equity.

In the end, Congress declared "that in voting for general officers, a due regard shall be had to the line of succession, the merit of the persons proposed, and the quota of troops raised, and to be raised, by each State." It was an ungainly compromise that threw the decisions back into the realm of prejudice and politics.

For example, John Adams said that a man's qualification for promotion should depend on his "Morals, his Honour, and his Discretion." Then again, he thought, Congress might consider his "Genius, Spirit, Reflection, Science, Literature, and Breeding." Plus, he noted, the delegates could not "appoint Gentlemen whom they don't know"—so connections, friendships, and patronage would be prerequisites.

In the minds of the officers, who lived in a world of violence tempered by honor, this was a schoolboy's, or rather, a lawyer's notion. During a wilderness march, where the lives of a thousand men depended on one man's decisions and inspiration, that man had to have special qualities. When the chaos of a violent battle pushed men toward panic, only a gifted leader could find a path to victory. Those qualities were not easy to discern, especially for someone like Adams, whose nature was so antithetical to the bloody chaos in which the skills were required. Science, literature, and breeding didn't mean much amidst cannon fire and hand-to-hand combat.

Behind the delegates' tortuous thinking on the matter was their wariness of a standing army. For the more radical members, the threat of a permanent army that might seize power from the civil authority loomed larger than battlefield losses. History offered plenty of examples of armed men usurping elected leaders. Congress, which lacked both an executive arm and the power to tax, eyed the Continental Army, the only other national entity, with suspicion. When James Duane suggested Congress promote officers in consultation with their superiors, other delegates were outraged. Congress must not cede even that amount of power to the military.

Washington, who bent over backward to defend civilian control of the military, warned that the delegates were pushing the principle too far. Patriots need consider themselves as "one people, embarked in one Cause." The continual suspicion and disregard that Congress directed at the military would backfire. "The jealousy which Congress unhappily entertain of the Army," he said, was more appropriate to a mercenary army in peacetime than to a force of citizen-soldiers in the middle of a war.

ARNOLD GAVE NO credence to the idea that officers of the Continental Army might attempt to overthrow Congress. What he knew was that the actions of the delegates were interfering with the ability of soldiers in the field to win the war. "I think it betrays want of judgment, and weakness," he wrote, "to issue or deny promotions for trivial reasons." If it kept up, no gentleman would agree to risk his reputation in the service.

Like many issues, this one was, for Arnold, personal. "Had I been content with barely doing my duty," he argued, "I might have remained at ease and in safety, and not attracted the notice of the malicious, or envious." He had instead sacrificed his fortune and his reputation for the cause. He declared that "I sensibly feel the unmerited injury my countrymen have done me."

John Adams would not bend. "I have no fears from the resignation of officers if junior officers are preferred to them," he said. "If they have virtue they will continue with us. If not, their resignation will not hurt us."

The overworked congressman had too much else to contemplate. "I am wearied to death with the wrangles between military officers, high and low," he wrote to his wife, Abigail. "They worry one another like mastiffs, scrambling for rank and pay, like apes for nuts."

By JULY, IT was clear that Congress had no intention of restoring Arnold's seniority. He lost faith in politicians. They were hollow men, ignorant of the challenges that soldiers faced, of the code that sustained a man who was called to violent action.

His sentiments contained a suspicion that the entire Revolution had been turned on its head. While he faced the British in battle, enemies were attacking him from behind. The machinations of Brown and his ilk began to seem motivated by more than envy, the whims of Congress by more than caprice, and the injustice from his countrymen by outright malice.

When Congress had superseded him by the appointment of "a number of junior officers," it had been "an implied impeachment of my character." He was not leaving the service, he wrote, "from a spirit of resentment (though my feelings are deeply wounded), but from real conviction."

He went on to declare, "Honor is a sacrifice no man ought to make." He treasured it as a birthright. "As I received, so I wish to transmit it inviolate to posterity." On July 11, he turned in his resignation as an officer in the Continental Army. In his view, his military career was over.

12

❧

Or Die in the Attempt

T HE NEWS ARRIVED AT PHILADELPHIA ON THE VERY DAY that Benedict Arnold submitted his formal resignation to Congress—Fort Ticonderoga had fallen.

During the two years since Arnold and Ethan Allen had seized the fort on Lake Champlain, Ticonderoga had stood as a symbol of protection against invasion from Canada. The defenders there had been sorely tried in 1776, but Arnold's delaying tactics and staunch resistance at Valcour Island had neutralized the threat. The bastion had gained a reputation as the "Gibraltar of the North."

The notion of an impregnable fort was a dangerous myth. Poorly placed, never completely repaired after years of neglect, inadequately manned and supplied, Ticonderoga had become a vulnerable outpost. In June 1777, General John Burgoyne set out from Canada with an army of crack British regiments and German mercenaries. They were joined by some five hundred Native American allies. More Indians would arrive later—some of them walked from the upper Great Lakes region in the west. His men came south by boat along an undefended Lake Champlain and during the first days of July wrapped the fort in a deadly embrace.

On the night of July 5, General Arthur St. Clair ordered his soldiers to abandon Ticonderoga without firing a shot. St. Clair used good judgment—his force was outnumbered and the enemy were in the process of surrounding him. By retreating, he saved his men from a hopeless situation. But the defeat cratered morale in the northern army and terrified residents of the region north of Albany.

The fall of Ticonderoga, George Washington said, was "an event of chagrin and surprise, not apprehended nor within the compass of my reasoning." Some suspected treason. General St. Clair and his superior, Philip Schuyler, were in league with the enemy. They were secret Tories. They had taken bribes. Others saw excess timidity. "I think we shall never be able to defend a post until we shoot a general," John Adams opined.

The loss disheartened patriots and gave joy to the enemy. When the news reached London, King George was reported to have burst into his wife's boudoir and announced to a naked Queen Charlotte, "I have beat them! I have beat all the Americans!"

Benedict Arnold was still in Philadelphia when the alarm sounded. On July 12, Congress received a request from General Washington. His words tart with irony, he suggested that "if General Arnold has settled his affairs, and can be spared from Philadelphia," he should be returned immediately to the northern army. "He is active, judicious, and brave, and an officer in whom the militia will repose great confidence." John Hancock passed on the compliment and told Arnold that the delegates "have directed you to repair immediately to headquarters to follow such orders as you may receive."

The clouds of bureaucratic wrangling, pettiness, and insult suddenly parted and the bright sun that was the prospect of action burst into Arnold's mind. On leaving, he took one more slap at the legislators in Philadelphia, asserting that "I shall be happy as a private citizen to render my country every service in my power." He would serve, but would not subject himself to the

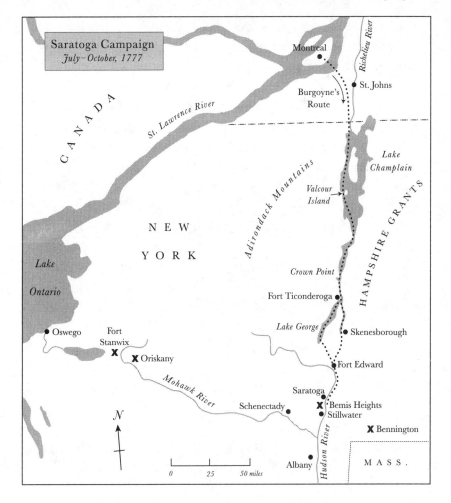

whims of Congress. The delegates ignored the comment and left his status in the army murky.

From Philadelphia, Arnold made the hard two-day ride to Washington's headquarters at Morristown. The commander asked him to waive "for the present, all disputes about rank." Arnold agreed to accept orders from General St. Clair if necessary.

Washington wrote to General Schuyler that he was sending Arnold north to help organize patriot resistance to the British juggernaut. "From his activity and disposition for enterprise I flatter myself, his presence and assistance in that quarter, will be attended with happy consequences."

Arnold finished his consultation at headquarters on the afternoon of July 18. He decided to head north immediately. Riding through the night, he covered nearly two hundred miles in four days, joining Schuyler on July 22. The beleaguered northern army was encamped at Fort Edward, the northern limit of navigation on the Hudson River halfway between Ticonderoga and Albany.

Burgoyne had chosen to bring his troops through Skenesborough and down the rugged path along Wood Creek. He shipped most of his heavy guns and supplies down Lake George, whose southern tip lay twenty-five miles by road from Schuyler's lines.

Fort Edward was a relic of the French and Indian War with only the deteriorating remnants of its fortifications. Schuyler had fewer than four thousand Continental soldiers to defend the post, including those who had escaped from Ticonderoga. His artillery consisted of two field pieces.

Burgoyne, on the other hand, commanded seven regiments of redcoats, backed by five battalions of German mercenaries, a total of nearly seven thousand men. In addition, he had two thousand Canadians and loyalists and at least a thousand Indians to serve as scouts and skirmishers. Even more ominously for the patriots, the British were hauling an artillery train of 138 heavy cannon.

Schuyler's only option was to retreat. He sent a thousand men to cut trees and reroute streams in order to obstruct the British Army's path along Wood Creek. The work of these woodsmen slowed the enemy advance, but the redcoats came relentlessly on.

The day after Arnold arrived, Schuyler moved his main force seven miles down the Hudson River from Fort Edward. He put Arnold in command of the army's left wing, leading two Massachusetts brigades. He was to occupy the territory between the two armies, convey intelligence of the enemy's movements, and check any sudden British advance.

The duty was not pleasant. Burgoyne's forces were intent on what the Baron von Riedesel, the commander of his German allies, called a "march of annihilation." A screen of Indians, rangers, and light infantrymen spread out through the thick woods far ahead of the main force in order to harass and terrorize both enemy soldiers and civilians. Patriots kept hearing "the cursed war hoop which makes the woods ring for miles," one officer wrote. "Our army at this post is weak and shattered, much confused, and the numbers by no means equal to the enemy."

The Indians were practiced at stimulating terror with eerie cries as well as by torturing prisoners and mutilating corpses. One patriot was found dead with the soles of his feet sliced open; another corpse was dismembered and festooned on a tree.

Arnold reported that one of his patrols had been taken, with five men killed and scalped. Two days later, the corpses of two officers were found closer to Fort Edward, also scalped. In a letter to George Washington, Arnold noted that "we are daily insulted by the Indians." He expressed his wish that "Colo. Morgan's rgt would be spared to this department." The Virginia backwoodsman's men, he felt, would be able to counter the skulking tactics of native warriors.

Four days later, Arnold reported that "our picket at Ft. Edward, where we have one hundred men advanced, was attacked by a large party of Indians and regulars." Five privates and a lieutenant were killed. Indians took two women prisoner from a "house near the fort" and carried them back to the regulars' camp. There, Arnold noted, "they were shot, scalped, stripped, & butchered in the most shocking manner, one of them, a young lady of family, who has a brother, an officer in the regular service."

This was the initial word of what would become one of the most notorious incidents in the campaign. Conflicting accounts were offered at the time, and more accumulated as the story mutated into legend.

It became clear that one woman, Mrs. Sarah McNeil, had been captured and carried to Burgoyne's camp alive. A cousin of British general Simon Fraser, she loudly complained of her treatment and demanded that vengeance be inflicted on her captors.

The other victim, Jane McCrea, was killed and scalped along the way. The atrocity was personal to Arnold. Less than a year ago, he had spent time with Stephen McCrea, brother of the victim. He had recruited the twenty-one-year-old to serve as surgeon on his Lake Champlain fleet. Stephen and his sister, who was twenty-five, were the children of a New Jersey minister. They had moved to Fort Edward after their father died. An older brother, John, lived in the area and had, like Stephen, taken the patriot side. Jane, perhaps because of her attachment to David Jones, a loyalist who had also moved north from New Jersey, had remained faithful to the crown. She was engaged to be married to Jones, who was now in a provincial corps marching with General Burgoyne.

The sketchy facts of the McCrea affair were lost in what would become a macabre web of myth. Jane was noted for her long, fair hair. The night of the murder, an Indian fighter danced around the fire in camp flaunting her easily recognizable tresses. Called to account, he claimed that pursuing patriot militiamen had accidentally shot the woman, killing her. Other stories held that two Indians fought over the valuable prisoner and that one slew her in anger.

The murder appalled British and German officers, but Burgoyne could not afford to punish the possessor of the scalp for fear of alienating his valuable force of native warriors. General Horatio Gates would later label the incident one that "will forever stain the Honour of the British Arms." He featured the atrocity in a propaganda campaign aimed at encouraging New York and New England militia to join the northern army.

SCRAMBLING WITH LIMITED resources to stop Burgoyne's legions, Philip Schuyler and Benedict Arnold were suddenly presented with a new threat. British general Barry St. Leger was leading an army from the west toward Schuyler's flank. If he could not be stopped, his force would serve as the anvil to Burgoyne's hammer.

Two paths, both mostly waterways, gave access from Canada to the colonies to the south. The Champlain-Hudson corridor was the front door. The back door passed from Lake Ontario along streams and lakes to the Mohawk River, which flowed into the Hudson just north of Albany. St. Leger had started down this route in late June with three hundred redcoats, more than six hundred loyalist volunteers, and a thousand Indians.

The only significant obstacle to his advance was Fort Stanwix, another post dating from the French and Indian War, which guarded the portage that separated the western streams from the Mohawk River. St. Leger had assumed this wilderness fort to be crumbling and undermanned, but Schuyler had stationed the 3rd New York Regiment of Continentals there under the leadership of Colonel Peter Gansevoort. The troops had rebuilt the compact but sturdy bastion and renamed it for Schuyler. The limited battery of cannon that St. Leger's men were hauling through the wilderness would have little effect on the earth-and-log structure.

The twenty-seven-year-old Gansevoort, son of a prominent Albany brewer, received a message from his younger brother stating that he was sure Peter would "not be a disgrace to New York arms" and relaying their father's sentiment that Peter would "conquer or die."

On August 2, St. Leger surrounded Fort Stanwix and began

his siege. The fort's seven-hundred-man garrison faced an enemy more than twice as numerous. To keep up spirits inside, American soldiers gathered scraps of cloth to create the arrangement of stars and stripes that Congress had recently approved as the national emblem. "The flag was sufficiently large and a general exhilaration of spirits appeared on beholding it wave," noted Colonel Marinus Willett, the fort's second-in-command. It was the first display of the American flag in battle.

GENERAL ST. LEGER had been optimistic that the substantial population of active loyalists in the Mohawk Valley would soon swell his ranks. But these hopes were dimmed by an incident during his approach to Fort Stanwix. A small band of Indian scouts crept near the fort and hid in the brush as four armed patriot soldiers marched past. A few minutes later, they surprised three teenage girls picking berries barely two hundred yards from the bastion's walls. The assailants killed and scalped two of them, while the third ran for her life. She escaped with two musket balls through her shoulder.

News of the butchery had a powerful effect on the tightly knit patriot community along the Mohawk. Combined with the threat of St. Leger's invasion, it spurred men, day by day, to take up their firearms and report to their town militia units. Their anger and thirst for revenge would contribute to one of the bloodiest incidents of the entire war.

TO THE EAST, Burgoyne's army had reached Fort Edward. To advance farther, he needed to accumulate provisions. In addition to throwing up obstacles, Schuyler's troops had been conducting a scorched-earth campaign as they fell back, taking with them or destroying as much grain, livestock, and animal forage as they could. Their efforts created a challenge for Burgoyne, who had to rely on a lengthening and ever more vulnerable supply line that stretched back to Canada. He needed to feed his seven thousand men, along with a contingent of camp followers. He also required forage for the hundreds of horses and oxen required to pull baggage wagons and cannon through enemy territory.

To be on the safe side, Burgoyne decided he would amass thirty days of supplies before making his thrust for Albany. That important town was only forty-five miles away and his army could have reached it in three days of hard marching. But to do so meant crossing the river and fighting their way past the rebel army. The experienced British commander was reluctant to break away from his tenuous supply line without sufficient provisions to maintain his army if anything went wrong.

His sluggish pace had little to do with patriot opposition. By late July, General Schuyler had moved his own army over to the west side of the Hudson and retreated as far as the village of Saratoga. Although this was the site of his extensive country estate, he barely hesitated there before giving up more territory and withdrawing southward another twelve miles to Stillwater. By the middle of August, he had fallen back even farther, taking a stand at the juncture of the Mohawk and Hudson Rivers, a place called Van Schaick's Island. Albany was now only ten miles to his rear.

IN THE FIRST days of August, a piece of intelligence came to Burgoyne's headquarters that promised at least a partial solution to his supply problems. At the town of Bennington, thirty-five miles to the southeast, the rebels were building a large supply depot. The food, forage, and livestock seemed ripe for the taking. Burgoyne dispatched Brunswick colonel Friedrich Baum with seven hundred men to march toward the town.

Baum needed to move swiftly and quietly through the countryside and mount his attack before the rebels could gather a force of defenders. Instead, he trudged along, announcing his presence with blaring band music. He allowed his Indian allies to raid surrounding farms, raising further alarm and anger among local residents.

Unknown to Baum, Bennington was already well defended by a large force of New Hampshire militiamen. Their commander, John Stark, had distinguished himself at Bunker Hill and had fought in the critical battles at Trenton and Princeton. Like Benedict Arnold, he had been stung when Congress failed to promote him to brigadier general. They preferred another man from his state, although Stark's rank and achievements should have given him preference.

"I am apprehensive that your Promotion will cause Colo. Stark to resign," George Washington had written to Congress. He was right. Stark declared, "I am bound on Honour to leave the service." He told a colleague, "An officer who would not maintain his rank, was unworthy to serve his country." He resigned, went home, and later agreed to return to duty only to lead his state's militia forces.

Coincidentally, General Stark and 1,500 of his militiamen had just taken post in Bennington. On the steamy morning of August 16, they went out to confront Baum's detachment. The result was a startling patriot victory. Instead of gaining supplies, Burgoyne lost two hundred men killed, Baum included. Rebels took hundreds of enemy soldiers prisoner and captured their equipment, including several cannon.

The defeat had the effect of discouraging Burgoyne's native allies, especially the western Indians. About three-fourths of them soon departed, leaving the British with few experienced scouts to screen their advance.

Although Burgoyne asserted, "I do not yet despond," the battle at Bennington was a costly blow. "The great bulk of the country is undoubtedly with Congress, in principle and zeal," he admitted to authorities in London. "The Hampshire Grants in particular . . . abounds in the most active and rebellious race on the continent, and hangs like a gathering storm on my left."

TEN DAYS BEFORE the conflagration at Bennington, St. Leger's campaign in the west exploded in even deadlier violence. Stirred by the threat to Fort Stanwix and the murder of the two girls there, Mohawk Valley militiamen prepared to march to relieve the fort's garrison. General Nicholas Herkimer, one of the valley's richest men, gathered nearly a thousand soldiers. He set out on August 4 to cover the thirty miles along the river to Fort Stanwix. By the next night his men were camped near the Oneida Indian village of Oriskany, ten miles from the besieged fort. Their numbers included a contingent of the Oneida, the only Iroquois tribe to side with the patriots.

Against his better judgment, Herkimer was persuaded to push the column forward on the morning of August 6 rather than wait to establish communications with the fort. The men spread out in a line more than a mile long as they slogged through the oppressive heat. Although sweating profusely and tormented by swarms of mosquitos and biting flies, the citizen-soldiers were excited by the prospect of what they were sure would be a victorious action once they reached the fort.

About ten o'clock, the forward units crossed a corduroy road through a swampy ravine. As they emerged onto higher ground, the quiet morning erupted into an explosion of gunshots and otherworldly screams. A force of loyalists attacked the front of the column. Indian fighters, who had hidden themselves in brush and leaves, appeared with a suddenness that seemed almost magical. Glistening with red, black, and yellow war paint, they rushed in from all sides. Bullets whistled through the steamy air.

Early in the melee, a ball shattered General Herkimer's leg bone and brought his horse down on top of him. Two men dragged him from under the dying animal and got him to a roadside tree. Smoking his pipe, he calmly issued orders amid the chaos. The Americans, mostly farmers, found themselves caught up in one of the most vicious battles of the war.

The fighting continued for four grueling hours, interrupted only when the sky darkened and a deluge of rain poured down on the combatants. Finally, the enemy withdrew and the patriot force was left to claim the field of battle. It was no victory—almost four hundred patriot militiamen lay dead.

The fight erased a good part of an entire generation of young men from the Mohawk Valley. Those left behind would mourn long into the future—the Oneidas would refer to the battlefield as a "Place of Sorrows."

WITH BURGOYNE MASSING for a drive against the outnumbered patriots and the garrison at Fort Stanwix still under siege, delegates in Philadelphia were determined that someone should take the blame for the loss of Fort Ticonderoga. Philip Schuyler, so recently exonerated for the 1776 campaign, became the lightning rod for their accusations.

Congress told George Washington that, "in our opinion," he should replace Schuyler with Horatio Gates. Washington, who was marching his army to Pennsylvania to be in a position to counter an attack by General Howe, asked to be excused from issuing the order. On August 4, the delegates made the switch themselves. John Adams was overjoyed, sure that Gates would "restore our affairs in that department."

So inept was the delegates' handling of the affair that if Schuyler had followed congressional orders, he would have left the army leaderless—Gates had yet to appear to relieve him. Feeling he had a duty to remain, the general continued to work feverishly to coordinate the patriots' defenses.

During the past two years, Benedict Arnold had developed a close relationship with the courtly Schuyler. He wrote to Washington asserting that Schuyler had "done everything a man could do in his situation. I am sorry to hear his character has been so unjustly aspersed and calumniated."

THE DEVASTATION VISITED on Herkimer's relief column threw the survival of the garrison at Fort Stanwix into doubt. Provisions were dwindling. The enemy kept up a steady bombardment. Although their cannon had yet to breach the walls, the firing was unnerving to those inside. Sharpshooters drawn from the Tory and Indian forces picked off careless sentries.

The one encouraging event for the patriots happened during Herkimer's battle. While the fighting raged, a force of Continentals had sallied from the fort and sacked the camp of the Indians, looting and destroying all they could. In the process the patriots found the scalps of the two teenage girls who had been murdered as the siege began, one with the hair still in a braid. The raid infuriated the Indians, who were already discontent with St. Leger's leadership.

The possibility that Stanwix, like Ticonderoga, would fall haunted Philip Schuyler. Still in charge until Gates arrived, he was determined to reinforce the garrison and save the Mohawk Valley, with its rich farmland, from falling into enemy hands.

His officers were far more concerned with the threat from Burgoyne's soldiers. The patriots felt that dividing their outnumbered army at this point would be suicidal. Some suggested that a weakening of their position was just what Schuyler, a secret loyalist, had in mind.

Schuyler called a council of war on August 13, a week after the carnage at Oriskany. He announced he was sending a detachment of Continentals on the one-hundred-mile march to Stanwix. Benedict Arnold volunteered to lead the expedition.

"It gives me great satisfaction," Schuyler wrote to Arnold, "that you have offered to go and conduct the military operations in Tryon county."

The next day, Arnold left with eight hundred Continental infantrymen, all volunteers. Along the way, he met Marinus Willett. Colonel Gansevoort had sent his second-in-command out of Stanwix to plead with Schuyler for relief. Willett and another soldier had evaded sentries, crept through the enemy camp, and carried the word down the valley.

At the fort, loyalist officers sent out a proclamation warning that even a delay in surrendering would enrage the Indians and that they would "put every soul to death, not only the garrison, but the whole country, without any regard to age, sex, or friends." In response, Gansevoort ordered that all troops report to their alarm posts at two A.M. to guard against a possible night attack.

Arnold used his celebrity status at each small town along the valley to urge the local militiamen to join him. After the catastrophe that had engulfed the first attempt, few were willing to shoulder arms. He stopped briefly at Herkimer's farm to pay his respects to the wounded militia general. He left his own surgeon behind to treat him, but Herkimer died the following day.

On August 17, Arnold and his brigade were at Fort Dayton, thirty miles east of Stanwix. He had fewer than 1,000 soldiers to face the 1,700 redcoats and Indians besieging the outpost. To relieve the garrison, his force would have to march along the same route as Herkimer's.

On August 20, Arnold issued his own proclamation accusing "a certain Barry St. Leger . . . at the Head of a Banditti of Robbers, Murderers, and Traitors" of committing "atrocious Crimes." He offered to pardon any loyalists who would lay down their arms and swear allegiance to the United States.

The next day, his officers expressed their qualms in a council of war. Oneida Indians had told them the British invading force was twice as numerous as the patriot battalion. Arnold sent back to headquarters asking for more troops and decided "not to hazard our little army" until they arrived.

Instead, Arnold arranged for a stratagem. St. Leger had sent loyalist leader Walter Butler and a small group of soldiers down the valley. Butler spoke at a local tavern, urging loyal residents to join St. Leger's force. Word of the meeting reached Fort Dayton, and Arnold dispatched a force of Continentals to arrest the men.

The group included a young man named Hon Yost Schuyler, a Tory militiaman who lived in the area and may have been a distant relative of Philip Schuyler. He was sentenced to be punished with a hundred lashes, but a rumor circulated that he would be hanged. His mother and brother, who lived nearby, pleaded with Arnold to spare him.

Arnold decided to send Hon Yost to Fort Stanwix with false information. Hon Yost had married an Oneida woman and spoke two native dialects. He was well known to many of St. Leger's Indians. He agreed to the ruse. His brother would be held hostage until he accomplished it. For good measure, several bullets were fired through his coat to make it seem he had narrowly escaped the rebels. The young man set out, accompanied by two Oneida Indians who would back his story.

Growing ever more impatient, Arnold received word that St. Leger's guns were approaching the fort's wall. Continual firing could now open a breach. In spite of the reluctance of his officers, he was "determined, at all events, to hazard a battle rather than suffer the Garrison to fall." He rallied his men and they set off on a forced march to Stanwix. He wrote to General Gates: "You will hear of my being Victorious or no more."

On the march, they had to pass the scene of Herkimer's battle.

The heat had bloated and burst the bodies of the patriot dead. The stench made men grimace and gag.

For St. Leger, events took a sudden turn on August 21. That day, he heard of the earlier disaster at Bennington. Then, he found that two hundred of his Indian allies had already headed home. The rest threatened to desert unless he immediately began a retreat.

At this critical moment, Hon Yost came into the British camp with a tale of an approaching army of more than three thousand led by the patriots' most notorious general, Benedict Arnold. Seeing his situation crumbling, St. Leger had little choice but to retreat. The Indians, now disgusted by the entire campaign, "seized upon officers' liquor and clothes . . . and became more formidable than the enemy."

The next day, the British expeditionary force left their camp-fires burning and fled. Colonel Gansevoort marveled at the turn of events when scouts reported that "St. Leger with his army was retreating, with the utmost precipitation."

At the fort, twelve defenders had been killed, twenty-three wounded. The wife of soldier Dennis McCarthy had endured the ordeal while in the last weeks of her pregnancy. During the final British bombardment, a shell fragment had struck Mrs. McCarthy in the hip, gouging "a piece of flesh as large as a Man's fist." In spite of her injury, the night the enemy departed she gave birth to a healthy girl, known as the "siege baby."

The men of the garrison saluted Arnold's relief force with cheers and musket blasts as they marched into Fort Stanwix. Arnold quickly rushed forward to attack St. Leger's retreating battalion, but caught up with the enemy only as they had already begun rowing their boats back to Canada. The threat to Fort Stanwix was over.

NOW IT WAS Benedict Arnold's turn to endure the judgment of the politicians in Philadelphia. The delegates took up an amend-

ment that justified restoring his seniority in the military hierarchy "on account of his extraordinary merit and former rank in
the army." After a long and contentious debate, sixteen delegates,
including John Adams, opposed the measure. Only six voted in
favor.

James Lovell, a Massachusetts schoolteacher before being
elected to Congress, asserted that "it was really a question between monarchical and republican principles." Congress would
not be dictated to by the military men who thought Arnold worthy of the honor. General Arnold, he said, was "at liberty to
quit" if he didn't like the decision.

South Carolina delegate Henry Laurens, on the other hand,
declared the decision pure politics. He found the delegates' reasoning "disgusting." Congress had denied Arnold his deserved
rank "not because he was deficient in merit . . . but because he
asked for it." What was at stake was not any deep republican principle, simply the delegates' notion of "the honor of Congress."
The ill-considered action would probably deprive the nation of
Arnold's services "and may be attended by further ill effects in
the army."

Although angered and disappointed, Arnold nevertheless
decided to delay putting his resignation back into effect. With
Burgoyne's army bearing down on the patriot forces, the prospect
of action was too pressing for him to walk away. He wrote to
Horatio Gates that no action by Congress, "no public or private
injury, or insult, shall prevail on me to forsake the cause of my injured and oppressed country, until I see peace and liberty restored
her, or die in the attempt."

HORATIO GATES HAD spent a leisurely two weeks traveling to Van
Schaick's Island to take over the northern army—Arnold had
made a similar journey in three days. After joining his command

on August 19, Gates called a council of war with his officers, notably excluding General Schuyler, who had been standing in opposition to the British invasion for more than a month and who possessed extensive knowledge of the terrain and situation.

The day before, Daniel Morgan and his regiment of Virginia riflemen had marched into camp. Although reluctant to part with one of his best fighters, George Washington had sent him to stiffen the resistance to Burgoyne's onslaught. Militiamen from across the northeast had begun to join the Continentals even before Gates took over. Now they arrived in even larger numbers.

On September 7, having retreated continuously for two months, the northern army made its first movement toward the enemy. Gates led them the fifteen miles back to Stillwater. After surveying the nearby territory with Arnold and engineer Thaddeus Kosciuszko, the commander determined that the three-hundred-foot-high tablelands to the west of the river would be the best place to confront the enemy. The ravine-scarred plateau was known as Bemis Heights, after a tavern on the River Road below owned by loyalist Jotham Bemis.

"Our people are in high spirits, and wish for action," Arnold wrote to his old artillery colonel John Lamb. "I heartily wish your regiment with us, as a few days, in all probability, will determine the fate of Gen. Burgoyne's army, or that of ours."

13

⁂

Freeman's Farm

T HE GROUND WAS "IN VERY IMPERFECT CULTIVATION, THE surface broken and obstructed with stumps and fallen timber." The meager farm had been carved from rugged hill country in the hinterlands of New York State. In the late summer of 1777, two armies would clash on this plot of land in a fight that a participant called "one of the Greatest Battles that ever was fought in America."

The farm on Bemis Heights was the product of years of hard labor by John Freeman and his family. They cut timber, girdled trees to bring light to the ground, plowed through roots, opened grazing areas, erected rail fences. They built a log home, a barn, a few sheds.

The plot represented something distinctively American. Unlike crofters and peasants in Europe, Freeman was not working land passed down through generations. He had confronted a wilderness and mastered it.

Freeman had lately relinquished the lease to another farmer, but the parcel was still known as Freeman's Farm. Stands of brush-clogged pine, chestnut, and maple separated it from the nearby hardscrabble holdings. Freeman and his son, both loyal to the crown, had joined the British invasion army now bearing down on their former home.

[182]   GOD SAVE BENEDICT ARNOLD

On September 13, 1777, that army under General John Burgoyne crossed over a floating bridge of boats spanning the Hudson. It took two days to get the troops, provisions, baggage, artillery, and procession of camp followers to the west side of the river. The troops flashed bayonets and marched in step to bright band music. An observer wrote that it was a spectacle, "reminding one of a grand parade in the midst of peace."

Soldiers took the bridge apart. They loaded supplies onto bateaux and rafts to float down the river parallel to the line of march. The move severed the army's communication with Canada and committed Burgoyne to reach Albany by the road that ran along the narrow plain bordering the Hudson River.

First, they would have to defeat the rebel army arrayed in front of them. Burgoyne "burned with impatience to advance on the enemy." He still commanded a lethal force of nearly seven thousand professional soldiers. If the rebel army, which had continually retreated before him, were to take a stand, his disciplined regiments would surely defeat them.

After crossing, the British soldiers were relieved to encounter terrain that included open fields and dwellings rather than the endless forest and underbrush they had been marching through for two months. They set up camp at Philip Schuyler's large estate near the village of Saratoga. Burgoyne made Schuyler's mansion his headquarters. He ate off Schuyler's china while soldiers harvested Schuyler's grain and ground it in Schuyler's mill. By the time the army marched on, the place had been "reduced to a scene of distress and poverty" by the invaders.

As they proceeded south along the river, the redcoats crossed a succession of streams that flowed down from the high ground to the west. Patriots had destroyed the bridges, so British workmen had to repair each span to allow passage for horses, wagons, and guns. The work slowed the advance to only a few miles a day.

The army reached the Swords farm, five miles south of Saratoga, on September 17. Thomas Swords was an Irish immigrant who had recently spent eight months in a patriot prison for his loyalist sentiments. American deserters gave Burgoyne a sketchy picture of Gates's army, which was entrenched on high ground four miles to the south. Near Bemis Tavern, the Americans had gouged a deep ditch across the River Road and backed it with a breastwork. A battery of artillery guarded the position; a swamp west of the road protected the barrier's flank; and cannon on the heights could rake the road at will.

Burgoyne ordered General Simon Fraser, a Scottish native with two decades' military experience, to deploy on the British right. Fraser's advance guard of 2,500 light infantrymen and grenadiers formed the hard spearpoint of the army. General James Hamilton, another Scot, would command the center with four regiments of foot soldiers totaling 1,600 more fighters. General Friedrich Riedesel's 3,000-man force of German mercenaries, accompanied by the heavy guns, would advance along the river. The artillery was under the direction of British general William Phillips, a gunnery expert who was also second-in-command to Burgoyne.

The British soldiers had marched through miles of rugged country since leaving Skenesborough in July. Their uniforms were ragged, their provisions were dwindling, yet their mood was buoyant. Earlier in the campaign, Burgoyne had stated in a general order, "This Army must not Retreat." The British soldiers had come all this way to fight, and they sensed that a fight was near. They were certain they could sweep aside the enemy. They could taste victory.

AMERICAN RANGERS WERE taking the pulse of the enemy. Benedict Arnold had been sending men from Morgan's rifle regiment to roam the highlands, slip through the woods, and chart the primitive roads and trails. They slept in the open and learned the complex layout of hollows and ravines. Burgoyne stationed pickets, lines of armed observers, to detect and deter an enemy approach, but he now lacked the screen of Indians who could have given him more detailed intelligence.

Commanding the patriot left wing, Arnold was always eager for information about the enemy. He went out with Morgan to make contact with enemy troops and grab prisoners. He sent a contingent from his division to the east side of the river—patriots had built their own bridge of boats just south of Bemis Tavern. Arnold's men crossed over and took a position on high ground opposite the Swords farm where they could observe the enemy's daily activity.

The brilliant volunteer Thaddeus Kosciuszko continued to direct the troops and laborers who were fortifying the American camp on Bemis Heights. General Gates later said "the great tacticians of the campaign were hills and forests, which a young Polish engineer was skillful enough to select for my encampment."

On three sides of the half-mile-long camp, Kosciuszko ordered breastworks of dirt, logs, and fence rails constructed. They would be fronted by abatis—tangles of cut trees with sharpened limbs pointing outward. Ravines in front and behind the position offered further protection.

Inside the camp an orderly array of tents sheltered the American soldiers. Several farmhouses served as headquarters for top officers. Arnold's forces on the left or west side were the strongest. Morgan's riflemen and regiment of light infantry led by Colonel Henry Dearborn, who had followed Arnold over the Maine mountains, a thousand men in total, gave him a mobile strike force. The muscle of his division came from two infled of 1,200 men each led by Generals Enoch Poor and Ebenezer Learned. Gates personally commanded the three additional brigades, led by Generals John Glover, John Nixon, and John Paterson, which guarded the River Road. General Benjamin Lincoln led a militia force on the east side of the Hudson. Including militia support, Gates's force totaled nearly nine thousand fighters.

THE FIFTY-YEAR-OLD GATES was an affable man, fond of jokes that went "beyond the nice limits of dignity." When angered, he could swear in a way that made "a New Englandman's hair almost stand on end." By temperament, he was conservative and calculating. As he led his first independent command, his watchwords were discipline, order, and preparation. He favored a defensive stance over a rash attack on the enemy.

A veteran of the British Army, Gates had great respect for the murderous efficiency of redcoat regiments. He knew his troops could not match the enemy in training and discipline. He counted on his extensive barricades to give his men confidence. He knew that Burgoyne could not advance his army, with its baggage and artillery, except along the River Road. Blocking that route became his first priority. He also knew that every delay would erode Burgoyne's provisions and narrow his options. Gates was content to wait.

Benedict Arnold was fourteen years younger than his commander, his personality and way of thinking far more aggressive. While he was not reckless, taking the battle to the enemy was always his first inclination. He had done so in his capture of Ticonderoga and his attack on Quebec. He had boldly challenged the Royal Navy at Valcour Island.

In the current situation, he saw an advantage to hitting the British before they could reach a position in front of the American camp. The enemy, with their heavy guns, could besiege the patriot army if they were allowed to approach the unfinished fortifications. If they breached the American breastworks, they might spark a panic. He also saw the danger of a flanking move to the west by the powerful enemy right wing. Go out to meet them, Arnold argued, where trees and brush favored the open formations of Morgan's riflemen. If his troops had to retreat, they could still fall back behind the fortifications for protection.

On September 15, General Gates had written a letter to Congress, declaring that he intended to "defend the main Chance; to attack only by detail; and when a precious advantage offers." He noted that Burgoyne's own attack, if it was coming, was only "a few days, perhaps a few hours" away.

The next morning, Gates raised an alarm at three A.M., calling out his men to stand with arms ready until after daylight. Two days later, on the eighteenth, he again roused the army before dawn. This time he ordered the soldiers to strike their tents and pack them in wagons, a standard maneuver in the face of battle. If Burgoyne launched his attack that day, the army would be ready to move forward or to retreat, depending on the outcome of the fight.

That night, Gates doubled the rum ration for his stressed troops. As they sought sleep under a star-spangled sky, their minds rehearsed the battle all knew was imminent.

A COLD, CLEAR morning broke on September 19—harvest weather. The American troops were up before dawn, fingering icy musket barrels in the dark, waiting. The whispering daylight revealed blankets of fog nestled in the river valley. Utter stillness.

Soon after the sun began to sparkle through the chill forest, the prickly crackle of musket fire broke out along the river. Officers and troops on Bemis Heights came alert. The enemy was on the move, pushing back American pickets.

As Gates had suspected, the British were mounting their attack along the all-important River Road. Hessian rangers had slipped south to probe the American position near Bemis Tavern. Some had climbed onto the higher terrain where they had a view of the American defenses. Burgoyne had set his invasion army in motion.

Gates sent three hundred Continental soldiers from John Nixon's brigade scrambling eastward down the slope. They were able to kill thirteen enemy soldiers and take thirty-five prisoners. The German attackers pulled back, regrouped, and tried another advance. The Massachusetts men repelled them again.

The shooting died down. But from the east side of the Hudson came reports that all the troops in the British camp had struck their tents and were preparing to move. A substantial part of the army was marching up the Great Ravine, a deep hollow that lay between the two armies. From there, they could turn left and advance on the American camp. Men from Morgan's unit reported that British rangers and pickets were stalking through the woods to the west.

About eight in the morning, General Gates told Arnold to put Morgan's troops on alert. The riflemen were to watch for an enemy advance and, if it came, to "hang on their front and flanks, to retard their march, and cripple them as much as possible."

While the German soldiers made their push beside the river, the remainder of Burgoyne's troops had gained the heights and were advancing in two additional columns. On the right was the large advance corps led by General Fraser. Moving through the woods and broken farmland in the center came the four infantry regiments under the command of General Hamilton. Gates, now suspecting the action along the River Road was a feint, waited.

At ten o'clock, American officers heard the distant thunder of cannon fire, perhaps a signal to coordinate the various British units. The attack was gathering momentum. Benedict Arnold told Gates that it was "my opinion that we ought to march out

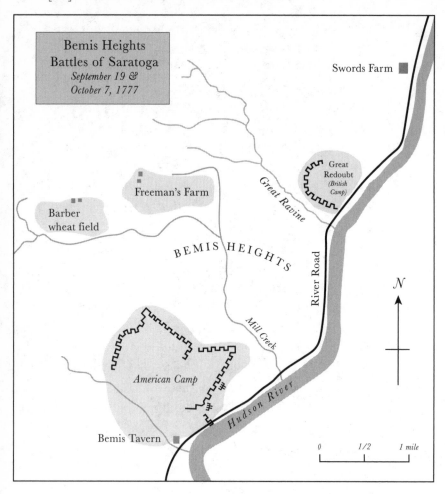

Bemis Heights
Battles of Saratoga
September 19 &
October 7, 1777

Swords Farm

Great Redoubt *(British Camp)*

Freeman's Farm

Great Ravine

Barber wheat field

BEMIS HEIGHTS

River Road

N

Mill Creek

American Camp

Hudson River

Bemis Tavern

0   1/2   1 mile

and attack them." Gates partly agreed. He told Arnold to have Morgan seek out the enemy, "observe their direction, and harass their advance," but avoid an all-out battle.

Morgan's men trotted north along a farm lane through the forest. The mostly wooded, scrub-laden uplands complicated the movement of large bodies of men. Muddy wagon tracks or forest footpaths offered the only passages. Troops had to march in narrow, stretched-out columns and could easily become disorganized.

In less than half an hour, Morgan's riflemen reached the edge of the open ground at Freeman's Farm, which would likely lie in the path of the British advance. The plot, barely a quarter mile east to west and two hundred yards deep, comprised about fifteen acres. The fields, some cultivated, some pasture, were now abandoned and "choked up with weeds," a witness said. A ragged rhythm of gunfire was sounding in the clearing. American pickets, finding cover in Freeman's house and behind trees and stumps, were shooting at their enemy counterparts, who were advancing in front of the main body of troops. Observing a paltry number of redcoats out in the open, Morgan's men rushed forward.

Now a steady *rat-a-tat* of firing began in the farm clearing. The British skirmishers made easy targets for the riflemen. Excited by their success, Morgan's troops sprinted up the open slope after the retreating enemy. Hunters from an early age, they were eager to run down their quarry.

The loud blast of each rifle shot was answered by the scattered booming of musket fire from the redcoats exposed in the open field. Before the fight, Morgan had reminded his troops, "Boys, shoot at those who wear epaulettes rather than the poor fellows who fight for sixpence a day."

The idea that it was unethical to take deliberate aim at an officer was a notion left over from feudal times. The British believed it. George Washington frowned on what he saw as assassination rather than war. But to Morgan and the rough frontiersmen who made up his corps, that type of restraint was nonsense. Who better to kill than officers? Some of the men climbed trees for a better vantage.

True to Morgan's word, British officers were the first to fall.

Americans would later learn that the British pickets were commanded by Major Gordon Forbes of the British 9th Regiment of Foot. An American marksman hit Forbes, a twenty-year veteran, wounding him. Patriots shot down every other officer in the unit before the skirmishers disappeared into the woods to the north.

Suddenly, the riflemen were themselves struck by heavy firing from the west. Surprised, they fell back in confusion. General Fraser's advance corps of light infantry, moving ahead on the British right, had heard the shooting and now crashed into the Americans' flank. Some of the riflemen were hit, a few taken prisoner. The rest sprinted back the way they had come, the downward slope and surge of adrenaline giving their feet wings. They ran along the uneven ground until they reached the cover of the forest that bordered the cleared land.

Colonel Dearborn's light infantry had filtered through those woods and now approached the west side of the battlefield. They too ran into Fraser's battalions. Dearborn pulled back to a knoll a quarter mile southwest of the farm and set up a defensive position. The fight made Freeman's Farm explode in a roar of echoing gunfire.

THEN, ALMOST AS quickly as it had broken out, the shooting tapered off. The calm of a late summer day began to sneak back into the clearing. From time to time the quiet was scarred by the angry crack of a rifle. Men from both sides peered across the clearing into the distant woods, trying to make sense of movement and shadow.

Benedict Arnold, with Gates's concurrence, ordered the seven-hundred-man 1st New Hampshire Regiment, part of General Poor's brigade, to march toward Freeman's Farm. Populated by veterans whose service went back to Bunker Hill, the unit had been raised and led by John Stark. When Stark resigned from the Continental service, Colonel Joseph Cilley replaced him.

Cilley, who had fought in the French and Indian War, maneuvered his regiment into position on the left of Morgan's riflemen, who were still in the process of regrouping. Opposite them, the men could watch the deployment of three British regiments from Hamilton's brigade. The lines of redcoats outnumbered the Americans. Even more worrying, British gunners were wheeling cannon into the two gaps between their battalions of infantry. Troops from both sides marched onto the field and opened fire.

Cilley summed up the battle that followed: "The engagement began very closely, and continued about 20 minutes, in which time we lost so many men, and received no reinforcement, that we were obliged to retreat."

While pulling back, Cilley encountered fresh troops coming forward. Arnold had dispatched the 3rd New Hampshire Regiment. Led by Colonel Alexander Scammell, a thirty-year-old Harvard-educated lawyer, these infantrymen took up positions along the margin of the forest. Heartened, Cilley turned his regiment around and rejoined the battle.

With a surge of firing, the fracas mounted to a new height of intensity. The American regiments tried to push into the gap between Hamilton's infantry and Fraser's advance guard. Carefully monitoring the fight from behind the lines, Arnold sent forward two veteran New York Continental regiments. He deployed each unit to a position where the fresh troops could best support the American line.

The British had rolled several 6-pounder cannon into the gaps between their own regiments. Just the sound of their gut-punching booms was enough to unnerve a man. A soldier of the era had observed that on facing heavy guns, "all of a sudden I was overtaken by a fear which deprived me of all my courage, and a terror which set my limbs a-trembling." Questioning his comrades, he found that all had, at one time or another, been overcome by "cannon-fever."

The New Hampshire men formed in front of the tree line and began to march forward. The enemy were doing the same— the 62nd Regiment advancing up the center. Artillerymen moved the big guns forward until they could no longer keep up with the infantry and had to cease their fire.

Now came the ghastly pattern that would be repeated through-out the afternoon. The two sides marched to within fifty yards of each other. British soldiers closed ranks to make up for the men who had been dropped by the American riflemen's sniper fire. They stopped, presented their muskets, and fired a stupendous volley. The Americans reeled backward. The British advanced again and fired another volley. Officers screamed orders. A deadly clank of metal as each man fixed his bayonet. *Charge!* The British infantrymen came forward at a run, their hoarse screams erupting from the smoke-clogged air.

The bayonet enjoyed a mystique in the British Army. Bur-goyne was convinced that, while any coward could fire a musket, "the onset of bayonets in the hands of the valiant is irresistible." He referred to the sixteen-inch-long triangular bayonet as the "national weapon" and encouraged his officers to rely on it.

It was true that even hardened troops could be intimidated by an oncoming wall bristling with shining death. The New Hamp-shire men were no exception. They turned and ran, retreating to the relative safety of the forest. The British attacks quickly pe-tered out as the charging men encountered the trees, brush, and ravines in the wooded areas. The Americans regrouped and coun-terattacked, driving the enemy back across the open field.

"The conflict was grievous to behold," wrote a British cap-tain. "The rebels fled at every charge deeper still into the woods; but when the British troops returned to their position, they were slowly followed, and those who had been the most forward in the pursuit were the first to fall."

The fight surged. The forces of both sides advanced, fought in the open field, pulled back. One man dropped in a loose heap, his life suddenly extinguished. Another stumbled and rolled onto the ground, clutching at a wound.

IT BECAME CLEAR that for now General Fraser was not about to break off and make a sweep around the western side of the American position. Arnold felt confident sending more, then more of his division into the battle at the clearing. These fresh troops heartened the patriots even as they discouraged the British, who had few additional men to call on. "Reinforcements successively arrived and strengthened the American line," lamented one British soldier.

Between three and four P.M., the battle reached a crescendo. Gunfire echoed for miles through woods that had never known such a roar. "Both armies seemed determined to conquer or die," observed American general John Glover. The noise of muskets and cannon swelled like an organ in church. General Enoch Poor, whose brigade was now fully committed to the fight, later recounted that "the blaze from the artillery and small arms was incessant, and sounded like the roll of the drum. By turns the British and Americans drove for each other . . . often mingling in a hand to hand wrestle and fight. Scammell fought like a hero."

Hand to hand. The fight was both violent and intimate. Emotions without names swallowed men whole. Honor, pity, country, life—all words and all ideas were consumed in the tumult of action.

The noise was unimaginable. Lieutenant William Digby, an infantryman with Fraser's column, described "an explosion of fire I never had any idea of before, and the heavy artillery joining in concert like great peels of thunder, assisted by the echoes of the woods, almost deafened us with noise." The uproar continued undiminished until sunset. The men's numbed ears gave them a sense of fighting underwater. The dangerous, haze-filled air turned the sunlight rancid. At times the smoke grew so thick that it obscured the scene entirely. Breathless men inhaled the sulfurous fumes.

"We beat them back three times," remembered Benjamin Warren, a captain in the 3rd New Hampshire, "and they reinforced and recovered their ground again, till after sunset without an intermission."

The pastoral field had become a scene of hellish pandemonium. Wounded men lay screaming, quivering, weeping. The dead stretched in immodest postures. Bodies were torn open, limbs ripped off, skulls shattered like eggshells. A militia officer noted the musket balls that "whistled their thousand different notes around our heads." The field's clipped shafts of rye and wheat were smeared red. Leaves and twigs from the surrounding oak and maple trees, torn by bullets, rained down on those taking cover in the woods.

THE BRITISH CANNON became a locus of struggle. In action, they had been effectively fending off American attempts to encircle the enemy. But Morgan's marksmen kept picking off the soldiers who worked the big guns. Forty-eight British gunners were assigned to the cannon. Before long, more than thirty of them lay dead or wounded.

The two sides contested the cannon "with small arms and at the point of the bayonet . . . with alternate slaughter on both sides." At least three times, patriot soldiers rushed forward and gained possession of the guns. But they didn't have the equipment to turn them on the enemy. Nor, having shot the artillery horses from a distance, could they draw the cannon off. British counterattacks regained the prizes.

British lieutenant James Hadden, assigned to a battery atop a knoll, saw nineteen of his twenty-two gunners struck down. The patriots were moving to take his field pieces. He hurried to General Hamilton and begged him for a force of infantrymen to protect the battery. "While speaking to him," he noted, "my cap was shot through in front." Hamilton ordered Captain Thomas Jones to join Hadden with guns from another battery. Returning to the field, the two men found that soldiers from the 62nd Regiment, attempting to retake the cannon, had been overwhelmed in the melee. Patriots had taken more than two dozen of the enemy prisoner.

Captain Jones put his guns into action to beat back the Americans. He was soon shot down himself, along with almost all of the fresh gunners. Hadden tried to keep Jones on his feet while the infantrymen were forced back, leaving the guns behind. Jones collapsed and Hadden carried him to a nearby hut. The building was so crowded with wounded men that the lieutenant could not find space on the floor. When he was finally able to lay Jones down, the captain coughed out his last breath. Only the intervention of the 20th Regiment kept the entire British line from being attacked on the flank and rolled up.

"Few actions," one British officer judged, "have been characterized by more obstinacy in attack and defence."

GENERAL GATES WAS accused by some of dereliction during the September 19 battle for remaining in camp during the entire event. But it was logical for the commanding general to position himself where he could communicate with all his forces and be found by couriers. If he went onto the battlefield, he put himself temporarily out of touch and risked being wounded or killed unnecessarily.

Arnold, as a major general in command of a division, also remained behind the lines, positioning troops and relaying orders to the generals and colonels beneath him. While he rode out more than once to survey the field during the battle, it's most likely that Arnold directed his forces from a distance. After the battle, he was critical of some of his junior officers, whose "zeal and spirit" induced them to expose themselves to enemy fire "when their correct place was in the rear."

Persistent myths have pictured Arnold storming around the field in person. Colonel Scammell was reported to have said that "Arnold rushed into the thickest of the fight with his usual recklessness, and at times acted like a madman." Scammell even recounted the improbable sight of Arnold grabbing a firelock from one of the riflemen in order to take a potshot at the enemy. Ebenezer Wakefield, an officer in Dearborn's battalion, reported many years later that he had seen Arnold "riding in front of the line, his eyes flashing." It might be that these heroics were performed not by Arnold in the flesh but by the ghost of his oversized reputation, which inspired his men to fight even as it disheartened the enemy.

More important than Arnold's position on the battlefield was the fact that his tactical instincts and his management of the fight had paid off. The intervention of his division had stopped the British center before they were able to bring their cannon to bear on the American fortifications. The steady flow of fresh troops that Arnold had so skillfully fed into the fight held Burgoyne's army in place and prevented Fraser's men from turning the American flank.

Burgoyne admitted as much. He had expected that Gates would let the British bring the fight to the Americans. Benedict

Arnold disrupted the plan when he "chose to give rather than receive the attack." Burgoyne commended Arnold for his "perseverance in the attack on his lines."

By FIVE P.M. the sun was dropping toward the west, its face a red disk through the battlefield smoke. American commanders and soldiers alike began to hope that there was time left to utterly defeat the persistent enemy. The British 62nd Regiment, the enemy's anchor on the eastern edge of the field, had suffered grievous casualties. The patriots, joined by even more reinforcements, pressed them with renewed determination. But now they heard in the distance a new sound. Were they imagining it? Drums approaching from behind them? Men yelling? Men singing?

Suddenly, a sharp volley of musket fire hit them from the woods to the east. Almost immediately came the boom of cannon. The men twisted their heads. A new hostile force was attacking them.

General Riedesel, stationed near the river, had been worried all afternoon by the rattle of small arms and the pounding of artillery from the uplands. Late in the afternoon, Burgoyne sent him new orders: He should secure the baggage and artillery accompanying his column and bring as many troops as he could spare up the heights to attack the Americans' right flank. Riedesel immediately led a regiment up the slope, joined by his gunnery captain, Georg Pausch, with several cannon. Riedesel told his men to make as much noise as possible to give the Americans the impression of a larger force.

The arrival of five hundred fresh soldiers coincided with the renewed attack of the 20th Regiment and the last stand of the 62nd. The combined effect was enough to turn the tide of the fight.

The Germans came on "with great vigor." At the same time, Pausch's guns "directed a murderous grapeshot fire against the enemy." The Englishmen, who had teetered on the verge of defeat, now "bellowed one hurrah after another."

Caught in the middle, the Americans on the right quickly fell back. Exhausted men, their faces blackened from gunpowder, stumbled across a field descending into darkness. Some of the Americans turned to fire the last of their ammunition at faintly perceived targets in the gloom. They sought the safety of the woods, leaving the British to occupy the open ground. The shooting subsided—a tremulous calm descended on the place of battle.

As SOON AS the sun slipped out of sight, the field assumed the coolness of an autumn evening. Men who had sweated for hours felt a sudden chill. Most American troops staggered back to their encampment. Colonel Scammell's men stayed out observing the enemy until almost midnight.

On both sides, officers tallied the casualties. Officially, 100 Americans had been killed, 325 wounded. British losses were 160 killed, 364 wounded. The real toll was not counted in numbers but in the loss of friends, relatives, comrades known intimately, faces never to be seen again.

According to the standards of war, the British had "won" the battle. They held the contested field while the Americans retreated. But it was, as British lieutenant Digby observed, a "dear bought victory." General Burgoyne would soon admit that "no fruits, honour excepted, were attained with the preceding victory."

His men had it hardest that night. Lacking food and tents, they formed in ranks and lay down on the ground, each man clutching his musket. If the Americans launched an attack in the dark, they would be ready to respond instantly. "We remained in our ranks," Lieutenant Digby recorded, "and though we heard the groans of our wounded and dying at a small distance, yet could not assist them till morning."

Their sleep was hardly restful. The temperature dropped below freezing. In the black of night, the zone of battle became a replica of hell. Some of the dead had been hurriedly dragged into mass graves, but bodies and parts of bodies still littered the ground. The stench of spilled blood and disemboweled men turned the air septic. The groans, wails, and calls for help seemed to seep up from the stubbled ground itself. Spectral figures— wives searching for missing husbands, camp followers taking the opportunity to loot dead bodies—flitted through the shadows. Wolves, attracted by the prospect of fresh carrion, skulked down from the hills.

AND SO, ON a day in September, by the strange alchemy of war, an event at a tiny clearing in an obscure woodland along the Hudson River had shaped the history of America. The outcome, so favorable to the patriots, was largely the result of the aggressive energy of Benedict Arnold and the men he led.

The war, even the struggle at Saratoga, was far from over. But those on both sides would not think of the conflict in the same way again. A shadow passed over British prospects for victory— the hearts of American patriots glowed with renewed hope.

Now or Never

"THE COURAGE AND OBSTINACY WITH WHICH THE AMERI-
cans fought were the astonishment of everyone," wrote
British lieutenant Thomas Anbury after the battle that Benedict
Arnold led on September 19. He concluded, "They are not that
contemptible enemy we had hitherto imagined them."

A German soldier would marvel about the patriots, "I question whether any war has ever witnessed regular troops withstand
hostile fire so courageously and stubbornly as these farmers and
burghers." American general John Glover suggested the reason:
The patriots were fighting "for their all."

When the sun rose on September 20, both sides waited
nervously for a renewal of combat. General Gates preferred to
suspend fighting until he was able to replenish his supply of gunpowder from Albany, which he did a day later. General Burgoyne
hoped that a rapid attack would crack the enemy line, but the
sheer exhaustion of his troops required that he too wait a day to
reorganize. By the following day, he had his own reason to delay.

GENERAL WILLIAM HOWE, the overall British commander in
America, had decided to strike Philadelphia. His thinking was

that a threat to the American capital would require George Washington to commit his army to a climactic battle. A British victory would win the war. Washington was puzzled. Why didn't Howe make the more obvious move and attack northward along the Hudson River to support Burgoyne and split the colonies?

After weeks of preparation and hesitation, Howe loaded fifteen thousand troops onto ships at New York City and headed for the Chesapeake Bay. At the end of August, he landed his army fifty miles from the rebel capital. Congress made a hasty retreat into the Pennsylvania hinterlands. On September 11, 1777, Howe fought Washington's army at Chadds Ford on Brandywine Creek and defeated the patriots with heavy casualties. He would capture Philadelphia on September 26. His success made it even more crucial that patriots hold the line at Bemis Heights.

Howe left Sir Henry Clinton, a glum, quarrelsome officer with little enthusiasm for the war in America, to maintain the British position in New York City. He gave Clinton vague instructions to make a move "in favor of General Burgoyne's approaching Albany," once more troops from England reinforced New York.

Acknowledging Burgoyne's pleas for help, Clinton had written to him: "You know my good-will and are not ignorant of my poverty. If you think 2000 men can assist you effectively, I will make a push . . . in about ten days." The push he referred to was an attack on the American forts guarding the Hudson Highlands. If he could get past them, he could sail on up to Albany to cooperate with Burgoyne, or perhaps draw some of Gates's troops south. The encrypted message, sent on September 11, arrived at Burgoyne's camp on the twenty-first, two days after the fighting at Freeman's Farm. Although Clinton's tone was hardly optimistic, Burgoyne decided to await the hoped-for reinforcements.

Both sides hurried to fortify their positions on Bemis Heights. Men cut down trees and drove spades into the clay-thick earth to build protective barriers. For the next fifteen days, the armies would maintain a tense standoff barely two miles apart, so close that each could hear the enemy's drumrolls and the boom of their morning cannon. Soldiers from both sides would man their barricades before dawn, grip their muskets, and stare into the thick morning mist for an attack that did not come.

THE MAIN BRITISH position was a fortified camp stretching from their base on the river up to the highlands. In front of these works, just south of the Great Ravine, Burgoyne established a long line of breastworks facing the American position. To prevent the Americans from circling around Freeman's Farm and attacking eastward into his camp, he had his men build two large field fortifications. The first, known as the Balcarres Redoubt, was a log-and-earth wall twelve feet high that ran across high ground nearly a quarter mile north to south, enclosing the western end of Freeman's Farm and incorporating the Freeman house and barn. It bristled with eight cannon. Two small outworks on nearby knolls offered extra protection.

A quarter mile to the northwest of this fort, Burgoyne established Breymann's Redoubt. This fortified camp, manned by German grenadiers, comprised two zigzag walls of timber seven feet high. Cannon stared menacingly from embrasures. The camp behind it was protected by earthen breastworks. Canadian volunteers stood guard in two reinforced log cabins to protect the lowland between these major redoubts.

The Americans, who had already begun extensive fortifications, kept improving them until they had built a solid line from the river up onto Bemis Heights. Every day, the American soldiers struck their tents and prepared for battle. But General Gates was not content to simply wait for an enemy attack. He ordered a campaign of harassment intended to speed the erosion of British fighting strength.

Daniel Morgan and Henry Dearborn had their men in the field almost continuously, ranging around the outskirts of the enemy positions, sniping at British sentries and ambushing forage parties. Other regiments sent out scouts, groups of sixty to a hundred men, to keep an eye on the enemy and suppress British patrols. These forces would venture as far as Saratoga Lake, six miles to the west. One mission went all the way to the village of Saratoga, which lay on the Hudson River ten miles north of the British lines. They destroyed a bridge there to hamper any attempt by the enemy to retreat. A British soldier complained that "picquets and advanced parties were almost continually firing and skirmishing, so much so that the officers and men refreshed and slept exposed to the enemy's fire."

Good news kept American morale high. Within a week of the battle, three thousand militiamen came into camp from New York and New England, men eager to join a force poised for victory. Abraham Ten Broeck, one of the wealthiest men in the region, brought 1,300 soldiers of the Albany militia— practically every able-bodied man in the area. These troops, although green, were eager to protect their homes only thirty miles away.

Altogether, six thousand militiamen arrived, bringing Gates's total number of rank-and-file troops to more than twelve thousand. And more kept coming. A hundred Oneida tribesmen volunteered. They ranged around the British camp; during one night they captured twenty-nine prisoners.

The days grew shorter, the nights colder; the hardwood trees flamed out in vermillion and gold. Burgoyne's prospects of success seemed dimmer every day. Waiting only compounded his problems. Desertion plagued the British Army. The daily password often had to be changed in the middle of the day because of the danger that deserters would reveal it to the Americans.

Conditions for his troops were steadily deteriorating. A portion of his men occupied the Freeman battlefield. After the fighting, heavy rains opened the shallow graves, and the stench of rotting corpses reminded the living soldiers of their possible fate. Worn-out British tents were letting in water. Provisions for the men—salted beef and flour—were steadily dwindling. Just as alarming was the lack of fodder for the thousand horses on which the army's movement depended. Twenty tons of grass and hay were needed daily. Without it, the animals, already emaciated, would starve.

"Our grass was ate up and many horses dying for want," a British soldier wrote. That meant that hundreds of foragers had to go out regularly to gather feed. A large force of armed troops was needed to protect these laborers from rebel patrols. The longer the army stayed in one place, the scarcer the fodder became. Burgoyne ordered a new bridge of boats built so that he could send foraging expeditions to the east side of the river. These missions were menaced by General Lincoln's militiamen, who were camped on that bank.

General Gates's situation was promising but his duties were daunting. His camp soon took on the proportions of the fourth largest city in America. Every day he had to oversee the incorporation of new troops into his units, the assignment of camping areas, the maintenance of sanitary facilities, the distribution of provisions. He enforced military justice. He drew up orders for a steady flow of raids, probes, and patrols into no-man's-land. Meanwhile, he continued to evaluate intelligence from spies, scouts, and deserters and kept up a high level of security around the camp.

It was the type of organizational work at which Gates excelled. Burgoyne had created many of his own problems, but the trap he found himself in had been carefully planned by Horatio

Gates. His defensive strategy, combined with Arnold's stunning action at Freeman's Farm, was working.

THE SOLUTION TO one potentially damaging problem eluded Gates. For two weeks after the Freeman's Farm battle, he and Benedict Arnold engaged in a heated feud that generated discord within the American command. It began with the report of the Freeman's Farm battle that Gates sent to Congress on September 22. In it, he lauded the good behavior of the troops and wrote that "to discriminate in praise of the Officers would be Injustice, as they all deserve the honour and applause of Congress." He singled out for special mention the two lieutenant colonels who had been killed in the fight.

Arnold was told of this letter by one of his aides, probably Richard Varick. Reveling in his first independent field command, Gates had been stingy with the glory. His narrative suggested that Gates himself had initiated all the troop movements.

Such after-action accounts followed a pattern that routinely highlighted the role of key subordinates. Because Arnold's division had carried most of the action, he should have received more credit. To him, Gates's letter was demeaning. To emphasize the snub, Gates issued an order after the battle that put Morgan's and Dearborn's regiments under his own command rather than Arnold's.

It didn't take long for the touchy Arnold to work himself into a lather. The same day that Gates's report went out, Arnold proceeded the half mile from his cabin, burst into Gates's headquarters, and set off a heated argument with his superior. He started by saying he wanted justice done to his division "as well as particular Regiments and Persons."

The tone went downhill from there. "High words and gross language" ensued. Gates erupted in anger. Knowing exactly what would most irritate Arnold, he mentioned the imminent return to camp of General Lincoln, one of the officers who had been promoted over Arnold in February. In the heat of the moment, Gates said that he knew nothing about Arnold being a major general, since Arnold had resigned his commission before the military crisis had begun. In fact, he went on, Arnold had no command in the army at all. Gates would himself take over the American left wing and Lincoln could manage the right.

A furious Arnold demanded a pass that would allow him to proceed to Philadelphia. He was determined to find a situation where he would be appreciated. To his surprise, Gates agreed to let him go. With the enemy only minutes away and another attack imminent, it seemed preposterous that the commander of the northern army was dismissing his most valuable fighting general.

Arnold stomped back to his quarters and wrote out a long letter summarizing the disagreement. Some of his complaints were puerile. He had "been received with the greatest coolness at headquarters," he wrote. Such treatment would "mortify a person with less pride than I have." He said he still wanted to serve his country, "though I am thought of no consequence in this department."

When word got out that Arnold might quit the army, General Enoch Poor was alarmed. He suggested that the American officers sign an "address" to thank Arnold "for his past services, and particularly for his conduct during the late action," while "requesting him to stay in camp." Eventually the petition was signed by every general officer in camp except Lincoln and Gates.

The dynamics of this unfolding drama involved two emotional officers manipulated by those around them. Arnold was ill-served by the young men, protégés of Philip Schuyler, whom he had taken on as aides. Henry Brockholst Livingston, twenty years old, and Varick, twenty-four, sent headquarters gossip to Schuyler and deliberately cultivated Arnold's animus toward Schuyler's enemy, Gates. James Wilkinson, also twenty, played a similar role as

General Gates's Iago, at one point referring to Arnold in writing as "a certain pompous little fellow." Eventually Livingston and Varick were pressured by senior officers to leave camp and did.

By September 26, four days after the blowup, Arnold had decided to stay in service. The busy General Gates, amiable by nature, had also cooled off. Arnold sent his commander one last written salvo on October 1. Although he accused Gates of "jealousy," he assured him that he was not trying to "command the army, or to outshine you." He was, he wrote, willing to "sacrifice my feelings" for the cause.

The dispute, although potentially dangerous, had few lasting consequences. It revealed Gates's tendency toward pettiness and bureaucratic maneuvering and Arnold's oversensitivity to slights and insults. Both men had been under tremendous stress for a month even before the cataclysmic battle on the nineteenth, and it was hardly surprising that they were subject to emotional outbursts and frayed nerves.

"The fatigue of body, and mind," Gates wrote to his wife, Elizabeth, during the ordeal, "is too much for my age and constitution." He added that "a general of an American army must be everything, and that is being more than one man can long sustain."

The dispute was detailed in letters composed by the aides who were busy fomenting it in the first place. The extensive written record they left behind cemented the controversy in the historical record. While the quarrel did no credit to the reputation of either Gates or Arnold, its importance was negligible. None of the other American officers who left behind accounts of the Saratoga campaign even mentioned the dispute. By the first week in October the friction had smoothed—Arnold and Gates were back on speaking terms and eating dinner together.

* * *

COLONEL ALEXANDER SCAMMELL wrote a letter to a friend on September 26, using as a return address *Camp Now or Never*. He reported that "we expect another severe Battle every Hour."

With the coming of October, everyone who was gathered on the heights above Bemis Tavern sensed that a crisis was approaching. No "officer or soldier ever slept during that interval without his cloaths," Burgoyne wrote. No general or regimental commander "passed a single night without being upon his legs occasionally at different hours, and constantly an hour before daylight."

On October 3, Burgoyne ordered that the food ration for each of his soldiers be cut by a third, to a single pound of bread or flour. The clock was ticking, and whether he advanced or retreated, the British general would have to do so before his dwindling provisions ran out.

That same day, in his general orders, he noted that "there is reason to be assured that other powerful Armies of the King are actually in cooperation with these Troops." He was referring to the battalions of General Clinton. Burgoyne could not easily communicate with Clinton—his messages were almost always intercepted during their long journey through enemy territory. He may have fabricated the hopeful information purely to raise morale in his army. Or Burgoyne may have been interpreting Clinton's tentative proposal to help him as a promise of redemption for his beleaguered army.

One fact, had it been known to British commanders on Bemis Heights, would have demolished their hope of relief. General Clinton, whose first priority was to defend New York City, had not dared move north until he received reinforcements from England. That same October 3, when Burgoyne issued the reassuring order, Clinton was just starting out on his diversionary mission. By a clever feint, he captured the two patriot forts guarding the Hudson Highlands fifty miles north of the city. A few days later, he overcame the defenses at West Point. Only then did he write to Burgoyne that there was now "nothing between us but Gates. I sincerely hope this little Success of ours may facilitate your Operation."

But that was all the effort Clinton made before he returned to New York City. A week later, he sent a force of redcoats farther up the river to burn the town of Kingston, which was being used as the seat of government by New York State officials. But Clinton had no intention of proceeding an additional fifty miles to Albany or of actually cooperating with Burgoyne. Nor was Horatio Gates tempted to send even a detachment of his men south. The situation remained unchanged. Gates was effectively, step-by-step, narrowing his enemies' options.

ON OCTOBER 4, Burgoyne held a council of war with Generals Phillips, Fraser, and Riedesel. He had a plan. They would leave eight hundred men to guard the supplies, artillery, and hospital along the Hudson. The rest of the army, some four thousand troops, would sweep to the west and hit the patriots' left flank with all they had.

Some meaningful looks, no doubt, flashed among Burgoyne's three subordinates. General Riedesel, who had helped save the army from catastrophe at Freeman's Farm, spoke up. First, he explained, eight hundred soldiers could not hold off the large force that the Americans could send against his troops along the river. If the enemy broke through and the provisions were lost, the army would be lost.

In addition, if they made the move that Burgoyne outlined, they would be proceeding blindly. Because of heavy American patrolling, they had little intelligence about the lay of the land west of the Americans' fortified camp. They did not know where the roads led. They did not know how strongly the rebels had fortified their position. Just moving so many men and their supplies and guns through unfamiliar territory would take three or four days, ample time for the enemy to react.

"I attempted to present the danger of our situation," Riedesel later wrote. He urged a retreat at least to the Batten Kill, a stream on the east side of the Hudson River opposite the village of Saratoga. There they could take up a strong defensive position and await General Clinton—if he was in fact on his way.

Fraser agreed with Riedesel, Phillips offered no opinion. Burgoyne said they should go and survey the supply depot and artillery park to determine if the force he suggested would be enough to defend it. They did so and agreed that Riedesel was right, Burgoyne's plan was too dangerous. They would meet again in the morning.

Burgoyne should have seen that his options were steadily narrowing. "However," Riedesel noted, "we waited, nourished by hope."

THAT SAME DAY, General Gates wrote a letter to New York governor George Clinton, informing him that affairs in his department "have a pleasing appearance." Of Burgoyne, he predicted that "perhaps his Despair may dictate to him, to risque all upon One Throw. He is an Old Gamester, and in his Time, has seen all Chances."

His words hint at the satisfaction this former British Army major took in his duel with one of Britain's most illustrious generals. All he had to do was to wait for Burgoyne's final throw of the dice. The odds were in Gates's favor.

AT THE NEXT council of war, Burgoyne proposed a compromise. The following day, October 7, they would leave most of the army in place to defend their position and guard the supplies. They would select 1,500 of their best troops—grenadiers and light infantrymen—to march around to the west in a reconnaissance maneuver. Another five hundred loyalists and Canadians, along with the few Indians remaining, would guard their flank. To give the mission spirit, Burgoyne would lead the troops personally. With ten cannon, they would proceed to a ridge that gave a view of the left end of the American line. If conditions there were favorable, they would bring up more units of the army, more guns, and attack on October 8. If not, the whole army would retreat northward.

The plan recognized both Riedesel's concerns and Burgoyne's reluctance to pull back. If they had to abandon their position, Burgoyne noted, they should go only as far as Fort Edward so that the Americans would not feel free to rush south to attack General Howe and perhaps end the war. In addition, this reconnaissance foray might allow them to collect the forage they desperately needed to keep their horses alive and their army mobile.

Burgoyne's plan was complicated, vague, and riddled with unknowns. It was just what Gates had predicted, a throw of the dice.

The weather at Bemis Heights had turned balmy. The days took on the warmth that Americans called Indian summer. Birdsong had faded, but bees still probed the wildflowers blooming optimistically along the edges of fields. At evening, however, the glassy air quickly chilled. As the stars embellished the darkness on October 6, several cannon shots sent booms rolling out from the British camp. Rockets soared high into the blackness and exploded in red and yellow flame. To the patriots, the display was a mystery. A rumor went around Burgoyne's camp that it was a signal to Henry Clinton—deliverance was finally at hand.

"At no time," a German officer remembered, "did the Jews await the coming of their Messiah with greater expectancy than we awaited the coming of General Clinton."

15

We Will Have Some Fun

THEY WERE WET AND COLD AND TIRED. DANIEL MORGAN and his riflemen had spent the night of October 6 on an extended patrol around the British lines. Heading back with a half dozen prisoners, they made a wrong turn and became disoriented in the dark. Wary of coming too close to the enemy, they slept in the woods under a black rain. Now they huddled around fires to dispel the chill and ate a welcome breakfast. The rising sun illuminated the wet sheen of autumn leaves.

The morning passed quietly. At midday, General Horatio Gates sat down to dinner. Among those partaking of ox heart at his table were Benedict Arnold and John Brooks. Benjamin Lincoln probably joined them as well. The twenty-five-year-old Brooks, a doctor in civilian life and now colonel of the 8th Massachusetts Regiment, had accompanied Arnold on the relief expedition to Fort Stanwix. The animosity between Arnold and Gates, if not forgotten, had subsided. Brooks remembered that the now familiar debate about whether to await Burgoyne's attack in camp or venture out to meet him continued, with Arnold insisting on the more aggressive option.

Gates was confident. He commanded forty-three regiments, almost thirteen thousand men. Six thousand of his troops were proven Continentals. They were well supplied—Philip Schuyler, even after being relieved of command, continued to send ample provisions from Albany. Gates assigned incoming battalions of eager militiamen to reinforce the Continental brigades.

The men at Gates's table were used to hearing the pop of musket shots echoing through the forest day and night as pickets and scouts on both sides fired nervously to deter the enemy. At one o'clock in the afternoon, the pulse of that firing quickened. The officers glanced to the northwest, trying to judge where the commotion was coming from.

Next they heard a distant drumroll. Then another, closer. It was the urgent tattoo that signaled "to arms." The camp began to come alive with the clank of metal, the footsteps of men running, the barked orders of sergeants. Having already struck their tents, the men ran to their alarm posts and stood waiting with muskets in hand.

The officers all rose. In one account, Arnold asked Gates, "Shall I go out and see what is the matter?"

General Gates stared at him for a moment in silence. "I am afraid to trust you, Arnold."

"Pray, let me go," Arnold answered. "I will be careful. And if our advance does not need support, I will promise not to commit you."

Gates relented and Arnold went to prepare his regiments.

The commanding general ordered his aide, James Wilkinson, to ride out and bring back word on the cause of the shooting. Wilkinson returned less than an hour later to report that a substantial body of British troops, accompanied by a number of carriage guns, had marched out from their fortified lines around Freeman's Farm. They moved west and south until they reached the next hardscrabble plot, which was owned by a man named Barber. They halted at a downward-sloping clearing planted in wheat just below a small group of outbuildings. Foragers began harvesting the grain. The British deployed their brass cannon, including a couple of massive 12-pounders, on the rise in front of the buildings. American pickets had fallen back but continued to observe the enemy from the woods.

What was going on? The number of troops and the presence of heavy cannon seemed to indicate more than a simple expedition to acquire forage. But the maneuver did not resemble the full-scale attack of September 19.

"They are foraging, and reconnoitering on your left," Wilkinson reported, "and I think sir they offer you battle."

Gates turned to his division commanders. General Lincoln was concerned that it might be another attempt to break into the American fortifications from the west. General Arnold wanted to hit the enemy before they could advance. Gates decided to repeat the tactics of the earlier battle. Arnold would move regiments of his left wing to intercept the enemy advance. He could employ additional troops from the ample patriot ranks if needed.

As usual, the first move fell to Morgan. Arnold ordered the riflemen, accompanied by Dearborn's light infantry, to head north and reconnoiter the enemy position. Morgan's men shook off their weariness and circled westward along familiar paths to gain a position on the enemy's right. Their destination was a hill west of the Barber wheat field. Arnold sent the light infantry out, Henry Dearborn remembered, to "ascend the eminence and then advance to meet any part of the enemy that might be moving in that direction." General Poor's battle-hardened brigade of New Hampshire men would take a more direct route and confront the British occupying the wheat field head-on.

As Morgan and Poor moved toward the enemy, they picked up information from pickets and scouts. The British advance included a surprisingly small portion of their army, maybe 1,500 men in total. Fraser's light infantry and 24th Regiment of Foot marched on the British right, west of the wheat field; General

Riedesel and a portion of his German mercenaries advanced in the center; British grenadiers under Major John Acland guarded the left flank. The entire force had been slowed by their dozen cannon, which they had to haul along rough terrain, throwing a bridge over every stream and hollow.

Now they were arrayed on the rise that overlooked the field of grain. Some officers—could it be Burgoyne himself?—had climbed to the roof of an abandoned farm building and were studying the landscape through their spyglasses. Foragers were swinging their scythes and loading the wheat into wagons. British and German gunners had unlimbered their cannon and set them up facing south.

The British officers could not see far beyond the quarter-mile strip of cultivated land being laid to stubble. The American pickets spotted some Indians and rangers moving southward through the woods. The rest of the enemy troops sat down in ranks, their muskets propped between their knees, and waited, far from home under a rich blue sky.

Quite suddenly, the atmosphere at the wheat field changed. The day remained balmy, the sun continued to smile, but experienced soldiers were alert to the new rhythm of the small arms fire.

Major Acland may have sensed the change first. He was the thirty-one-year-old scion of a family of aristocrats from Devon on England's southwest corner. A member of Parliament and an outspoken Tory, he had crossed the Atlantic a year earlier with his elegant wife, Lady Harriet. A hard-drinking, rather coarse man in spite of his courtly background, he commanded the elite British grenadiers.

Assigned to the eastern sector of the field, Acland kept peering into the trees down the slope and to his left. What was it?

The empty woods beyond the fields seemed less empty. Acland glimpsed a flicker of movement between tree trunks, detected a rustling of bushes. He heard a horse neighing somewhere off to the left. The bucolic landscape was stirring.

Participants agreed that it was about three o'clock when the wheat field exploded. Enoch Poor and his experienced New Hampshire regiments had approached through the woods along the edge of a ravine. They were led by Colonels Joseph Cilley and Alexander Scammell, who had been in the thick of the fighting on the nineteenth.

The British grenadiers were an imposing sight to the men peering from behind trees at the bottom of the slope. They were big men and their high miter caps trimmed in bear fur made them seem even taller. The bouncing "Grenadiers March" was familiar to all, an insistent tune screamed out by fifes riding the pounding tom-tom drums.

Here come the Grenadiers, my boys, who know no doubts or fears!

Then sing tow, row, row, row, ro-ow, row, for the British Grenadiers.

Now the drums set these redcoats into motion. They fell into line behind the two 12-pounder cannon. The gun crews stood ready.

The New Hampshire men just inside the wood line watched great billows of white smoke erupt from each muzzle. An instant later the thunderclap hit. The air went electric, canister shot whizzed, twigs rained down. Fortunately for them, the trees made aiming the big guns difficult and the slope caused most of the shot to pass over their heads.

After more blasts, the grenadiers formed in front of the guns. Their scarlet coats had faded during the long campaign, but the men made a stark impression: broad-shouldered, armed, and defiant. On an order, they began to march down the slope as if on parade.

What Acland couldn't see from where he stood was the number of men opposing them. General Poor was positioning 1,600 soldiers in the woods, more than Burgoyne's entire detachment. Acland's 266 grenadiers marched straight toward them and halted. A portion of the Americans fell into line in front of the forest. The British soldiers leveled their muskets. The first volley of the day ripped the air and raised a cloud of white smoke.

Acland thought he saw the American line waver. He remembered Burgoyne's endorsement of the bayonet. Now was the time to drive the rebels back. At an order, the men lowered their lethal steel points. At an order, they came charging forward.

But now more and more Americans were filing into line. Still more. The Britons rushed toward them, their mouths issuing guttural *huzzahs* and animal screams.

A coordinated American volley cut down the redcoats almost as efficiently as the scythes that had been sweeping through the wheat. Still the enemy advanced. More firing. The British attack faltered. The grenadiers who remained standing swiveled their heads to see what had become of their comrades. Another volley. Now it was the Americans who were running. Up the hill they came, their own bayonets seeking soft flesh.

THE REALITY OF combat always exceeds the boundaries of imagination. Every battle is an amalgamation of a thousand personal battles, and each man's fight a kaleidoscope of sights, sounds, and smells that burn into his consciousness and echo for as long as his life lasts.

A man excited to rage runs across a smoky stubble field. One moment he is bounding ahead on eager legs. A second later he is shocked to find the ground leaping up to dash him rudely in the mouth. His teeth clack, he tastes the gritty soil. He gasps for air. Hot liquid seeps ominously from his belly. Sounds echo and recede. An idea quivers on the edge of his mind. A word forms on his dry tongue. No breath to voice it. The sun shines on him from a night sky.

MORE TROOPS POURED from the woods. The British soldiers, the army's best fighters, turned. They were running away. Some didn't make it. Knees sagged, bodies crumpled in disheveled death. One observer described a fifteen-yard section of the field littered with almost twenty dead and dying grenadiers.

Near the woods, James Wilkinson came upon an excited fourteen-year-old patriot soldier pointing his musket and threatening with cracking voice a wounded British officer. The injured man was Major Acland. Patriot fire had struck the well-bred officer in both legs. Wilkinson dismissed the boy. He and his orderly helped Acland onto a horse and led him back toward the American camp.

As POOR'S MEN were routing the grenadiers, a new commotion broke out on the British right. It began with the dangerous crackle of rifle fire. Men of the British light infantry battalion commanded by Major Alexander Lindsay found themselves under intense fire. They spotted forms moving through the trees. Lindsay was a Scottish lord, the 6th Earl of Balcarres. Although only twenty-five, he had been in the army for ten years and now served directly under General Simon Fraser.

Daniel Morgan's four hundred men "poured down like a torrent from the hill." Firing as they came, they hit Balcarres's troops from the right and rear. Minutes later, Dearborn's musketmen crashed squarely into the British advance guard's opposite flank. The enemy heaved backward without orders.

What had seemed a limited foray by the British was turning into a full-scale battle. As he had during the Freeman's Farm battle,

General Gates supervised the fight at the wheat field from the American camp, occasionally venturing out to assess the situation.

New Hampshire militiaman Nathaniel Bacheller, stationed behind the lines, wrote to his sister two days after the battle. He reported that "General Arnold soon went out into the woods on horseback with his aide-de-camp to view the enemy which then engaged with the riflemen."

General Gates soon arrived at the spot where Bacheller waited and asked about Arnold. The commander "was told he was out of the lines to view the enemy." Gates sent an officer on horseback to go to General Arnold and make sure his riflemen did not fire on Colonel Scammell's regiment as they maneuvered—the ever more crowded battlefield posed a danger of friendly fire accidents.

While Gates was sending orders to Scammell to attack the British left, Arnold returned. The militiaman continued his account: "General Arnold says to General Gates, 'It is late in the day but let me have men and we will have some fun with them before sunset.'" Bacheller concluded, "Soon a very heavy fire began."

Have some fun. Arnold, engrossed in the unfolding events, knew well how war let loose the reins of his imagination. It allowed his mind to romp. In battle, anything was possible.

THE BATTALIONS OF enemy troops manning the center felt themselves dangerously exposed. The rebel onslaught pressed toward them. "They rushed on with loud shouts," a British lieutenant remembered. "We drove them back a little with so great a loss to ourselves that it evidently appeared a retreat was the only thing left for us."

The gunners touched off another blast, a spray of canister shot. Their rote actions the product of endless drills, the men loaded and fired until the barrels of the big guns became too hot to touch. American musket fire dropped artillery horses. The wheat field had become a smoke-clogged terrain shaken apart with a continuous, deafening clamor. Parched throats screamed, the acrid air stung watery eyes. German infantrymen began to edge backward. Soon, the gunners were stranded seventy-five yards in front of the line. "The smoke was very dense," one man noted.

General Burgoyne tried to bring order to the increasingly chaotic situation. Several musket balls pierced his coat as he rode up and down the British position shouting orders. Rebels were appearing from all directions. He knew his men could not stand much longer against far greater numbers of enemy soldiers. He told his aide, Sir Francis Clerke, to announce to the other commanders a general retreat. As Clerke rode off to deliver the message, he was shot from his horse. Patriot troops swooped in to capture him. It didn't matter that the order was never delivered, the British and German troops were retreating on their own.

Captain Pausch moved to the rear with his guns, trying to gather enough infantrymen to make a stand. The plan "proved delusive and was totally dispelled," he wrote. He found the road back to his lines occupied by enemy troops. "They came towards us on it; the bushes were full of them." Pausch saw that the situation was irretrievable. "I called on my few remaining men to save themselves." They all headed for the nearest British fortification.

THE NEW HAMPSHIRE regiments fought their way up the hill in the face of the cannon fire. As the big guns fell silent, the Americans surged ahead. Colonel Joseph Cilley, animated by a kind of battle ecstasy, leapt onto the carriage of one of the 12-pounders and claimed it for his regiment. His men were able to drag the gun around and fire at the retreating Germans. Other guns on the rise changed hands two or three times before the enemy were finally driven off.

As the fight became an inferno, Benedict Arnold charged into the action at the head of General Learned's brigade. It was a timely push against the British center. Connecticut militia general Oliver Wolcott noted that "Genl Arnold came up with a reinforcement about four, upon which the fire of musketry became violent and incessant."

Passing a regiment of Connecticut militia on the way, Arnold had recognized men he knew from his youth in Norwich and New London. "Now come on, boys," he yelled, "if the day is long enough we'll have them all in hell before night!"

FOR THE BRITISH and German troops remaining in the wheat field, hell had already arrived. Many of these stalwart soldiers stood up to wave after wave of fresh American troops. General Abraham Ten Broeck's large brigade of Albany militia came in beside Learned and pressed the British hard.

General Fraser saw that the men at the front were in danger of being overrun. He ordered his 24th Regiment of Foot, which had been assigned the reserve position, to fill in and steady the line in order to prevent a panicked retreat. While he was rallying his troops, a bullet, probably from the gun of one of Morgan's riflemen, slammed into his belly. Fraser slumped. He was helped down from his horse, his wound a throbbing, bloody gash.

Fraser was a model warrior, unflinching in the face of the enemy. By advancing into the fray he had inspired his men and stabilized their morale at a time when many of them balanced on the tightrope of panic. Now that he was wounded, perhaps fatally, doubts ricocheted through the regiment. The entire British line began to crumble.

One of his officers wrote that Fraser's shooting "helped turn the fate of the day."

JUST PAST FOUR in the afternoon, the fighting at the wheat field was over. General Burgoyne watched his troops scramble back the way they had come. They soon gave up any attempt to form a line or to halt the onrushing rebels. Most simply ran for the shelter of the fortifications.

"Finding us in their rear, the main body gave way," American colonel Henry Dearborn wrote about the enemy. "They then all retreated with great precipitation and confusion."

Burgoyne rode ahead to the Balcarres Redoubt, the strong point anchoring his line. Hundreds of soldiers from the collapsed reconnaissance expedition were piling inside. He gave orders that the post be held to the last extremity—if the men gave way, his whole command would be threatened. He then hurried to his headquarters to issue alarms to all sectors of the army.

BENEDICT ARNOLD HAD promised to dispatch the enemy before dark. Shadows were lengthening across the open fields as the sun sagged westward. Having led General Learned's brigade in their charge against the British center, he continued on with them as they pushed the enemy northward. More than three thousand men from his division were in the fight. Gates had let him have 1,400 more fresh troops from Paterson's brigade, officially assigned to the American right wing, and still more men from Glover's battalions.

Arnold had what he wanted, a substantial portion of the patriot army behind him and a retreating enemy in front. The reinforcements and his own instincts convinced him that with one final effort they could break through Burgoyne's lines and score a victory for the ages.

Like the British, the Americans had lost much of their order. Fighting at close range, surging ahead when the enemy gave way, the patriot troops became a roaring wave rolling toward the enemy fortifications. Some men had the strange sensation, as they sprinted across the ground, that they were rooted to the earth—it was their surroundings that were moving, dreamlike, past them.

Shoving and scrambling, the British and German soldiers crowded through the openings into the relative security of the redoubt named for Lord Balcarres, who now commanded in the place of General Fraser. The soldiers immediately turned to deliver a steady fire from openings and over the top of the walls. They put their eight cannon to work, blasting canister shot point-blank into the mass of patriot soldiers.

The firing checked the progress of the attack. Surveying the scene, Arnold sent an aide to the right to tell General Poor to "bring his men into better order." After an initial charge forward, Poor's men had found they could not advance against the hailstorm of projectiles. They sought cover in nearby trees and kept up their own fire from a distance. The regiments from the brigades of Paterson and Glover joined them, as did Ten Broeck's militiamen.

"The Americans stormed with great fury the post of the light infantry," remembered British lieutenant Thomas Anbury, who was inside the redoubt, "rushing close to the lines, under a severe fire of grapeshot and small arms. This post was defended with great spirit, and the enemy, led on by General Arnold, as gallantly assaulted the works."

Although the initial assault was repulsed, the Americans' relentless firing kept the soldiers in the redoubt pinned down and unable to counter American moves. Light was fading. General Arnold surveyed the chaos and instantly settled on a new tactic.

ON A HUMP of land a quarter mile to the northwest lay the zigzag rail wall that formed the west side of the fortified camp called Breymann's Redoubt. This loose system of fortifications offered a more vulnerable target for the mass of patriot troops than did the heavier stronghold they were currently attacking. Some men of Learned's brigade had already veered in that direction. The Canadians who defended the gap between the two redoubts stared nervously from their fortified cabins. Once past these obstacles, the attackers would be able to rush the lightly defended breastworks and sally ports of the German camp.

Daniel Morgan had already begun to position his troops and Dearborn's light infantry behind a low hill west of Breymann's fort. Arnold spurred his horse and crossed the front through fire from both sides. He quickly advised his subordinates of his plan: Morgan would attack the rail wall head-on. Arnold would lead men from John Brooks's 8th Massachusetts Regiment, accompanied by a band of riflemen, into the gap and past the Canadian cabins. If they could make it to the rear of Breymann's Redoubt, the defenders would find themselves assaulted from two directions.

Time was running out. The iron disk of the sun was becoming entangled in the limbs of trees in the west.

IN MOMENTS OF stress, reality roars. Some are overwhelmed by the rush of events. Others arrive at a place of sudden clarity unfiltered by thought. Excitement burns away the inessential. Time seems to slow. The warrior flows calmly through his experience, his thoughts bounding ahead of the tumult.

When Arnold was a child, he and his companions would play around a Norwich gristmill. One of his favorite stunts was to leap onto the massive undershot wooden waterwheel and ride it down and through the millrace, holding his breath underwater. If he lost his grip, he would drown. Holding on for his life, he endured the heart-pounding moments. Then he was resurrected, heaved skyward by the turning wheel. Stories of this prank, of his attraction to risk, were told years later. Now the thrill of childhood became play for mortal stakes. Now, Colonel Brooks said, Arnold's "energy gave spirit to the whole action."

THE CANADIAN DEFENDERS of the cabins did not stand long to the assault directed at them. As Arnold and his band of soldiers rushed up the gap between the two forts, the path to the rear of the redoubt fell invitingly open.

Arnold spurred his horse. The beast, terrified but intent, responded with a leap forward. Waving his sword, the general plunged through the sally port and into the redoubt. A rifleman noted that "Genl Arnold was the first who Entered." He found himself on the rocky expanse of the fortified camp crowded with German mercenaries.

In slow motion, he gripped the leather reins and waved his sword. The last gleam of sunlight winked and went out.

At the front of the fort, Morgan and his riflemen, accompanied by Dearborn's light infantry, rushed forward. They faced the fire of two cannon in the center and of muskets along breastworks, but they sprinted so rapidly across the 150 yards that the defenders could get off only a single volley. The rangy backwoodsmen, gripping rifles, tomahawks, and scalping knives, came piling over the rail wall.

Only two hundred of the German grenadiers had been left to defend this position. Their companions had joined the reconnaissance and were now sheltering in the other redoubt. Like their British counterparts, the German grenadiers were big men. They were decked out in high-peaked brass helmets.

Now they found themselves outnumbered and attacked from front and back, an alarming position for any soldier. Overwhelmed, they began to push to the rear. Lieutenant Colonel Heinrich von Breymann, enraged by his men's hesitancy, tried to restore their spirit by striking at them with the flat of his sword, even stabbing them. One of his men, determined to retreat, shot him dead.

The fort descended into a melee, war at its most basic. In the hand-to-hand struggle, amid the smoke, men struck each other down, left enemies bleeding.

Twilight was casting the scene into ever deeper shadow. One final spasm of intense violence consumed the darkening compound. Smoke fumed the air with brimstone, bright flames burst from muzzles. Amid shouts and screams, musket butts cracked heads, bayonets plunged into flesh, fists pounded faces.

In the midst of the pandemonium, a ball tore through Benedict Arnold's left leg just above the ankle. Another shot plunged into his horse's vital organs, bringing it stumbling to its knees. The massive animal fell and rolled. Arnold was pinned to the ground.

More and more Germans pushed their way out of the fort and ran. The Americans were tempted by the baggage left behind: tents, gunpowder, clothing, even pots still simmering over fires.

Soldiers helped drag Arnold from under the horse now trembling in death. The general's wound was in the same leg that a bullet had ripped open at Quebec. He knew the shinbone was shattered. The leg would not support him, the pain came on quickly. Blood flowed.

Lying on the ground in the dusky gloom, Arnold swore between gritted teeth. The frustration at being laid low infuriated him. There was more to do. The enemy were on the run. This was the moment. His men must continue their attack. They did not have much time. He ached to plunge back into the action.

But even now, the darkness of night was seeping into the corners of the fortification. Gradually, the noise quieted, leaving the men with ringing ears. The fight was over.

THE CAPTURE OF Breymann's Redoubt put Burgoyne's entire forward line in imminent jeopardy. During the night, he ordered all his men to withdraw north of the Great Ravine and gather in the main camp overlooking the river.

The British spent the next day burying their dead—more than 180 had been killed. Their hospital overflowed with 260 freshly wounded soldiers, many of whom had to be stretched on the ground outside. Rain threatened.

Combined casualties on the American side came to fewer than two hundred. The heavy loss of officers was particularly damaging to the British—Burgoyne was grieved by the death of General Simon Fraser, a friend who went to his rest after an excruciating night. Sir Francis Clerke was dead. The wounded Major Acland was in the hands of the enemy.

On the night of October 8, the Britons did what Burgoyne had said they must never do—they marched north through the darkness, away from their victorious enemy. A heavy, ice-cold rain drenched them. The starving draft animals dropped dead at such a rate that the army teamsters had to abandon and burn many of their wagons. Each of the soldiers was burdened with carrying his own share of the diminished rations.

When the dismal, rain-soaked troops reached the village of Saratoga two days after the battle, they found themselves cut off. John Stark, recently promoted to Continental brigadier general for his Bennington victory, had taken a position north of them.

His New Hampshire militia blocked the Hudson crossings. Additional American troops had occupied Fort Edward. General Gates, cautious as always, followed behind with his entire army.

Burgoyne's officers finally forced their commander to face reality. They could not proceed farther north. To reverse direction and reach Albany was equally impossible. They were surrounded. A fleeting notion that General Clinton might save them, based on faulty intelligence, dissolved as quickly as it appeared. If the Americans were to attack them, they might have a chance to win a fight in spite of being outnumbered, but Gates was content to wait until dwindling provisions brought on his enemies' doom. Steadily, patiently, he had narrowed Burgoyne's options to one—surrender.

Burgoyne asked for a truce on October 13. During three days of negotiations, he demanded liberal terms. Gates agreed. The British would be allowed to depart their camp with the "honors of war." They could return to England if they agreed not to fight in America again. The document of surrender would be called a "convention," not a capitulation.

At nine A.M. on October 17, Burgoyne's troops marched between long lines of silent American soldiers. The redcoats and Germans stacked their muskets for the last time.

Word shot through the new country. Patriots were delirious, loyalists stunned. When the news crossed the Atlantic, Britons could not believe it. For the first time in their history, an entire British army had surrendered. An account of the battle reached the ears of the French on December 4. In less than two weeks, King Louis XVI had agreed to declare war on his perennial rival. In early February 1778, he formally pledged to support the independence of the United States.

While Horatio Gates basked in glory, Benedict Arnold lay in an Albany hospital suffering searing pain. He rejected a doctor's advice that his leg be amputated. In his dispatch to Congress,

Gates championed all of his officers, including the "gallant Major General Arnold."

Gates's own handling of the campaign was worthy of praise. He had held the line against the enemy juggernaut, brought Burgoyne to a standstill, and worn him down until the Americans could win a clear victory.

BUT PATIENCE AND planning, caution and defense, can only accomplish so much. Sooner or later, as George III himself had said early in the rebellion, "blows must decide whether they are to be subject to this Country or independent."

When the issue came to blows, it was Benedict Arnold who had made the decisive contribution. During both battles on Bemis Heights, he had directed much of the action. When needed, he had risked his life to bring about victory. Saratoga would prove the pinnacle of his career as a soldier, the moment of greatness he had yearned for all his life.

Part Four

Downfall—1780

Benedict Arnold, 1780
(Library of Congress Prints and Photographs Division)

16

Trust

"IT THUS CAME ABOUT, THROUGH A SINGULAR INSTANCE OF THE irony of fate," wrote historian Gardner Allen in 1913, "that we owe the salvation of our country at a critical juncture to one of the blackest traitors in history."

In September 1780, George Washington was close to despair. The past three years had failed to deliver on the promise of the great victory at Saratoga. The Continental Army had endured the awful winter at Valley Forge, when men's legs turned black from frostbite for lack of blankets. In a blistering letter to Congress, Washington had berated the delegates, who "seem to have little feeling for the naked and distressed Soldier, I feel superabundantly for them."

During 1778 and 1779, the fighting had abated and American patriots began to sense that the war was nearly over. Enthusiasm for continuing the conflict waned. The French alliance helped, but Congress so neglected the army that in May 1780, Continental soldiers from Connecticut mutinied to protest a lack of food. Morale in the army hit rock bottom, desertion prevailed. Disgruntled officers, Washington wrote, "brood over their discontent, and have lately shown a disposition to enter into seditious combinations."

"There never has been a stage of the war," he continued, "in which the dissatisfaction has ever been so general or alarming." The enlistments of half the soldiers serving under him were due to expire the first of January 1781.

The British, meanwhile, were renewing the war. In May 1780 they took Charleston, the major port city of the South. They captured five thousand patriot soldiers there, along with tons of supplies. Congress sent Horatio Gates to lead a force against the army of British general Charles Cornwallis in South Carolina. Gates suffered a disastrous defeat at Camden in August. A thousand more Continentals and militia were taken prisoner while the hero of Saratoga retreated in disgrace. The French had finally landed troops in Newport in July, but their army included only five thousand men and its commander, the Comte de Rochambeau, was not inclined to take the field. He was appalled by the ragtag Continental Army, only ten thousand poorly equipped men. "Do not depend on these people," the veteran advised his superiors.

The fate of the Revolution balanced on a knife-edge. By the first week in September, Washington was sending militia volunteers home—with the shortage of provisions, he had no way to feed them. He feared that if he left camp, his army guarding the crucial Hudson Highlands above New York might disintegrate altogether. He put off meeting Rochambeau for two months. When Lafayette urged him to respond to the French commander's desire to confer with him, Washington said, "There is nothing I should more ardently desire." But his presence in camp was necessary to keep the army "going on at all."

On September 17, he finally rode to Hartford in central Connecticut to meet the French officers. Washington presented his idea of mounting a joint French-American campaign to retake New York City. Privately, the French commander thought the plan absurd, given the patriots' weakness. Publicly, he said he would need more troops before he could undertake any mission.

Although the conference accomplished little, the change of scene lifted Washington's spirits. At towns along the way, cheering crowds turned out to greet him. Cannon salutes and fireworks signaled the patriotic fervor he inspired.

ON MONDAY, SEPTEMBER 25, 1780, Washington rose early to begin the next leg of his return trip. He had spent the night at Fishkill, New York, not far from the Hudson River. The day was sunny and dry. As the mist lifted, he and his entourage enjoyed a lovely vista of the broad river valley. Lafayette had accompanied him to Hartford to serve as interpreter. The corpulent Henry Knox, his artillery chief and adviser, rode with him, along with Washington's aide, Colonel Alexander Hamilton, additional staff officers, and two dozen horsemen as bodyguards.

The plan that morning was to meet with Major General Benedict Arnold at his home and headquarters, an elegant house on the east bank of the river, which the patriots had confiscated from a loyalist named Beverley Robinson. Arnold was now the commander of the lower Hudson region, which included the critical fort at West Point, two miles north of the Robinson house on the opposite bank.

The party planned to breakfast with Arnold, then inspect the West Point defensive works, which the general was in the process of strengthening. Washington joked with Lafayette that he and the other young officers were anxious to enjoy the company of Arnold's wife.

Arnold had fallen for Margaret Shippen in 1778 while still recovering from his Saratoga wound. Known, like his first wife, as Peggy, she was the eighteen-year-old daughter of Philadelphia magistrate Edward Shippen. "My public character is well known," he had assured her, "my private one is, I hope, irreproachable." In April 1779, the couple had married in a simple ceremony. Petite and refined, with a sparkling personality, Peggy was said to be one of the most beautiful women in America. She had borne Arnold a son in March 1780.

Duty came first. Washington decided to inspect several redoubts along the east bank of the river. He sent two aides, Majors Samuel Shaw and James McHenry, to inform the Arnolds that their breakfast guests would be delayed. These officers sat down to a meal and McHenry soon observed Arnold departing toward the river. The general, he later said, displayed "an embarrassment which I could not at that time account for."

Raising dust along the road, Washington's group arrived at the Robinson house just before ten thirty. As the officers sat down to eat, Major David Franks, Arnold's aide, expressed his deep regret that General Arnold had been called to West Point unexpectedly. He assured them that his superior would return soon, certainly in time for dinner. Unfortunately, Mrs. Arnold was feeling ill, as was Colonel Richard Varick, Arnold's principal assistant.

After breakfast, Washington decided to go ahead with his planned inspection of West Point. Taking Knox and Lafayette with him, he was rowed across the Hudson to the landing on the far side. The principal bastion there had been named Fort Arnold in recognition of the illustrious general. Washington expected the usual color guard and cannon salute, but no such welcome awaited. Instead, he encountered confusion. The fort's ranking officer, Colonel John Lamb, had not anticipated a visit from the commander in chief, nor had he seen Benedict Arnold that morning, or for the past two days.

Washington found this odd. What could it mean? "The impropriety of his conduct when he knew I was to be there," he said of Arnold later, "struck me very forcibly, and my mind misgave me; but I had not the least idea of the real cause."

As he walked and rode around the system of forts and gun emplacements on the rising ground above the point, Washington's anxiety grew. When Arnold had taken command of the post in June, he had assured Washington that he would expedite efforts to restore the deteriorating structures. Little of the work had been completed. Walls were collapsing. Ammunition supplies were low. Soldiers had been sent away to other duties.

After the tour, a worried and perplexed Washington returned to the Robinson house. Arnold was still not back. The general went to his room to rest. A messenger soon interrupted him with a packet of papers. The general examined the documents. Struggling to master emotions that gripped him by the throat, he called for Knox.

"Arnold," he said, "has betrayed us. Whom can we trust now?"

IT WAS THE worst sort of betrayal. Washington was acutely aware that trust formed the core of a republic—the trust that the people put in their representatives, that Congress put in the army, that officers and enlisted men shared among themselves.

"We mutually pledge to each other our Lives, our Fortunes and our sacred Honor," the signers of the Declaration had affirmed. Without "each other," there was no republic. Discarding the guidance of a divinely inspired king or a traditional aristocracy, the Founders relied on an informal but pervasive web of mutual trust among citizens. Treason struck at the very principle that held the nation together.

And George Washington loved Benedict Arnold. They were alike in their enthusiasm for the cause, in their assurance in battle, in their initiative and perseverance. The childless Washington looked on his young aides and officers as his family. Arnold's betrayal broke his heart.

AFTER THE MUSKET ball shattered his leg at Saratoga in October 1777, Arnold had spent several months in an army hospital at

Albany. By refusing amputation, he took his chances with gangrene. The leg slowly began to heal. His doctors found him "very peevish," a querulous and impatient patient. For months, he could barely sit up. His pain was unrelenting. By the time he was able to get out of bed, his wounded leg had shrunk by two inches. Walking was still an effort for him two years later.

Congress had proclaimed Horatio Gates to be the victor at Saratoga—they awarded him a gold medal for his effort. They also praised Generals Arnold and Lincoln for their contributions. In November 1777, the delegates voted Arnold his reward: They would finally restore him to the rank he had held before other generals were promoted over him following the Valcour campaign. Henry Laurens, now the president of Congress, sent him a letter with the long-sought good news, expressing his "very great respect and esteem." George Washington said the promotion was "necessary justice."

Rather than delight, Arnold displayed indifference. Two months passed before he got around to replying to Laurens. In his answer, he did not even mention the issue of rank.

His Saratoga injury continued to torment him. On March 12, 1778, five months after the battle on Bemis Heights, he wrote to George Washington to report that the wound had "broken out again," aggravated by splinters of bone that the doctors would have to extract. He nevertheless assured the commander in chief of his desire to "render every assistance in my power" to the patriot cause and of his hope of "seeing peace and happiness restored" to the country.

After months in Albany, Arnold was able to endure a move to a friend's house in Middletown, Connecticut, north of New Haven. It allowed him to recuperate closer to his sister and sons. While he was there, he tried to revive his courtship with Betsy DeBlois, the young belle of Boston. In his letters, he lamented that her "cruel indifference" had made him "languish in despair."

The wording suggested a real loneliness, but Arnold's hackneyed language failed to strike a spark. The seventeen-year-old still wanted nothing to do with him.

It wasn't until May 4, 1778, that Arnold was able to return to New Haven and enjoy a hero's welcome. Crowds turned out, his company of Foot Guards paraded in dress uniforms. Hannah and his three sons welcomed him home at last. That spring Arnold received a gift intended to cheer him. A French nobleman had given George Washington a gold sword knot and set of epaulets and suggested he bestow them on his favorite general. Washington sent them to Arnold "as a testimony of my sincere regard and approbation of your conduct."

On May 21, "to the great joy of the army," Arnold arrived in Valley Forge, where the men of the Continental Army had endured their dismal winter. Many attributed the supply shortages to a stingy and neglectful Congress. Connecticut general Samuel Holden Parsons would write, "The wretches who have crept into Congress are almost below contempt. Our country will never prosper in their hands."

Congress, wary of the discontent within the army and intent on rooting out potential loyalists, had dictated that officers swear an oath of allegiance to the United States. The soldiers had to acknowledge the nation's independence, abjure allegiance to King George, and oppose his "abettors, assistants and adherents." Arnold pronounced and signed the oath in front of Henry Knox on May 30, 1778.

The alliance with France was one bright point that spring. Facing war with their old rival, the British high command decided to adopt a more defensive strategy. With Britons tiring of war, Parliament also passed two bills of reconciliation. They sent peace envoys, known as the Carlisle Commission, to attempt a negotiated settlement with the Americans. The crown would agree to every colonial demand, including recognition of Congress, as long as the rebels were willing to renounce independence and rejoin the empire. But patriots were determined—no deal.

General Sir Henry Clinton, in command of all British forces in America following the departure of William Howe, now shifted his focus to the South. He positioned his troops closer to the West Indies—Britain's valuable islands there had suddenly become vulnerable to the French fleet. His army captured Savannah in December 1778. In June he had evacuated his forces from Philadelphia, which the British had held since the previous September. As the enemy forces marched across New Jersey toward New York, Washington's army stung them in a sharp engagement at Monmouth.

Knowing that Arnold was not yet fit to lead troops in the field, Washington decided to make him the military governor of the Philadelphia region. The stationary post required mainly administrative work as the city made the transition back to civilian rule. The assignment would keep his valuable officer busy until his health was restored. Normally astute at judging and assigning men, Washington was unknowingly making a grave error.

MANY PHILADELPHIANS HAD thrived under the British occupation. The city was home to no small number of loyalists and even more "neutrals." British officers had dominated the winter social season, dancing at balls and mounting theatrical productions. City merchants welcomed the chance to sell supplies to the enemy for hard cash rather than accept nearly worthless Continental currency. Farmers from the hinterlands also found the British Army a ready market.

After the British departure from Philadelphia, patriots took their revenge on those who had collaborated with the enemy. Three thousand loyalists left the city voluntarily with the departing regulars. Others were proscribed and forced to vacate their homes.

Leading the patriot faction was Joseph Reed, a successful, London-educated lawyer. Reed had vacillated politically early on, pushing for reconciliation with Britain even as he participated in the patriotic Committee of Correspondence in Philadelphia. He had served as Washington's aide and adjutant general early in the war, but had used the position to raise questions about his commander's competence. He was elected to Congress early in 1778. Before the end of the year, he would become the head of Pennsylvania's Supreme Executive Council, a post equivalent to governor.

After the reoccupation of the capital by patriots, Reed prosecuted almost two dozen Philadelphians for treason on slight evidence. He charged and convicted two elderly Quaker collaborators, ignored a clemency petition signed by religious and military leaders, and hanged them. Mob actions in the streets expressed the general anger against the city's high-toned citizens who were suspected of Tory leanings.

As the man assigned to manage this fraught situation, Arnold was entirely out of his element. The position required the skills of a diplomat, not a soldier. Arnold loathed politicians in general, resented insubordination in any form, and was far too blunt in dealings with city officials. He declared martial law and closed all shops during the first weeks of the reoccupation. Philadelphia's radical patriots resented his toleration of loyalists and bridled against military rule.

On June 19, 1778, the day after the British left, Arnold entered the city in a gala procession, riding in an ostentatious carriage. He surrounded himself with the luxuries he had missed during the long privation of his military life. He settled in the spacious John Penn house on Market Street, formerly occupied by British general Howe. He spent lavishly and reveled in dinners and entertainments that drew the city's elite. His extravagance elicited further animosity from austere patriots. Worse, he frequently socialized with suspected loyalists, including the family of Edward Shippen, a prominent Philadelphia lawyer and judge.

With the war in abeyance, many American citizens of means felt an urge to indulge in luxuries, including items manufactured in Britain. They ignored the principle of nonimportation, the patriots' earliest strategy for resisting British rule. The level of imports at New York reached prewar levels, and many of the products filtered out to rich Americans. "Speculation, peculation, and an insatiable thirst for riches seem to have got the better of every other consideration," Washington wrote to a friend. Benjamin Franklin was vexed to find that, in the middle of a war, even Congress was spending money on imported tea and on "gewgaws and superfluities." Avid patriots looked on Arnold's opulence as emblematic of the times.

Eventually Arnold became a target of Reed and his backers. The military governor, Reed asserted, was trying "to subvert the Whig interest" and coddling loyalists. The lawyer drew up eight charges against him. Some involved profiting from his position, others were as petty as allowing one of his aides to send a militia sergeant to fetch his barber.

It was true that Arnold had participated in the black market. Early in the occupation, he had used state-owned wagons to transport personal property he intended to sell. The ethical boundaries of profiteering were murky during the Revolution. Nathanael Greene, an officer of sterling reputation, took the usual one-percent commission on purchases he made during his time as quartermaster general. He funneled public spending to his family's business. "My appointment," he admitted, "is flattering to my fortune."

Reed became yet another enemy of Arnold, determined to prosecute him for his malfeasance. He filed formal charges in January 1779 and had them printed as a handbill. A committee of Congress tossed out half of Reed's accusations but ordered

Washington to hold a court-martial on four of them. Insulted and only partly vindicated, Arnold received permission from Washington to resign his command in Philadelphia. He told the commander in chief in March 1779 that he would be happy to rejoin the army when he was physically able.

To SOME, ARNOLD'S April 1779 marriage to the exquisite Peggy Shippen aroused further suspicion. During the British occupation, Peggy had danced the night away with enemy officers and was particularly friendly with Captain John André, who would later be promoted to major and named the British Army's adjutant general.

In writing to Edward Shippen asking for his daughter's hand, Arnold had downplayed their political differences. "I flatter myself the time is at hand," he wrote, "when our unhappy contests will be at an end and peace and domestic happiness be restored to everyone." It was a sentiment widely shared in the country.

Theirs was an attraction of opposites. Peggy reveled in art, poetry, and music. Arnold expressed little interest in high culture and wanted the education of his sons to be "useful rather than learned. Life is too uncertain to throw away in speculation." Yet their marriage was marked by a devotion that would withstand extraordinary adversity.

Although he wanted to return to active duty, Arnold was still held back by his leg injury. At his wedding, another officer stood at his side to help support him. He decided to take a leave from the army and settle into his new life with Peggy. He had borrowed money to buy a beautiful estate on the Schuylkill River. Unfortunately, he was so short of cash that he had to rent the mansion and move with his bride into a smaller home in the city.

Idleness was Arnold's enemy. In action, he inspired men, improvised brilliantly, and never flinched from the blows of adversity. During gaps in the fighting he brooded, squabbled with those around him, and dwelled on perceived injustices.

In one of his rare comments about his inner life in the days before their marriage, Arnold wrote to Peggy, "I am heartily tired with my journey and almost so with human nature. I daily discover so much baseness and ingratitude among mankind that I almost blush at being of the same species."

On May 5, he sent Washington a frantic appeal to hold the delayed court-martial that would allow him finally to clear his name. "If Your Excellency thinks me criminal," he wrote, "for Heavens sake let me be immediately tried and if found guilty executed." He reminded his commander that he had made every sacrifice of fortune and blood, "and become a Cripple in the Service of my Country." He complained of the "ungrateful Returns I have received of my Countrymen."

ON MAY 10, 1779, a nervous thirty-five-year-old glass and china salesman from Philadelphia walked into the New York office of Major John André, who had recently been named head of intelligence by his mentor, the British commander in chief Sir Henry Clinton. The visitor, Joseph Stansbury, was loyalist in his sentiments, although he had dutifully taken the oath of allegiance to the United States that was required of citizens when patriots regained control of Philadelphia from the British.

Stansbury could hardly pour out his story quickly enough. He had come under a "solemn obligation of secrecy." A very important Continental Army general, a man who had once purchased furniture from him for his Philadelphia mansion, wanted to convey "his intention of offering his services to the Commander-in-Chief of the British forces, in a way that would most effectually restore the former government." His name: Major General Benedict Arnold.

André was astounded. If the information proved authentic, it would be the most consequential defection of the war. If handled properly, it might go a long way toward assuring a British victory. He quickly set up a means to communicate with Arnold, involving code names, ciphers, invisible ink. The news excited the usually dour Clinton, who had been struggling to find a way to prevail in America since Burgoyne's disaster at Saratoga.

Because Arnold currently held no command, André and Clinton decided that it was best for him to remain in the Continental Army rather than join them openly. He could feed them intelligence while waiting for an assignment that would allow him to make the most helpful contribution to the British cause. The delay would also give Clinton a chance to make sure Arnold's offer was not a ruse.

When he did defect, Arnold would be risking his position and property in America. He insisted that the British adequately compensate him for his losses. André sent a letter back with Stansbury, assuring Arnold that if his efforts would lead to the defeat of rebel troops or the capture of important patriots, "then would the generosity of the nation exceed even his own most sanguine hope."

AFTER ARNOLD HAD taken the first step toward treason, events seemed to confirm him in his decision. Joseph Reed had repeatedly postponed Arnold's court-martial as he tried to gather evidence to prop up his case. When the panel of officers finally met in December 1779, they found Arnold guilty of two of the four charges and sentenced him to a simple reprimand. Washington wrote up the softest censure possible and sent it with a consoling letter. But Arnold, always thin-skinned, was stung.

Another blow came when the Treasury Board of Congress weighed in on his convoluted financial claims for distributions and outlays that went back to his service in Canada. Again, lost and nonexistent records became the basis for a judgment against his assertion that the government owed him a substantial amount of money. The finding was an injury piled on an insult. Arnold, in serious need of cash, felt it acutely.

The dismal record of Congress in supporting the Continental Army, along with the British military resurgence during 1780, further convinced Arnold, if he needed convincing, that he had been right in his decision to join the enemy.

FIFTEEN MONTHS PASSED after Arnold's initial contact with André. He occasionally sent the British information about American troop movements and operations, including a plan, never carried out, to renew the invasion of Canada using an army led by Lafayette. He also passed on word of the impending arrival of the French fleet and army in Providence, Rhode Island—the British did not move quickly enough to intercept them. He resisted Washington's suggestion that he might be ready to take on another field command. His leg wound, he said, would not allow it.

All this time, Arnold was playing a life-or-death game. One breach of secrecy within the British command, one betrayal, one intercepted message, would mean disgrace and an ignominious death by hanging.

During 1780, he set his sights on command of the Hudson Valley, including West Point. In that position, he could facilitate the British capture of one of the most strategic posts in America, along with a substantial garrison of troops. It was an offer that tantalized Henry Clinton.

Washington gave Arnold the command in June 1780. By September, everything was in place. Arnold had weakened West Point's defenses and sent detachments of defenders to other locations. General Clinton had made plans to rush transports loaded with his own troops up the Hudson River. He kept the target se-cret, letting on that the force would attack the Chesapeake region. Detailed information from Arnold would allow an easy victory at the undermanned fort.

All that was needed was a final meeting to solidify the ar-rangements and make sure the offer was genuine. André would go to meet his informant face-to-face and judge his trustworthiness.

It was never clear whether Arnold imagined that the British could move quickly enough to take Washington prisoner in the process of capturing the fort. "How far he meant to involve me in the catastrophe," Washington later wrote, "does not ap-pear by any indubitable evidence." He felt that Arnold would not have endangered the main objective of handing over West Point by trying to also arrange the simultaneous capture of the commander in chief, but such a double coup would certainly have pleased Sir Henry Clinton.

THE EVENTS THAT unfolded that last weekend of September 1780 were among the most dramatic of the Revolution. André came up the river on the British warship *Vulture* the night of Thursday, September 21, landed on the west bank of the Hudson, and met Arnold in a grove of fir trees. The two rode north on horseback to a house owned by Joshua Hett Smith. The thirty-one-year-old New York lawyer lived on a hilltop overlooking King's Ferry, the main crossing point to patriot-held Peekskill. Smith was suspected of having loyalist sympathies, and Arnold's aides had warned him against having any dealings with the man.

On the way, Arnold and André passed through a checkpoint from neutral ground into patriot-controlled territory—André had covered his scarlet regimental uniform with a blue cloak. It was a fatal error.

The two men discussed military details of the British seizure of West Point and finalized the terms of compensation for Arnold. If the operation was a success, André promised him a payment of £20,000 (around $4 million today). It was a substantial amount but, to Arnold, only fair recompense for the losses he would sustain for his action.

Their talk lasted until nearly dawn, too late for André to return to the *Vulture* under cover of darkness. Cannon fire from an American battery then forced the warship's captain to retreat down the river. Arnold convinced André to return to British lines that evening by land along the eastern bank. Smith would serve as guide.

The British major would have to disguise himself in civilian clothing. Arnold gave him plans and maps he had drawn up to help with the conquest of West Point. He told André to conceal the papers inside his stocking. The forcefulness of Arnold's personality overcame direct orders that General Clinton had conveyed to his aide not to venture into rebel-held territory out of uniform or to carry incriminating papers. In his enthusiasm for the plot, André had slipped from being a British officer under a flag of truce. He was now officially a spy.

Smith took André across on the ferry that Friday afternoon, and they headed south on horseback. They were stopped several times by patriot sentries and patrols. Each time, Smith showed passes written out by Arnold and convinced the questioners of his sincerity. The two men shared a bed at a roadside inn that night.

After breakfast on Saturday morning, Smith told his companion that he was turning back and that André should continue southward until he reached British lines. Smith headed north to the Robinson house to let Arnold know that André was safely on his way.

The adjutant general of the British Army found himself riding alone through the treacherous no-man's-land of Westchester

County. If he could make it to British lines, the long war in America might soon be over, and he a hero. If not, he might himself become a casualty of that war.

He rode through a dismal landscape of deserted farms, where irregulars from both sides operated. "Cowboys" were loyalists who served the British by stealing cattle. "Skinners" supported the patriot cause. Both groups raided farms and robbed travelers for their own benefit. New York governor George Clinton had recently offered a bounty for any cattle that patriots recovered from the cowboys.

André's horse plodded along the hilly, heavily wooded terrain that would be made famous as Washington Irving's Sleepy Hollow. Suddenly, three armed men appeared, blocking the back road Smith had told him to follow.

"Gentlemen," André said, "I hope you belong to our party."

One of the men asked, "What party?"

"The lower," said André, meaning the British to the south. Assuming they were loyalists, he now told the men he was an English officer.

"Get down," the stranger said, "we are Americans."

The men were members of a local militia unit and had been hoping to meet up with some of the cattle rustlers. Their leader was twenty-two-year-old John Paulding, a tall, sturdily built farmer.

André presented the pass from Arnold. The men ignored it, searched him, found the documents, took him prisoner, refused the bribe he offered for his release, and escorted him to an American outpost.

The officer in charge there sent a messenger to Arnold, the commander of the region, describing the suspicious circumstances. Then he had second thoughts and sent the papers found on André, including the plan of West Point, by another courier directly to George Washington. André, acutely embarrassed by being discovered out of uniform behind American lines, wrote a full confession, which was also sent in the packet that Washington would open at the Robinson house.

The message to Arnold arrived first. He immediately understood that the plot had been discovered. After a quick goodbye to his wife, he had eight privates row and sail his barge toward the *Vulture*, the British warship, which now lay well down the river.

"THE STRANGEST THING in the world has happened," General Henry Knox told the chief gunner at West Point. "Arnold has gone to the enemy."

Following his shocking discovery, Washington immediately sent Hamilton and another aide racing down the river with the distant hope of catching Arnold before he reached British lines. He issued a flurry of orders to bring a substantial portion of his army up the river to head off an enemy attack, which might already be in motion. Men were roused from sleep that night, hastily mustered and set marching northward.

Next, Washington had to address a domestic drama. Mrs. Arnold had fallen into a fit of hysteria. She had stripped off her clothes except for a scanty morning gown and paraded in front of an embarrassed Colonel Varick, ranting about the missing Arnold and insisting on seeing Washington. Although Washington, Alexander Hamilton, and other aides believed her both sincere and innocent, Varick later concluded that it was "a piece of splendid acting" intended to distract the officers and aid Arnold's escape.

By that time, her husband was approaching the *Vulture* waving a white handkerchief. At the last minute he announced to his crew his intention of changing sides. He offered them promotions if they would join him. Two of them did, but coxswain

James Lurvey, a five-year veteran, answered decisively, "No, Sir, one coat is enough for me to wear at a time."

ALL AGREED THAT Major John André had what Alexander Hamilton called "a becoming sensibility." Educated in England and Switzerland, he was adept at writing poetry and was a skillful artist. After his capture in a treasonous plot, he charmed American officers, Washington included, just as he had beguiled the ladies of Philadelphia. Some British officers, on the other hand, regarded the thirty-year-old adjutant as a "cringing, insidious sycophant." The favoritism shown him by Sir Henry Clinton incited jealousy and rumors of homosexuality.

Washington appointed a board of general officers in camp to hear André's case. The plot was uncovered on Monday, the board condemned him to death on Friday, and he was hanged the following Monday, October 2. Many contrasted the suave, honorable André, who went to his death gallantly, with the rough-edged, treasonous Arnold.

ARNOLD'S BETRAYAL SHOCKED and disappointed his friends. The artilleryman John Lamb, who had been wounded with him at Quebec and fought beside him at Ridgefield, witnessed the discovery of Arnold's treason firsthand at West Point. Among the officers who led troops to the Point during the emergency were Return Jonathan Meigs and Henry Dearborn, both of whom had endured the grueling march over the Maine mountains with Arnold, and Alexander Scammell, who had faced some of the hottest fighting at Saratoga by his side.

Eleazer Oswald, who had been Arnold's trusted aide from the earliest days of the war, said, "Let his name sink as low in infamy, as it was once high in our esteem." Patriots throughout the country were likewise stunned, then consumed by hatred. "The streets of every city and village in the United States," a New Jersey newspaper stated, "rung with the crimes of General Arnold."

The idea that one of the foremost heroes of the war had become a traitor was almost too much to bear. "The days of eternity would be too few to atone for his crime," a writer declared in the *New York Packet.* His betrayal "confounds and distresses me," Lafayette said, "and, if I must confess it, humiliates me."

Effigies of Arnold were paraded through the streets of many cities. The one in Philadelphia showed him with two faces and holding a mask for good measure. A devil stood behind to prod him to hell. In Norwich, Connecticut, patriots smashed the grave of Arnold's father, who shared his name.

ON SEPTEMBER 6, 1781, nearly a year after openly switching sides, Benedict Arnold sailed up the Thames River at New London, Connecticut. It was familiar territory for him, only twelve miles south of his birthplace at Norwich. That day, he was aboard a British warship, dressed in a scarlet uniform, and leading a force of loyalists, Americans who opposed the "anarchy" of the Revolution. Together with British regulars and Hessian mercenaries, his battalion totaled 1,700 men.

Both sides had suffered in the previous nine months. On New Year's Day, 1781, the Continental soldiers of the Pennsylvania line had mutinied, left their camp near Morristown, New Jersey, and begun a march to Philadelphia to enforce their grievances against Congress. In doing so, they let it be known that they were seeking fairness, not intending to become "Arnolds" by joining the enemy. Negotiations and concessions kept the mutiny from going too far. But a few weeks later an uprising by New Jersey Continentals ended with two soldiers being shot dead by a firing squad.

The British also struggled. Their campaign in the South was brilliantly thwarted by patriot troops under Nathanael Greene. General Cornwallis transferred his army to Virginia in May. By August he had taken refuge at Yorktown. Stranded there, he hoped to be rescued by the British fleet.

In New York, General Sir Henry Clinton had named Arnold a brigadier general in his army. At the end of December 1780, he had sent him to fight in Virginia. Arnold's "thundering excursions" of destruction at the head of two thousand regulars and loyalists spread "terror and alarm" through the state, a major provider of food and forage for patriot armies. He was so successful wearing a scarlet coat that he proved something of an embarrassment to British generals who had tried for similar results without success.

Now Clinton sent Arnold to raid the Connecticut coast. He wanted to create a diversion to draw rebel attention away from Cornwallis. He also saw value in cleaning out "the most detestable nest of pirates on the continent"—New London was a major port for the privateers who preyed on British shipping.

Arnold split his force, leading one battalion against New London and sending another across the river to assault Fort Griswold, a bastion on a hill overlooking the harbor. Troops confiscated supplies in New London and set fire to more. An explosion of a gunpowder cache spread the flames. Soon a good part of the city and docks were burning. In all, sixty-five homes, along with numerous stores, warehouses, and an Anglican church, burned to the ground.

At Griswold, the 160 militiamen and civilians defending the fort mounted a respectable resistance against 800 British and Hessian soldiers. Patriot militia colonel William Ledyard led the defense, but the enemy soon gained entry to the fort, forcing him to surrender. After handing over his sword, Ledyard was immediately stabbed to death. British soldiers shot down surrendering

Americans wholesale, killing most of them. Patriots labeled the actions a massacre.

Arnold had ordered his men to respect private property, and he was not on the scene when his troops stormed Fort Griswold. But he took no action to stop the town being burned, nor did he reprimand the officers who had condoned the killing at the fort.

It was a bloody, controversial outcome to the last battle of the Revolutionary War in the north. Six weeks later, Cornwallis surrendered his army to George Washington at Yorktown. The war for independence was effectively over.

On December 15, 1781, Benedict Arnold boarded the British warship *Robust* bound for England. He would never set foot in the United States again.

Explanations

HE HAD, OF COURSE, COMMITTED TREASON BEFORE. ALL who took up arms against the crown were subject to punishment for their insurrection. By returning his loyalty to King George, Benedict Arnold was joining the many thousands of Americans who had remained faithful all along, had supported and fought for the old order. Although these citizens were reviled, assaulted, and in many instances driven into exile, they were generally sincere in their beliefs.

But Arnold had violated a deeper principle of loyalty. He had joined a cause, led men to their deaths for shared beliefs, and formed deep bonds of friendship around mutual values. He betrayed those comrades as well as his country. He led enemy soldiers in warring against his fellow citizens. No excuse justified his treachery. His plot could have had important consequences for the outcome of the war. As it turned out, the seditious scheme, discovered and neutralized, had almost no effect. Patriots thanked Providence for thwarting the conspiracy.

Arnold had hoped that his change of sides would inspire many other American officers to do the same. It did not. Nor did it excite a new wave of fervor among patriots. Enlistments did not surge; desertion, even mutiny, remained a problem. Congressional delegates continued to neglect the needs of the soldiers; citizens still hungered for imported luxuries.

THE QUESTION ASKED about Benedict Arnold the day his treason was uncovered has been repeated for nearly 250 years: Why?

The editors of the *New York Packet* rendered the easiest and most obvious verdict: He had committed treason "for the base-born passion, love of gold." Although Arnold was adamant that he had not succumbed to mercenary motives, many of his contemporaries accused him of committing treason for profit. He was said to be obsessed with money. The British offered to compensate him handsomely. Certainly the £20,000 sterling that General Clinton promised if the plan succeeded was an attractive inducement. Even the £6,000 that Arnold received for the failed plot was considerable. Greed was the simplest, most understandable explanation for his crime.

There was a sense in which money did explain Arnold. All his life, he looked at the world with a businessman's eye. He peered through the surface toward what an item or transaction was worth in the market. He thought in terms of costs, expenses, and the potential for profit. He juggled debt and credit with a practiced hand. It was a habit of perception that he could not escape. Contemporaries interpreted it as avarice. British officers who knew him after his disaffection spoke of his "love of money, his ruling passion." Some modern historians have judged that Arnold changed sides "first and foremost for the money."

But while the instinct for lucre never left him, it's hard to imagine that he retreated from one of the highest peaks of achievement and renown to an infantile concern for pounds and pence. Arnold had never been attracted to money for its own sake, was never a hoarder. He wanted the luxuries it could buy because they represented for him the status he was always climbing toward. They measured the distance between himself and his father's ruin.

If he were motivated primarily by greed, why did he neglect his thriving business to put himself in harm's way in the first place? Why did he spend his own funds to supply and pay his men when Congress came up short? Why toss John Lamb a thousand pounds for enlistment bonuses? Even after deciding to switch sides, Arnold reached into his purse to help educate Joseph Warren's orphaned children, who had been "entirely neglected" by the state. Greed should be made of sterner stuff.

Did his wife make him do it? The Shippen family considered themselves neutrals rather than avowed loyalists—Peggy's father was on friendly terms with George Washington and after the war became the chief justice of Pennsylvania's Supreme Court. Peggy knew of the treason plot and, through her friendship with Major André, facilitated it. She doubtless supported and encouraged her husband once he made his decision, but nothing in his life or personality suggests she made it for him.

Other reasons put forth for Arnold's apostasy were more far-fetched. Some critics asserted that, however well documented his heroism, he had been a faux patriot from the beginning, his acts of courage "accidents." In fact, he had been a blackguard all his life. Absurd stories were bruited in early Arnold biographies about his disgraceful behavior as a child. It was his custom, one said, "to maim and mangle young birds" and to spread broken glass on pathways as a malicious joke. He was mad. He was a drunkard. He was in the grip of Satan.

A FEW DAYS after he went over to the enemy, Arnold published a document that suggested his own reasons for his change of heart. In this "Letter to the Inhabitants of America," he complained that congressional delegates—"Men who are Criminally protracting the War"—had failed to appreciate his achievements, had denied him promotion, and had proven themselves incompetent, faithless, and venal. Alexander Hamilton concurred that the main motive for Arnold's defection was "the ingratitude he had experienced from his countrymen." As far back as June 1775, during the imbroglio at Ticonderoga, Arnold had declared "the Congress are dubious of my rectitude or abilities, which is sufficient inducement for me to decline serving them longer."

He also blamed the French alliance for pushing him to switch sides. During his formative years, France had warred against Britain and her colonies. Like many New Englanders raised in a Puritan household, Arnold detested Catholicism. He considered the absolutist monarchy of Louis XVI "the enemy of the Protestant faith." The French were a bad match for Americans, and he suspected their motives.

He also wrote that his decision had turned on a hope for reconciliation between America and Britain, both of which he held in esteem. "A redress of grievances was my only object," he declared. He referred to the conflict as a "civil war," which needed to end as soon as possible. By assisting a British victory, Arnold later said, he was sure he would be rendering "the most essential service to both countries." To facilitate a compromise was the best way to save his comrades from further bloodshed. The belated peace overtures offered by the 1778 Carlisle Commission, Arnold implied, justified an immediate cessation of hostilities. The British government had offered to redress all grievances save independence. He had always opposed independence, he said, but in 1776 had been too busy fighting a war to take a stand against it.

It wasn't surprising that Arnold's explanations seemed formulated to excuse and absolve his treason rather than to expound on the deeply held beliefs that motivated it. The words of the public letter were not his. The document was written at Arnold's direction by William Smith, the royal chief justice of New York. Most of the complaints were standard loyalist propaganda. The language was that of a lawyer, not of a plainspoken soldier.

Few took Arnold's rationalizations seriously—the arguments were far too flimsy.

Arnold was not the only officer to be slighted by Congress. If he didn't like his treatment, he could have resigned with honor and left the army, as others did. In any case, by the time of his defection, he had been granted his long-sought promotion and officially praised for his heroism.

If he had disagreed with American independence, why did his most ardent efforts on behalf of the patriot cause come after the Declaration? He had never previously articulated any argument against breaking with Britain. Like many officers, he had been eager for the move, which served to inspire the troops.

He was far too experienced as a military strategist not to see that the French alliance was a necessary expedient for the resource-poor Americans. It signaled no embrace of papal religion or ratification of absolutist monarchy. Nor had he spoken out about his opposition to such an alliance before his defection.

As for his avowed hope of reconciliation, most patriots viewed the offer of peace as a ruse intended to divide the American populace and buy time. They dismissed the Carlisle Commission out of hand. "Silly and contemptible nonsense," Thomas Paine called it.

It was telling that Arnold could not find his own words to explain himself to his countrymen in what could have been the most important proclamation of his life. The fact was that his change of heart may have had a cause that he himself only dimly understood. It was a visceral impulse, not the product of careful reasoning. It was an act based on intuition rather than calculation. It was the final improvisation of his impassioned life.

FOR ALL HIS excuses, Arnold never thought of himself as treasonous. George Washington wrote that his subordinate was "lost to all sense of honor and shame" and had "no time for remorse." True, Arnold felt neither remorse nor shame. He cared about no one's judgment but his own, and he saw his actions, both before and after changing sides, as honorable. He repeatedly insisted on "the rectitude of my intentions." Circumstances had changed, not Arnold's dedication to his country. He had rebelled against the British government when they wronged him and his countrymen. He had returned to his former loyalty when they put forth their conciliatory offer.

Arnold only barely acknowledged that his actions might appear dishonorable. He wrote to Washington hours after his defection that he knew it was "a step, which the world may censure as wrong." Yet he asserted that the "principle of love to my country actuates my present conduct, however it may appear inconsistent to the world, who very seldom judge right of a man's actions."

If Arnold's motives for his treason seemed confused, so did the times. The upheaval of the Revolution strained the loyalties, even the mental stability, of many citizens. Centuries of tradition were being turned upside down. The well-marked road of honor had become a wilderness path of contention and new ideas. It was easy to lose one's way. Arnold had been one of the truest of true believers in the patriot cause, willing to sacrifice all, including his life. Yet his moral compass had failed him.

Washington, on reflection, may have best summed up Arnold's dramatic defection. It was, he said, "an unaccountable deprivation of presence of Mind in a Man of the first abilities."

THE REMAINDER OF Arnold's short, unhappy life contrasted sharply with the pageant of his war years. He and Peggy settled in London, now with two sons—two more boys and a girl would survive infancy. Some members of English society welcomed the former American general. He enjoyed a royal audience and offered King George military advice. Peggy received a generous annuity from the government "for her services" in the plot. Their boys, all of whom would enter military service, were assured officers' commissions.

Other Britons, disgusted by Arnold's treason or by his many contributions to the rebellion, scorned him and his family. Before he left America, according to a correspondent in London, he had "lost all his credit among the British troops, and the English shun to associate with him." In London, he and Peggy were sometimes hissed at when they attended the theater. He tried to obtain a commission in the military arm of the East India Company and was flatly refused. He fought a duel to extract an apology from a nobleman who had slighted him—no one was hurt.

In 1785, the Arnolds moved to Canada. They took up residence in St. John, a city on the coast of New Brunswick that had welcomed an influx of American loyalist exiles. Arnold returned to mercantile trade and plunged into land speculation. He did not succeed in amassing a large fortune, but his investments paid enough to support his family in comfort. He brought his sister, Hannah, and his three sons by his first wife to live with him in Canada. Richard, now in his late teens, helped run his father's store.

Arnold was as cranky as ever. Debts, disputes, and litigation soured his acceptance in St. John. The contention with his neighbors grew so heated that he was burned in effigy outside his own home.

After six years, Arnold and Peggy moved back to London, leaving his older sons to look after his Canadian interests. He again purchased ships and plunged into international trade, sailing mostly to the West Indies—he made thirteen trips to the Caribbean during the next eight years. During his voyages, Peggy, like his first wife, endured the loneliness of long absences. Nevertheless, she remained devoted to him and to her growing family.

When Britain went to war with revolutionary France in 1793, the high seas became a danger zone. In June 1794, Arnold sailed into the trading port at Guadeloupe, unaware that the island had been captured by the French. He tried to bluff his way out of trouble by claiming to be an American merchant. Suspicious French officials confined him on a prison ship in the harbor. He paid out part of the £5,000 he had gained from selling a cargo in St. Kitts to bribe his captors. He learned that the British were blockading the port and that the zealous French governor planned to have him guillotined. More bribes secured him a small raft. In the lush darkness of a Caribbean night, he put his money in a cask and set it afloat, shinnied down a rope, paddled the raft to an anchored skiff, and quietly rowed toward the harbor mouth. He managed to elude a French patrol boat in the process, accomplishing one final hairbreadth escape. He climbed onto a British ship, the *Boyne*, just before dawn. The cask containing his money washed up on a British-held beach, allowing him to recover what was left of his funds.

In succeeding months, he sailed as volunteer quartermaster with the British fleet and aided his fellow merchants in Guadeloupe. He and his family were granted more than thirteen thousand acres in Upper Canada as a reward for this service. But when he petitioned to be allowed to return to active military duty, the British government turned down his request.

His brief return to the action-filled life that he loved was balanced by tragedy. His eldest son, Benedict, now twenty-seven, had sought active duty in the war with France. In 1795, he was wounded while fighting in Jamaica. He refused to undergo an amputation, contracted gangrene, and died. He would be the last in a long line of Benedict Arnolds, a name now forever tainted.

"His death," Arnold wrote in a letter, "is a heavy stroke to me." Afflicted by the loss, he endured increasingly painful attacks of gout, which prevented him from accompanying his ships on their voyages. Asthma and heart failure wore down the aging soldier. In the spring of 1801, his health collapsed. He lost weight and became delirious. He died on June 14 at the age of sixty. Few took notice. An obituary printed in the *Gazette of the United States* conceded: "There is no doubt . . . but he was for some time, a real friend of the Revolution."

Peggy served as the executor of his estate and took pride in clearing up his typically convoluted finances, repaying his debts, and leaving the family free and clear. She lived only three years after him, dying of cancer in 1804.

18

❧

Life and Death

SAMUEL SHAW, A YOUNG AIDE TO HENRY KNOX, WROTE THAT "somehow or other, I cannot get Arnold out of my head." Americans have never been able to file Benedict Arnold's story away with those of the forgotten figures of a bygone age. He and his treason have troubled us down our history.

All knew that loyalty was at the heart of the matter, but loyalty to what? Just weeks after Arnold's treason, a writer admitted in the *Pennsylvania Packet* that a person's view of the general's guilt relied on his or her attitude. Arnold was "the ornament or the disgrace, the pride, or the pestilence of mankind" as the viewer's opinion dictated. Arnold himself wrote that "some may think I continued in the struggle of those unhappy days too long, and others that I quitted it too soon."

But avid patriots could not abide the suggestion that the worthiness of their cause was a matter of opinion. Zealots saw their principles as absolute, in all likelihood ordained by a higher power. Those who strayed from the faith were heretics, deserving of the severest condemnation.

The national conversation about loyalty and treason resurfaced eighty years after the Revolution when the nation plunged into the Civil War. In 1861, *Harper's Weekly* pointed readers' attention to "a few men directing this colossal treason, by whose side Benedict Arnold shines white as a saint."

After that war, national mythmakers depicted Confederate leaders with more magnanimity. One modern historian compared Arnold unfavorably to Robert E. Lee, who "declared his change of heart and simply shifted sides," rather than take money for doing so.

Lee justified his treason by asserting a higher loyalty to Virginia. "True patriotism," Lee wrote after the Civil War, "sometimes requires of men to act exactly contrary, at one period, to that which it does at another."

Yet Lee, the son of a heroic Revolutionary War officer, had sworn to defend the Constitution, just as Arnold had taken an oath of loyalty to his country. After shifting sides, Lee had no trouble transferring his allegiance to the Confederacy or waging war to destroy the United States. In order to create a new nation conceived in slavery, he oversaw the slaughter of tens of thousands of American soldiers, among them men he had trained as superintendent of the United States Military Academy at West Point.

In spite of their sedition, Confederate officers were long regarded as principled, even virtuous men. In time, they came to be honored alongside those who never betrayed the Union. Although more questions about the honor of their behavior have been raised in recent years and statues of them have fallen, they have avoided the blanket condemnation that has been the fate of Benedict Arnold.

"WE ARE A young Nation and have a character to establish," George Washington wrote to his younger brother in 1783 as he waited impatiently for the treaty that would formally end the Revolutionary War. "It behooves us therefore to set out right for first impressions will be lasting."

To guide the infant nation, citizens looked to the exemplary figures of the era. Washington himself became the central icon of the nation's founding. His image was immortalized, his conduct and demeanor held up as a model for his own and future generations. Other warriors and statesmen—Alexander Hamilton, Benjamin Franklin, Thomas Jefferson—entered the pantheon as examples of integrity and devotion to the public good. Over the years, myths turned them into idols. Their virtue was said to exclude all that was mean or dishonorable.

Villains too could serve as moral signposts. Just as Washington's image was inflated to extraordinary proportion, so Benedict Arnold was made out to be a treacherous character without peer, his virtues not just overshadowed but erased. His extraordinary betrayal became his central, and for many his only, attribute.

"We were all astonishment, each peeping at his next neighbor to see if any treason was hanging about him," Alexander Scammell declared in the aftermath of Arnold's failed plot. "We even descended to a critical examination of ourselves. This surprise soon settled down into a fixed detestation and abhorrence of Arnold."

The denigration of Arnold served a purpose. If patriots examined their own conscience and perceived a lack of public virtue, they could rest assured that at least they were more principled than the country's arch-traitor. And since genuine patriotism and social conscience are more or less lacking in every era, Arnold's reputation became a permanent, reassuring object lesson for citizens down the years.

We are no longer a young nation. We now see more clearly the cracks in our icons. Our champions enslaved human beings, tolerated political chicanery, conspired with enemies, and put personal profit above public benefit. We have come to understand that they were, after all, only human.

But what of Benedict Arnold?

In many ways, he was a typical American—cocky, restless,

grasping, perpetually optimistic, quick to take offense. He was a vivid example of the self-reliance and rugged individualism that would be celebrated by Americans from Ralph Waldo Emerson to Ronald Reagan. But self-reliance can swell to egoism, and confidence can beget arrogance. An impulse to write his own rules can make a man dangerous. And Benedict Arnold proved to be a dangerous man.

THE AMERICAN REVOLUTION was a product of ideas and war. Without the ideas, the war would have been a senseless insurrection—without the war, the ideas would not have gained a foothold in history. Before April 1775, Benedict Arnold's life was far from notable. He was a businessman on the make, a pushy and determined merchant, a man like many others. As soon as he entered the conflict, a new Arnold emerged.

Wars, Alexander Hamilton observed, "serve to bring to light talents and virtues which might otherwise have languished in obscurity." In the midst of combat, Arnold displayed a genius for strategy and tactics, for courage and leadership, that has been matched by few in our history. A light shined from him, a genius that threw the rest of his existence into shadow. Defying death inspired him. Violent action was more alluring than any idea, the rush of adrenaline more satisfying than any patriotic sentiment.

To most of the men who joined the Revolution, the war was the necessary means to achieve the Enlightenment ideals that inspired the rebellion. It's possible to imagine that for Arnold that logic was reversed. What excited him was not the abstract concepts but the fighting. The patriot cause was his pretext for violence. The immense, soul-transforming satisfaction he got from facing danger, overcoming adversity, and risking his life was more important to him than slogans or the prospect of a new political order.

If such a view holds truth, it's even possible to see his love of action, his addiction to violence and risk, as a motivation for—or at least an affirmation of—his treasonous plot. Disabled from sharing in the transcendence of battle, he may have searched for a way to live amidst danger and intrigue, and to play a role in great events. Treason offered such an opportunity. Having lurched down that path, he justified it to himself by the ingratitude and corruption of Congress or a multiplicity of other excuses. During the long months of plotting, he was in continual danger of detection. After the scheme collapsed, he became a marked man—Washington instigated a plan to kidnap and hang Arnold, which only barely missed succeeding. By committing treason, Arnold thrust himself back into the intoxicating game of life and death.

No single formula can encompass or explain Benedict Arnold. It can only hint at qualities that might have contributed to his actions and decisions. He remains, and perhaps will always remain, an enigma, his motives lost in the impenetrable alchemy of the human heart.

AFTER ARNOLD WENT over to the enemy, Eleazer Oswald, his early and faithful comrade in war, said, "Happy for him, and for his friends, it had been, had the ball which pierced his leg at Saratoga, been directed thro' his heart." Historians have echoed the sentiment down the years—if Arnold had died at Saratoga, he would have gone to his grave one of the most celebrated of American heroes.

Oswald's suggestion brings to mind another "if only" possibility. As a boy, Arnold had accompanied his father on sea voyages. The trips were a source of deep happiness—what boy would not exult in such watery adventures? Later, he went to sea himself in war and peace, and still later he took his own son with him on trading voyages.

Several times during the war, after his success at Valcour Island, Arnold tried to obtain a naval command. His Saratoga wound might prevent him from leading troops in the field, but a ship's captain need not move farther than his own quarterdeck. Arnold pleaded with Washington and with Congress to assign him to expeditions to the West Indies. His last request came on March 6, 1780, when he had already taken steps toward sedition.

A command at sea would have been ideal for the incorrigible general. He loved to operate independently; he yearned for battle; and he coveted a share in the valuable prizes that came from preying on the enemy's merchant fleet. Such an assignment would have canceled his idleness and returned him to the adventurous setting of his childhood. It might well have saved him from his final treason.

The prospect of him going to sea offers a vision of Arnold bounding over green waves in sunlight, facing down tempests, and losing himself in the thrilling, unpredictable action that was his forte. And when he returned—perhaps sailing into the harbor at New Haven after a long voyage—his wife and children would have awaited him at the wharf, his fellow citizens would have turned out to cheer, and someone might have shouted: "God save Benedict Arnold!"

Acknowledgments

I AM GRATEFUL FOR THE SUGGESTIONS, PROFESSIONAL CONTRI-butions, and support of the many folks who have helped me to deepen my understanding of Benedict Arnold and to research and write this book. I would particularly like to thank my editor, Elisabeth Dyssegaard, and the crack production and publicity teams at St. Martin's Press. Thanks to my agent, Eric Lupfer. Among those who have taken the time to help make this a better book, much thanks is due to Nina Sheldon, James Kirby Martin, Eric Schnitzer, Jeff Brouws, and especially Joy Taylor.

Notes

Some quotations have been altered from their original spelling and capitalization for readability.

Chapter 1: War

3. *"a company of"*: J. L. Bell, "'To Alarm the Country Quite to Connecticut.'" *Boston 1775*, May 1, 2010. https://boston1775.blogspot.com/2010/05/to-alarm-country-quite-to-connecticut.html.

4. *"A BLOODY BUTCHERY"*: Massachusetts Historical Society, "A Bloody Butchery, by the British Troops." https://www.masshist.org/database/viewer.php?item_id=467&pid=2.

5. *"He has had great luck"*: James Kirby Martin, *Benedict Arnold, Revolutionary Hero: An American Warrior Reconsidered* (New York: New York University Press, 1997), 55.

5. *"I was in easy"*: Isaac N. Arnold, *The Life of Benedict Arnold: His Patriotism and His Treason* (Chicago: Jansen, McClurg & Co., 1880), 34.

5. *"gentlemen of high respectability"*: Willard Sterne Randall, *Benedict Arnold: Patriot and Traitor* (New York: William Morrow and Company, 1990), 78.

6. *"the most accomplished"*: Martin, *Benedict Arnold*, 38.

7. *"gave him a little Chastisement"*: ibid., 43.

7. *"Good God!"*: Randall, *Arnold*, 68.

7. *"Deliver us from anarchy"*: Charles Mampoteng, "The Reverend Samuel Peters, M.A." *Historical Magazine of the Protestant Episcopal Church*, Vol. 5, No. 2 (June 1936).

7. *"The mobs of"*: Samuel Peters, *General History of Connecticut* (New York: D. Appleton & Co., 1877), 268.

8. *"How uncertain is life"*: Randall, *Arnold*, 64–5.

10. *"There wasn't any wasted"*: Nathaniel Philbrick, *Valiant Ambition: George Washington, Benedict Arnold, and the Fate of the American Revolution* (New York: Viking, 2016), 35.

10. *"none but the Almighty"*: Randall, *Arnold*, 83.

12. *"the greatest incendiary"*: Christian Di Spigna, *Founding Martyr: The Life and Death of Dr. Joseph Warren, the American Revolution's Lost Hero* (New York: Crown, 2018), 13.

12. *"Danger and war"*: Richard Frothingham, *Life and Times of Joseph Warren* (Boston: Little, Brown, 1865), 62.

13. *"No business but"*: Di Spigna, *Founding Martyr*, 11.

13. *"Our all is at stake"*: Nathaniel Philbrick, *Bunker Hill: A City, a Siege, a Revolution* (New York: Viking, 2013), 163.

Chapter 2: Fort Ticonderoga

16. *"boundless self-confidence"*: Christopher Ward, *The War of the Revolution* (New York: Macmillan, 1952), 64.

16. *"the Governor may stick"*: John J. Duffy and Nicholas Muller III, *Inventing Ethan Allen* (Hanover, NH: University Press of New England, 2014), 36.

16. *"rough and ready humor"*: Ward, *The War*, 64.

21. *"the great Jehovah"*: Randall, *Arnold*, 96.

21. *"sacrifice the whole"*: Allen French, *The Taking of Ticonderoga in 1775: The British Story* (Cambridge: Harvard University Press, 1928), 30.

21. *"deliver up his arms"*: ibid., 31.

21. *"The sun rising"*: Duffy and Muller, *Inventing*, 45.

22. *"everything is governed"*: James L. Nelson, *Benedict Arnold's Navy: The Ragtag Fleet that Lost the Battle of Lake Champlain but Won the American Revolution* (Camden, Maine: McGraw-Hill, 2006), 38.

22. *"When Mr. Allen"*: Benedict Arnold, "Benedict Arnold's Regimental Memorandum Book." *The Pennsylvania Magazine of History and Biography*, Vol. 8, No. 4 (Dec. 1884), 364.

24. *"in a small creek"*: Stephen Brumwell, *Turncoat: Benedict Arnold and the Crisis of American Liberty* (New Haven: Yale University Press, 2018), 41.

25. *"Had we been 6 hours later"*: NDAR, 1:367.

25. *"Several loyal Congress"*: Willard Sterne Randall, *Ethan Allen: His Life and Times* (New York: W. W. Norton, 2011), 320.

26. *"It appeared to me a wild"*: Randall, *Arnold*, 105.

26. *"It happened"*: Martin, *Benedict Arnold*, 76.

Chapter 3: Public Calamity

28. *"Deaths are multiplied"*: Clare Brandt, *The Man in the Mirror: A Life of Benedict Arnold* (New York: Random House, 1994), 5.

29. *"disabled in the use"*: Martin, *Benedict Arnold*, 30.

30. *"I have to inform you"*: Michael A. Bellesiles, *Revolutionary Outlaws: Ethan Allen and the Struggle for Independence on the Early American Frontier* (Charlottesville: University Press of Virginia, 1993), 118.

30. *"the last man that entered"*: Martin, *Benedict Arnold*, 97.

30. *"in the greatest confusion"*: Nelson, *Benedict Arnold's*, 37.

30. *"I think it my duty"*: Brumwell, *Turncoat*, 50.

30. *"be honorably acquitted"*: Martin, *Benedict Arnold*, 82.

31. *"Colonel Arnold has been"*: ibid., 98.

31. *"when the restoration"*: NDAR, 1:360.

32. *"Thus a War has"*: Samuel A. Forman, *Dr. Joseph Warren: The Boston Tea Party, Bunker Hill, and the Birth of American Liberty* (Gretna, LA: Pelican, 2012), 286.

32. *"The report of Ticonderoga's"*: NDAR, 1:562.

33. *"I have had intimations"*: Benedict Arnold, "Benedict Arnold to the Massachusetts Committee of Safety, May 19, 1775." *Northern Illinois University Digital Library.* https://digital.lib.niu.edu/islandora/object/niu-amarch%3A97639.

34. *"I took the liberty"*: Brumwell, *Turncoat*, 43.

34. *"discourage the enemies"*: Martin, *Benedict Arnold*, 92.

34. *"I am positive"*: NDAR, 1:672.

35. *"But as he produced"*: Benedict Arnold, "Benedict Arnold's Regimental," 363.

35. *"Had a rumor"*: ibid., 376.

36. *"uncommon vigilance"*: AA, 4th Series, 2:1088.

36. *"I find myself unable"*: Martin, *Benedict Arnold*, 100.

37. *"How soon our time"*: Randall, *Arnold*, 25.

37. *"Every recollection"*: Martin, *Benedict Arnold*, 102.

37. *"An idle life under"*: ibid.

Chapter 4: The Welfare of the Continent

38. *"were often obliged"*: Thomas A. Desjardin, *Through a Howling Wilderness: Benedict Arnold's March to Quebec, 1775* (New York: St. Martin's Press, 2006), 60.

40. *"so badly constructed"*: Kenneth Roberts, *March to Quebec: Journals of the Members of Arnold's Expedition* (New York: Doubleday, Doran & Company, 1938), 511.

40. *"What we most dreaded"*: ibid., 549.

40. *"very disagreeable"*: Martin, *Benedict Arnold*, 124.

40. *"Now," wrote Private*: Roberts, *March to Quebec*, 474.

41. *"I think he has deserved"*: Benson John Lossing, *The Life and Times of Philip Schuyler* (New York: Mason Brothers, 1860), 1:385.

41. *"Upon your conduct"*: Barry Wilson, *Benedict Arnold: A Traitor in Our Midst* (Montreal: McGill-Queen's University Press, 2001), 50.

42. *"the former harmony"*: Anonymous, "The Olive Branch Petition." *America's Homepage.* https://ahp.gatech.edu/olive_branch_1775.html.

42. *"that it is best to go"*: Wilson, *Benedict Arnold*, 47.

42. *"disagreeable to the Canadians"*: ibid., 48.

44. *"His manners were"*: North Callahan, *Daniel Morgan: Ranger of the Revolution* (New York: Holt, Rinehart and Winston, 1961), 65.

46. *"made an impression upon"*: Desjardin, *Through a Howling*, 38.

46. *"very simple and ignorant"*: Martin, *Benedict Arnold*, 122.

47. *"We have been obliged"*: NDAR, 2:443.

48. *"the officers, volunteers"*: Desjardin, *Through a Howling*, 10.

48. *"We were half leg deep"*: Wilson, *Benedict Arnold*, 64.

49. *"sons of ease"*: Roberts, *March to Quebec*, 512.

49. *"that our retreat may"*: Martin, *Benedict Arnold*, 126.

49. *"extremely bad"*: Desjardin, *Through a Howling*, 73.

49. *"The prospect is very"*: Wilson, *Benedict Arnold*, 68.

50. *"the greatest Difficulty"*: ibid., 67.

50. *"in a fortnight of having"*: ibid.

50. *"A dreary aspect"*: Roberts, *March to Quebec*, 522.

52. *"very wet and much":* James Thomas Flexner, *The Traitor and the Spy: Benedict Arnold and John André* (New York: Harcourt, Brace, 1953), 65.

53. *"came rushing at us":* Wilson, *Benedict Arnold,* 70.

53. *"This morning presented":* ibid.

53. *"from a Dead river":* Roberts, *March to Quebec,* 208.

54. *"We exerted every":* ibid., 207.

54. *"Happily," Arnold noted:* Martin, *Benedict Arnold,* 136.

55. *"Some of our men":* Roberts, *March to Quebec,* 551.

55. *"Our commander, Arnold":* ibid., 301.

57. *"the greater part":* George Washington, "From George Washington to John Hancock, 21 September 1775." *Founders Online.* https://founders.archives.gov/documents/Washington/03-02-02-0025.

58. *"I have to lament":* Lossing, *The Life and Times,* 1:424.

58. *"the sweepings of the York":* Robert McConnell Hatch, *Thrust for Canada: The American Attempt on Quebec in 1775–1776* (Boston: Houghton Mifflin, 1979), 82.

58. *"The instant I can":* ibid., 89.

58. *"as many of the best":* Arthur S. Lefkowitz, *Benedict Arnold's Army: The 1775 American Invasion of Canada during the Revolutionary War* (El Dorado Hills, CA: Savas Beatie, 2018), 144.

58. *"destitute of any eatable":* Martin, *Benedict Arnold,* 132.

59. *"disheartened and discouraged":* Roberts, *March to Quebec,* 137.

Chapter 5: Above the Common Race of Men

61. *"rejoiced to hear":* Lefkowitz, *Benedict Arnold's,* 165.

62. *"happy circumstance":* Brumwell, *Turncoat,* 54.

62. *"with inexpressible joy":* Roberts, *March to Quebec,* 523.

62. *"had the flesh worn":* ibid., 335–36.

62. *"Carri'd Back more":* ibid., 137.

63. *"was almost perished":* ibid., 138.

64. *"never perhaps was there":* ibid., 524.

64. *"After walking a few":* ibid., 554.

65. *"large, virtuous":* ibid., 337.

65. *"with tears of affection":* ibid.

65. *"the zenith of distress":* ibid., 218.

66. *"so faint and weak":* ibid., 478.

66. *"That sensation of mind":* ibid., 320.

66. *"the mercy of the woods":* ibid., 478.

66. *"left impressions":* ibid., 527.

66. *"My heart was ready":* ibid., 556.

67. *"still more unwell":* ibid., 139.

67. *"poor animal was instantly":* ibid., 219.

67. *"exceeding fine, clear":* ibid., 181.

67. *"I set out and marched":* ibid., 139.

68. *"This sudden change":* ibid., 529.

68. *"impiety, bigotry":* Martin, *Benedict Arnold,* 110.

68. *"to avoid all disrespect"*: ibid., 117.

69. *"shed tears of joy"*: Roberts, *March to Quebec*, 261.

69. *"echoes of gladness"*: ibid., 219.

69. *"bleaching bones"*: Martin, *Benedict Arnold*, 139.

69. *"knew my name"*: Roberts, *March to Quebec*, 347.

70. *"made a deep and wide"*: ibid., 346.

70. *"leaving us in such slight"*: Kevin Phillips, *1775: A Good Year for Revolution* (New York: Viking, 2012), 469.

71. *"so many of my brethren"*: Desjardin, *Through a Howling*, 107.

72. *"Surely, a miracle"*: Wilson, *Benedict Arnold*, 79.

72. *"I propose crossing"*: ibid.

74. *"will ever rank high"*: ibid., 80.

74. *"immediate surrender"*: Roberts, *March to Quebec*, 89.

75. *"the situation of our army"*: ibid., 481.

75. *"Most of the soldiers"*: ibid., 560.

75. *"Quebec must inevitably"*: Martin, *Benedict Arnold*, 150.

Chapter 6: The Most Terrible Night

76. *"The storm was"*: Desjardin, *Through a Howling*, 171.

77. *"headed mobs, excited"*: Hatch, *Thrust for Canada*, 53.

78. *"I am well acquainted"*: Michael Pearson, "The Siege of Quebec, 1775–1776." *American Heritage*, Vol. 23, No. 2 (Feb. 1972). https://www.americanheritage.com/siege-quebec-1775-1776.

79. *"peas would have"*: Martin, *Benedict Arnold*, 163.

79. *"our heap of nonsense"*: Roberts, *March to Quebec*, 589.

79. *"hard fate to be obliged"*: Hal T. Shelton, *General Richard Montgomery and the American Revolution: From Redcoat to Rebel* (New York: NYU Press, 1994), 67.

80. *"against my inclination"*: Rick Atkinson, *The British Are Coming: The War for America, Lexington to Princeton, 1775–1777* (New York: Henry Holt, 2019), 150.

80. *"I have not the talents"*: ibid.

80. *"'Tis a mad world"*: Shelton, *General Richard*, 78.

80. *"active, intelligent"*: ibid, 128.

81. *"The object was to"*: Roberts, *March to Quebec*, 561.

81. *"the most Terrible night"*: Lefkowitz, *Benedict Arnold's*, 247.

82. *"It was impossible to"*: Desjardin, *Through a Howling*, 173.

83. *"The main body"*: Roberts, *March to Quebec*, 190.

83. *"I know not if I shall"*: Simeon Thayer, *The Invasion of Canada in 1775* (Providence, RI: Knowles, Anthony, 1867), 57.

84. *"called to the troops"*: Martin, *Benedict Arnold*, 171.

84. *"between the tibia"*: Roberts, *March to Quebec*, 234.

85. *"it was his opinion"*: ibid., 172.

85. *"ordered his pistols"*: Martin, *Benedict Arnold*, 173.

85. *"much distinguished"*: ibid.

85. *"Morgan now raised"*: James Graham, *The Life of General Daniel Morgan of the Virginia Line* (Cincinnati: Derby and Jackson, 1856), 96.

86. *"we found it impossible"*: Desjardin, *Through a Howling*, 180.
86. *"Betwixt every peal"*: ibid.
87. *"You can have no"*: Lefkowitz, *Benedict Arnold's*, 267–68.
88. *"Orders are given"*: ibid., 247.
88. *"the critical situation"*: Flexner, *The Traitor*, 92.
89. *"For God's sake order"*: Desjardin, *Through a Howling*, 183.
89. *"had the enemy improved"*: Martin, *Benedict Arnold*, 181.
89. *"exceeding painful"*: Wilson, *Benedict Arnold*, 108.
90. *"Arnold's March is"*: Lefkowitz, *Benedict Arnold's*, 264.
91. *"split a stone"*: Martin, *Benedict Arnold*, 190.

Chapter 7: On the Lake
96. *"well made and his face"*: Philbrick, *Valiant*, 59.
96. *"did not combine"*: Wilson, *Benedict Arnold*, 11.
97. *"a tolerable share of"*: Flexner, *The Traitor*, 317.
97. *"with an aching"*: Joyce Lee Malcolm, *The Tragedy of Benedict Arnold: An American Life* (New York: Pegasus Books, 2018), 63.
98. *"The junction of the"*: Martin, *Benedict Arnold*, 218.
98. *"I am sorry you did not"*: Wilson, *Benedict Arnold*, 125.
99. *"A horde of Tartars"*: Douglas R. Cubbison, *The American Northern Theater Army in 1776: The Ruin and Reconstruction of the Continental Force* (Jefferson, NC: McFarland, 2010), 138.
100. *"place the Rebel Army"*: Eliot A. Cohen, *Conquered into Liberty: Two Centuries of Battles Along the Great Warpath That Made the American Way of War* (New York: Free Press, 2011), 169.
100. *"unless Every nerve"*: ibid., 176.
102. *"I have committed the"*: Martin, *Benedict Arnold*, 237.
102. *"we shall have a very"*: ibid., 238.
102. *"want of seamen or marines"*: ibid.
103. *"of greatest importance"*: Randall, *Arnold*, 256.
103. *"As soon as all the vessels"*: Nelson, *Benedict Arnold's*, 245.
103. *"to see the spirits"*: Walter Hill Crockett, *A History of Lake Champlain* (Burlington, VT: McAuliffe Paper Co., 1937), 181.
104. *"life and spirit"*: Martin, *Benedict Arnold*, 237.
104. *"the northern entrance"*: ibid., 246.
104. *"obstinate a temper"*: Allan S. Everest, *Moses Hazen and the Canadian Refugees in the American Revolution* (Syracuse, NY: Syracuse University Press, 1976), 161.
105. *"unprecedented and I think"*: AA, 5th Series, 1:1272.
105. *"by no means withhold"*: Martin, *Benedict Arnold*, 241.
105. *"the warmth of general"*: ibid., 243.
105. *"every report to your prejudice"*: ibid., 258.
105. *"fought and bled"*: Philbrick, *Valiant*, 334.
106. *"he says he will pay"*: Martin, *Benedict Arnold*, 249.
106. *"you surely must be out"*: NDAR, 6:215.
107. *"without a Scruple"*: ibid., 223.
107. *"now seems"*: ibid., 234.

107. *"it is a defensive War"*: Cubbison, *The American*, 218.

108. *"I am sorry to hear"*: Malcolm, *The Tragedy*, 146.

108. *"Preventing the enemy's"*: Cubbison, *The American*, 218.

Chapter 8: Stained with Blood

109. *"most Genteel feast"*: Philbrick, *Valiant*, 334.

110. *"attacked by a Party"*: NDAR, 6:734.

111. *"there is a ship"*: ibid., 884.

112. *"particulars of the affair"*: ibid., 838.

112. *"a greater part of those"*: Nelson, *Benedict Arnold's*, 276.

112. *"seamen (no land lubbers)"*: Randall, *Arnold*, 278.

113. *"When you ask for"*: ibid., 238.

113. *"Where it is not"*: NDAR, 6:1117.

113. *"I am greatly at a loss"*: Randall, *Arnold*, 281.

113. *"I am surprised by"*: John R. Bratten, *The Gondola Philadelphia and the Battle of Lake Champlain* (College Station: Texas A&M University Press, 2002), 54.

113. *"I cannot but think it"*: Martin, *Benedict Arnold*, 244.

114. *"Little Hal sends"*: Randall, *Arnold*, 262.

114. *"an exceeding fine"*: NDAR, 6:926.

115. *"zeal for the public Service"*: Randall, *Arnold*, 284

115. *"not half finished"*: Martin, *Benedict Arnold*, 263.

115. *"full of pranks"*: Randall, *Arnold*, 26–27.

116. *"We had alarm"*: Donald H. Wickman, ed., "A Most Unsettled Time on Lake Champlain: The October 1776 Journal of Jahiel Stewart." *Vermont History*, Vol. 64, No. 2 (Spring 1996), 92.

116. *"I gave it as my opinion"*: AA, 5th Series, 2:1224.

119. *"During the affair"*: Cubbison, *The American*, 239.

119. *"flesh and brains"*: Stephen Darley, *The Battle of Valcour Island: The Participants and Vessels of Benedict Arnold's 1776 Defense of Lake Champlain* (North Haven, CT: Darley, 2013), 106.

119. *"A prudent man"*: Denise Janet Choppin, *Godfrey Nims: A History of Colonial New England* (Markham, Canada: Stewart Pub & Print, 2002), 49.

120. *"we have a very"*: Martin, *Benedict Arnold*, 22.

120. *"Our decks were stain'd"*: Darley, *The Battle*, 106.

120. *"The Doctors cut off"*: Bratten, *The Gondola*, 64.

120. *"The Enemy Fleet"*: Darley, *The Battle*, 111.

121. *"he was our fighting"*: Arnold, *The Life*, 29.

121. *"obliged . . . to point"*: Martin, *Benedict Arnold*, 277.

121. *"the rebels directed"*: Cubbison, *The American*, 249.

121. *"Five broadsides"*: Philbrick, *Valiant*, 336.

122. *"To our utter"*: Nelson, *Benedict Arnold's*, 312.

123. *"exceedingly fatigued"*: Brumwell, *Turncoat*, 73.

123. *"well acquainted with"*: Martin, *Benedict Arnold*, 286.

124. *"the season is so far"*: ibid., 285–86.

125. *"fiery, hot, and impetuous"*: Bratten, *The Gondola*, 111.

125. *"conducted himself"*: Martin, *Benedict Arnold*, 287.

125. *"it has pleased"*: ibid.

125. *"defense he made"*: Arnold, *The Life*, 120.

125. *"animated scarecrows"*: John Ferling, *Almost a Miracle: The American Victory in the War of Independence* (New York: Oxford University Press, 2007), 165.

126. *"I think the game"*: Martin, *Benedict Arnold*, 293.

126. *"after his very long"*: ibid., 290.

Chapter 9: Dearer Than Life

131. *"I should be fond"*: Flexner, *The Traitor*, 119.

132. *"under the most anxious"*: Martin, *Benedict Arnold*, 303.

132. *"unless your Strength"*: Philbrick, *Valiant*, 100.

132. *"We have lately had"*: ibid., 90.

133. *"at a loss whether"*: Martin, *Benedict Arnold*, 308.

133. *"I fear your late"*: Nathanael Greene, "To John Adams from Nathanael Greene, 3 March 1777." *Founders Online*. https://founders.archives.gov/documents /Adams/06-05-02-0053.

133. *"most infallibly"*: Brumwell, *Turncoat*, 77.

133. *"Surely,"Washington*: Martin, *Benedict Arnold*, 308.

134. *"their promoting"*: Arnold, *The Life*, 127.

134. *"Every personal"*: Brumwell, *Turncoat*, 77.

134. *"sport or pastime"*: Martin, *Benedict Arnold*, 311.

134. *"no gentleman who"*: Flexner, *The Traitor*, 121.

135. *"I confess this"*: ibid., 124.

135. *"Miss De Blois has"*: ibid.

Chapter 10: Devilish Fighting Fellow

137. *We are alarmed*: Fairfield Museum, "The Battle of Ridgefield: April 27, 1777." *American Revolution & Colonial Life Programs*. https://www.fairfieldhistory.org /wp-content/uploads/BattleofRidgefield.pdf.

138. *"General Wooster is in our"*: Hatch, *Thrust for Canada*, 210.

140. *"leave all the western"*: Robert F. McDevitt, *Connecticut Attacked: A British Viewpoint, Tryon's Raid on Danbury* (Chester, CT: Pequot Press, 1974), 11.

140. *"stupid, cowardly"*: Brumwell, *Turncoat*, 78.

142. *"being a very zealous"*: McDevitt, *Connecticut*, 38.

142. *"the streets, in many"*: George E. Scheer, ed., *Private Yankee Doodle* (Boston: Little, Brown, 1962), 63.

144. *"Come on, my boys"*: McDevitt, *Connecticut*, 52.

144. *"the best disposition"*: ibid., 60.

147. *"You are my prisoner"*: Malcolm, *The Tragedy*, 182.

150. *"as soon as they were"*: McDevitt, *Connecticut*, 61.

150. *"Mr. Arnold endeavored"*: ibid.

151. *"Here again,"*: Silvio A. Bedini, *Ridgefield in Review* (Ridgefield, CT: Ridgefield 250th Anniversary Committee, 1958), 85.

151. *"having completely"*: William Edgar Grumman, *The Revolutionary Soldiers of Redding: Connecticut and the Record of Their Services* (Hartford, CT: Hartford Press, 1904), 51.

152. *"the spirit of opposition":* McDevitt, *Connecticut,* 66.

152. *"pleasing proof that":* Brumwell, *Turncoat,* 81.

152. *"many of the officers":* ibid., 81.

152. *"tho ignorant of":* McDevitt, *Connecticut,* 47.

153. *"the enemy gives":* Brumwell, *Turncoat,* 82.

153. *"General Arnold's promotion":* Arnold, *The Life,* 134.

153. *"But what will be done":* Martin, *Benedict Arnold,* 323.

Chapter 11: A Faithful Soldier

155. *"I longed more":* John E. Ferling, "'Oh That I Was a Soldier': John Adams and the Anguish of War." *American Quarterly,* Vol. 36, No. 2 (Summer 1984), 259.

155. *"violent and ill-founded":* Flexner, *The Traitor,* 114.

155. *"a man of honour":* Carl Van Doren, *Secret History of the American Revolution* (New York: The Viking Press, 1941), 155–56.

156. *"put to death by fire":* Flexner, *The Traitor,* 115.

156. *"Money is this man's":* Martin, *Benedict Arnold,* 324.

156. *"more than he chooses":* ibid.

156. *"It is universally":* ibid., 325.

157. *"his vigilance":* Brumwell, *Turncoat,* 82.

157. *"sufficient to make":* Philbrick, *Valiant,* 99.

157. *"every sacrifice":* Brumwell, *Turncoat,* 84.

157. *"gallant conduct":* Martin, *Benedict Arnold,* 325.

159. *"assassinate the":* Brumwell, *Turncoat,* 85.

159. *"given entire":* ibid., 85.

159. *"deprived of his rank":* Martin, *Benedict Arnold,* 333.

160. *"that in voting":* ibid., 305.

160. *"Morals, his Honour":* Richard D. Brown, "Where Have All the Great Men Gone?" *American Heritage,* Vol. 35, No. 2 (Feb./Mar. 1984). https://www.americanheritage.com/where-have-all-great-men-gone.

161. *"one people, embarked":* George Washington, "From George Washington to John Banister, 21 April 1778." *Founders Online.* https://founders.archives.gov/documents/Washington/03-14-02-0525.

161. *"I think it betrays":* Martin, *Benedict Arnold,* 311.

162. *"I have no fears":* Brown, "Where Have All the Great Men Gone?"

162. *"I am wearied to death":* Randall, *Arnold,* 336.

162. *"a number of junior":* Brandt, *The Man,* 124–25.

Chapter 12: Or Die in the Attempt

164. *"an event of chagrin":* Ron Chernow, *Washington: A Life* (New York: Penguin Press, 2010), 301.

164. *"I think we shall never":* John S. Pancake, *1777: The Year of the Hangman* (Tuscaloosa: University of Alabama Press, 1977), 125.

164. *"I have beat them":* Richard M. Ketchum, *Saratoga: Turning Point of America's Revolutionary War* (New York: Henry Holt, 1999), 206.

164. *"if General Arnold":* Arnold, *The Life,* 138.

164. *"have directed you":* Malcolm, *The Tragedy,* 194.

164. *"I shall be happy"*: Martin, *Benedict Arnold*, 343.

165. *"for the present"*: Philbrick, *Valiant*, 124.

166. *"From his activity"*: Martin, *Benedict Arnold*, 344.

167. *"march of annihilation"*: Max Von Eelking, ed., *Memoirs, and Letters and Journals, of Major General Riedesel during His Residence in America* (Albany, NY: J. Munsell, 1808), 125.

167. *"the cursed war hoop"*: Philbrick, *Valiant*, 123.

167. *"we are daily insulted"*: Brandt, *The Man*, 126.

167. *"our picket at Ft. Edward"*: Philbrick, *Valiant*, 125–26.

168. *"will forever stain"*: Kevin J. Weddle, *The Compleat Victory: Saratoga and the American Revolution* (New York: Oxford University Press, 2021), 175.

169. *"not be a disgrace"*: ibid., 188.

170. *"The flag was sufficiently"*: Philbrick, *Valiant*, 131.

172. *"I am apprehensive"*: Richard V. Polhemus and John F. Polhemus, *Stark: The Life and Wars of John Stark, French and Indian War Ranger, Revolutionary War General* (Hensonville, NY: Black Dome Press, 2014), 239.

172. *"I do not yet despond"*: Pancake, *1777*, 139.

173. *"The great bulk"*: ibid., 145.

174. *"restore our affairs"*: Martin, *Benedict Arnold*, 355.

175. *"done everything"*: ibid., 353.

176. *"It gives me great"*: Gavin K. Watt, *Rebellion in the Mohawk Valley: The St. Leger Expedition of 1777* (Toronto: Dundurn Press, 2002), 221.

176. *"put every soul"*: ibid., 228.

176. *"a certain Barry St. Leger"*: ibid., 238.

177. *"not to hazard our little"*: Martin, *Benedict Arnold*, 365.

177. *"determined, at all"*: Flexner, *The Traitor*, 166.

177. *"You will hear"*: Weddle, *The Compleat*, 213.

178. *"seized upon officers'"*: Pancake, *1777*, 145.

178. *"St. Leger with his"*: Weddle, *The Compleat*, 215.

178. *"a piece of flesh"*: Chip Twellman Haley, "'Siege Baby' Was Born at Fort Stanwix as British Bombed." *Rome Sentinel*, September 6, 2020. https://romesentinel.com/stories/siege-baby-was-born-at-fort-stanwix-as-british-bombed,103347.

179. *"on account of"*: Martin, *Benedict Arnold*, 356.

179. *"it was really"*: ibid.

179. *"not because he was"*: Flexner, *The Traitor*, 167.

179. *"no public or private"*: Arnold, *The Life*, 267.

180. *"Our people are"*: Martin, *Benedict Arnold*, 268.

Chapter 13: Freeman's Farm

181. *"in very imperfect"*: Ketchum, *Saratoga*, 354–55.

181. *"one of the Greatest"*: Weddle, *The Compleat*, 286.

182. *"reminding one"*: Paul David Nelson, *General Horatio Gates: A Biography* (Baton Rouge: Louisiana State University Press, 1976), 114.

182. *"burned with"*: Martin, *Benedict Arnold*, 373.

182. *"reduced to a scene"*: ibid.

183. *"This Army must"*: Dean Snow, *1777: Tipping Point at Saratoga* (New York: Oxford University Press, 2016), 76.
184. *"the great tacticians"*: William A. Griswold and Donald W. Linebaugh, eds., *The Saratoga Campaign: Uncovering an Embattled Landscape* (Hanover, NH: University Press of New England, 2016), 105.
185. *"beyond the nice"*: Nelson, *General Horatio*, 6.
186. *"defend the main"*: Weddle, *The Compleat*, 264.
187. *"hang on their front"*: Snow, *1777*, 84.
187. *"my opinion"*: John Luzader, *Saratoga: A Military History of the Decisive Campaign of the American Revolution* (El Dorado Hills, CA: Savas Beatie, 2014), 388.
188. *"observe their direction"*: Snow, *1777*, 162.
189. *"choked up with"*: Rupert Furneaux, *The Battle of Saratoga* (New York: Stein and Day, 1971), 173.
189. *"Boys, shoot"*: Snow, *1777*, 91.
191. *"The engagement"*: John Scales, *Life of Gen. Joseph Cilley* (Manchester, NH: Standard Book, 1921), 32.
191. *"all of a sudden I"*: Christopher Duffy, *The Military Experience in the Age of Reason* (London: Routledge, 1987), 187.
192. *"the onset of bayonets"*: Ketchum, *Saratoga*, 137.
192. *"The conflict was"*: Eric Schnitzer and Don Troiani, *Don Troiani's Campaign to Saratoga—1777: The Turning Point of the Revolutionary War in Paintings, Artifacts, and Historical Narrative* (Guilford, CT: Stackpole Books, 2019), 175.
193. *"Reinforcements successively"*: Luzader, *Saratoga*, 243.
193. *"Both armies"*: Ketchum, *Saratoga*, 363.
193. *"the blaze from"*: ibid.
193. *"an explosion of fire"*: ibid., 366.
194. *"We beat them back"*: ibid., 367.
194. *"whistled their thousand"*: Robert Middlekauff, *The Glorious Cause: The American Revolution, 1763–1789* (New York: Oxford University Press, 2005), 503.
194. *"with small arms"*: Schnitzer and Troiani, *Don Troiani's*, 180.
195. *"While speaking"*: Weddle, *The Compleat*, 280.
195. *"Few actions"*: Snow, *1777*, 151.
196. *"zeal and spirit"*: Weddle, *The Compleat*, 285–86.
196. *"Arnold rushed"*: Martin, *Benedict Arnold*, 379.
196. *"riding in front"*: ibid.
197. *"chose to give rather"*: ibid., 382.
197. *"with great vigor"*: Weddle, *The Compleat*, 283.
198. *"dear bought victory"*: Ketchum, *Saratoga*, 369.
198. *"no fruits, honour"*: Weddle, *The Compleat*, 284.
198. *"We remained in"*: John R. Elting, *The Battles of Saratoga* (Monmouth Beach, NJ: Philip Freneau Press, 1977), 55.

Chapter 14: Now or Never
200. *"The courage and"*: Martin, *Benedict Arnold*, 382.
200. *"I question whether"*: Weddle, *The Compleat*, 284.
200. *"for their all"*: Ketchum, *Saratoga*, 369.

201. *"in favor of General"*: Hoffman Nickerson, *The Turning Point of the Revolution or Burgoyne in America* (Boston: Houghton Mifflin, 1928), 340.

201. *"You know my"*: Luzader, *Saratoga*, 256.

203. *"picquets and advanced"*: Weddle, *The Compleat*, 309.

204. *"Our grass was"*: ibid.

205. *"to discriminate in praise"*: Schnitzer and Troiani, *Don Troiani's*, 207.

205. *"as well as particular"*: Weddle, *The Compleat*, 289.

205. *"High words and"*: Martin, *Benedict Arnold*, 387.

206. *"been received with"*: Flexner, *The Traitor*, 174.

206. *"for his past services"*: Martin, *Benedict Arnold*, 390.

207. *"a certain pompous"*: Brumwell, *Turncoat*, 94.

207. *"command the army"*: Weddle, *The Compleat*, 293.

207. *"The fatigue of body"*: Martin, *Benedict Arnold*, 388.

208. *"we expect another"*: Snow, *1777*, 190.

208. *"officer or soldier"*: Max M. Mintz, *The Generals of Saratoga: John Burgoyne & Horatio Gates* (New Haven: Yale University Press, 1990), 205.

208. *"there is reason to"*: Watt, *Rebellion*, 296.

209. *"nothing between us"*: Ketchum, *Saratoga*, 385.

210. *"I attempted to"*: Luzader, *Saratoga*, 276.

210. *"we waited, nourished"*: ibid., 276.

210. *"have a pleasing"*: Snow, *1777*, 222.

211. *"At no time,"*: Ketchum, *Saratoga*, 382.

Chapter 15: We Will Have Some Fun

213. *"Shall I go out"*: Mintz, *The Generals*, 208.

214. *"They are foraging"*: Snow, *1777*, 244.

214. *"ascend the eminence"*: Schnitzer and Troiani, *Don Troiani's*, 232.

218. *"poured down"*: Callahan, *Daniel Morgan*, 143.

219. *"General Arnold soon"*: Steven E. Clay, *Staff Ride Handbook for the Saratoga Campaign, 13 June to 8 November 1777* (Fort Leavenworth, KA: Combat Studies Institute Press, 2018), 254.

219. *"They rushed on with"*: Furneaux, *The Battle*, 227.

220. *"The smoke was very"*: ibid., 230.

220. *"proved delusive"*: Schnitzer and Troiani, *Don Troiani's*, 238.

221. *"Genl Arnold came"*: Weddle, *The Compleat*, 322.

221. *"Now come on"*: Snow, *1777*, 253.

222. *"helped turn the fate"*: Michael Stephenson, *Patriot Battles: How the War of Independence Was Fought* (New York: HarperCollins, 2007), 309.

222. *"Finding us in their"*: Henry Dearborn, *Revolutionary War Journals, 1775–1783*. Edited by Lloyd A. Brown (Chicago: The Caxton Club, 1939), 108.

223. *"bring his men into"*: Schnitzer and Troiani, *Don Troiani's*, 241.

223. *"The Americans stormed"*: Thomas Anburey, *Travels through the Interior Parts of America* (London: William Lane, 1789), 441–42.

225. *"energy gave spirit"*: Furneaux, *The Battle*, 238.

225. *"Genl Arnold was the"*: Weddle, *The Compleat*, 324.

229. *"gallant Major General"*: Ketchum, *Saratoga,* 419.
229. *"blows must decide"*: Ward, *The War,* 22.

Chapter 16: Trust

233. *"It thus came about"*: Gardner W. Allen, *A Naval History of the American Revolution* (Boston: Houghton Mifflin Company, 1913), 179.
233. *"seem to have little"*: Philbrick, *Valiant,* 188.
233. *"brood over their"*: Andy Trees, "Benedict Arnold, John André, and His Three Yeoman Captors: A Sentimental Journey or American Virtue Defined." *Early American Literature,* Vol. 35, No. 3 (2000), 247.
233. *"There never has been"*: ibid.
234. *"Do not depend on"*: Chernow, *Washington,* 373.
234. *"There is nothing"*: ibid., 376.
235. *"My public character"*: Flexner, *The Traitor,* 236.
236. *"an embarrassment"*: Brumwell, *Turncoat,* 273.
236. *"The impropriety"*: Chernow, *Washington,* 382.
237. *"Arnold," he said:* ibid.
238. *"very peevish"*: Martin, *Benedict Arnold,* 404.
238. *"very great respect"*: Brumwell, *Turncoat,* 119.
238. *"necessary justice"*: Martin, *Benedict Arnold,* 416.
238. *"broken out again"*: Brumwell, *Turncoat,* 120.
238. *"render every assistance"*: Martin, *Benedict Arnold,* 417.
238. *"cruel indifference"*: Flexner, *The Traitor,* 235.
239. *"as a testimony of"*: Martin, *Benedict Arnold,* 423.
239. *"to the great joy"*: Brumwell, *Turncoat,* 121.
239. *"The wretches who"*: ibid., 240.
239. *"abettors, assistants"*: Brandt, *The Man,* 147.
242. *"Speculation, peculation"*: Philbrick, *Valiant,* 230.
242. *"gewgaws and superfluities"*: Charles Royster, "The Nature of Treason." *The William and Mary Quarterly,* Vol. 36, No. 2 (April 1979), 174.
242. *"to subvert the Whig"*: Brumwell, *Turncoat,* 137.
242. *"My appointment"*: Terry Golway, *Washington's General: Nathanael Greene and the Triumph of the American Revolution* (New York: Henry Holt, 2005), 192.
243. *"I flatter myself the"*: Wilson, *Benedict Arnold,* 151.
243. *"useful rather than"*: Flexner, *The Traitor,* 255.
244. *"I am heartily tired"*: Wilson, *Benedict Arnold,* 152.
244. *"If Your Excellency"*: Brumwell, *Turncoat,* 153.
244. *"solemn obligation"*: Flexner, *The Traitor,* 276.
245. *"then would the generosity"*: Brumwell, *Turncoat,* 159.
247. *"How far he meant"*: Randall, *Arnold,* 562.
249. *"Gentlemen," André said:* Russell M. Lea, *A Hero and a Spy: The Revolutionary War Correspondence of Benedict Arnold* (Westminster, MD: Heritage Books, 2006), 480.
250. *"The strangest thing"*: Brumwell, *Turncoat,* 284.
250. *"a piece of splendid"*: ibid., 280.

251. *"No, Sir, one"*: ibid., 276.
251. *"a becoming sensibility"*: Sarah Knott, *Sensibility and the American Revolution* (Chapel Hill: University of North Carolina Press, 2009), 160.
251. *"cringing, insidious"*: Flexner, *The Traitor*, 267.
251. *"Let his name"*: Brumwell, *Turncoat*, 300.
252. *"rung with the crimes"*: Royster, "The Nature," 188.
252. *"The days of eternity"*: Brumwell, *Turncoat*, 299.
252. *"confounds and distresses"*: Eric D. Lehman, *Homegrown Terror: Benedict Arnold and the Burning of New London* (Middletown, CT: Wesleyan University Press, 2014), xv.
253. *"thundering excursions"*: Barbara W. Tuchman, *The First Salute: A View of the American Revolution* (New York: Alfred A. Knopf, 1988), 192.
253. *"the most detestable"*: Matthew Reardon, "Disastrous Leadership: Lt. Colonel Joseph Harris at the Battle of New London." *Journal of the American Revolution* (December 10, 2014). https://allthingsliberty.com/2014/12/disastrous-leadership-lt-colonel-joseph-harris-at-the-battle-of-new-london/.

Chapter 17: Explanations

256. *"for the base-born"*: Brumwell, *Turncoat*, 299.
256. *"love of money"*: Lehman, *Homegrown*, 134.
256. *"first and foremost"*: Philbrick, *Valiant*, 241.
257. *"entirely neglected"*: Brumwell, *Turncoat*, 136.
257. *"to maim and mangle"*: Martin, *Benedict Arnold*, 12.
257. *"Men who are Criminally"*: Malcolm, *The Tragedy*, 339.
258. *"the ingratitude"*: Brumwell, *Turncoat*, 163.
258. *"the Congress are"*: Flexner, *The Traitor*, 55.
258. *"the enemy of the"*: Randall, *Benedict Arnold*, 574.
258. *"A redress of"*: Arnold, *The Life*, 330.
258. *"the most essential"*: Brumwell, *Turncoat*, 326.
259. *"Silly and contemptible"*: Kevin T. Springman, "Notes and Documents: Thomas Paine's Response to Lord North's Speech on the British Peace Proposals." *The Pennsylvania Magazine of History and Biography*, Vol. 121, No. 4 (Oct. 1997), 358.
260. *"lost to all sense"*: George Washington, "From George Washington to Lieutenant Colonel John Laurens, 13 October 1780." *Founders Online.* https://founders.archives.gov/documents/Washington/03-28-02-0282.
260. *"a step, which the world"*: Benedict Arnold, "Benedict Arnold to George Washington, 25 September 1780." *Founders Online.* https://founders.archives.gov/documents/Hamilton/01-02-02-0867-0002.
260. *"principle of love"*: Martin, *Benedict Arnold*, 5.
261. *"an unaccountable"*: Brumwell, *Turncoat*, 284.
261. *"lost all his credit"*: D. A. B. Ronald, *The Life of John André: The Redcoat Who Turned Benedict Arnold* (Havertown, PA: Casemate Publishers, 2019), 249.
263. *"His death ... is"*: Wilson, *Benedict Arnold*, 217.
263. *"There is no doubt"*: Lehman, *Homegrown*, xii.

Chapter 18: Life and Death

264. *"somehow or other"*: Trees, "Benedict Arnold," 246.

264. *"the ornament or the"*: ibid., 247.

264. *"some may think I"*: Arnold, *The Life*, 332.

264–265. *"a few men directing"*: Brian F. Carso, Jr., *"Whom Can We Trust now?"*: *The Meaning of Treason in the United States, from the Revolution through the Civil War* (Lanham, MD: Lexington Books, 2006), 201.

265. *"declared his change"*: Philbrick, *Valiant*, 241.

265. *"True patriotism"*: Emory M. Thomas, *Robert E. Lee: A Biography* (New York: W. W. Norton & Company, 1995), 370.

265. *"We are a young"*: Trees, "Benedict Arnold," 249.

266. *"We were all"*: Andro Linklater, *An Artist in Treason: The Extraordinary Double Life of General James Wilkinson* (New York: Walker, 2009), 67.

267. *"serve to bring"*: Ron Chernow, *Alexander Hamilton* (New York: Penguin Press, 2004), 284.

268. *"Happy for him"*: Lehman, *Homegrown*, 96.

Selected Bibliography

Abbreviations used:

AA—*American Archives,* edited by Peter Force. Washington, DC: M. St. Clair Clarke and P. Force, 1853.

NDAR—*Naval Documents of the American Revolution,* edited by William Bell Clark et al. Washington, DC: Naval History and Heritage Command, 1964–.

Allen, Gardner W. *A Naval History of the American Revolution.* Boston: Houghton Mifflin Company, 1913.

Allen, Thomas B. *Tories: Fighting for the King in America's First Civil War.* New York: HarperCollins, 2010.

Anburey, Thomas. *Travels through the Interior Parts of America.* London: William Lane, 1789.

Anonymous. *Orderly Book of the Northern Army, at Ticonderoga and Mt. Independence from October 17th, 1776, to January 8th, 1777.* Albany: J. Munsell, 1859.

———. "The Olive Branch Petition." *America's Homepage.* https://ahp.gatech .edu/olive_branch_1775.html (accessed Sept. 1, 2022).

Arnold, Benedict. "Benedict Arnold's Regimental Memorandum Book." *The Pennsylvania Magazine of History and Biography,* Vol. 8, No. 4 (Dec., 1884).

———. "Benedict Arnold to George Washington, 25 September 1780." *Founders Online.* https://founders.archives.gov/documents/Hamilton /01-02-02-0867-0002 (accessed Sept. 7, 2022).

———. "Benedict Arnold to the Massachusetts Committee of Safety, May 19, 1775." *Northern Illinois University Digital Library.* https://digital.lib.niu.edu /islandora/object/niu-amarch%3A97639 (accessed Sept. 1, 2022).

Arnold, Isaac N. *The Life of Benedict Arnold: His Patriotism and His Treason.* Chicago: Jansen, McClurg & Co., 1880.

Atkinson, Rick. *The British Are Coming: The War for America, Lexington to Princeton, 1775–1777.* New York: Henry Holt, 2019.

Baldwin, Jeduthan. *The Revolutionary Journal of Col. Jeduthan Baldwin.* Bangor, ME: The De Burians, 1906.

Barbieri, Michael. "Infamous Skulkers: The Shooting of Brigadier General Patrick Gordon." *Journal of the American Revolution,* September 11, 2013. https://

allthingsliberty.com/2013/09/infamous-skulkers-shooting-brigadier
-general-patrick-gordon/ (accessed Aug. 30, 2022).

Bedini, Silvio A. *Ridgefield in Review.* Ridgefield, CT: Ridgefield 250th Anniversary Committee, 1958.

Bell, J. L. "'To Alarm the Country Quite to Connecticut.'" *Boston 1775,* May 1, 2010. https://boston1775.blogspot.com/2010/05/to-alarm-country-quite -to-connecticut.html (accessed Aug. 30, 2022).

Bellesiles, Michael A. *Revolutionary Outlaws: Ethan Allen and the Struggle for Independence on the Early American Frontier.* Charlottesville: University Press of Virginia, 1993.

Bellico, Russell P. *Sails and Steam in the Mountains: A Maritime and Military History of Lake George and Lake Champlain.* Fleischmanns, NY: Purple Mountain Press, 1992.

Berleth, Richard. *Bloody Mohawk: The French and Indian War & American Revolution on New York's Frontier.* Hensonville, NY: Black Dome Press Corp., 2010.

Billias, George A., ed. *George Washington's Generals.* Westport, CT: Greenwood Press, 1967.

Black, Jeremy. *Crisis of Empire: Britain and America in the Eighteenth Century.* New York: Continuum, 2008.

———, ed. *Warfare in Europe 1650–1792.* Burlington, VT: Ashgate, 2005.

Bobrick, Benson. *Angel in the Whirlwind: The Triumph of the American Revolution.* New York: Simon & Schuster, 1997.

Brandt, Clare. *The Man in the Mirror: A Life of Benedict Arnold.* New York: Random House, 1994.

Bratten, John R. *The Gondola Philadelphia and the Battle of Lake Champlain.* College Station: Texas A&M University Press, 2002.

Brown, Richard D. "Where Have All the Great Men Gone?" *American Heritage,* Vol. 35, No. 2 (Feb./Mar., 1984). https://www.americanheritage.com /where-have-all-great-men-gone (accessed Sept. 6, 2022).

Brumwell, Stephen. *Turncoat: Benedict Arnold and the Crisis of American Liberty.* New Haven: Yale University Press, 2018.

Bush, Martin H. *Revolutionary Enigma: A Re-appraisal of General Philip Schuyler of New York.* Port Washington, NY: I. J. Friedman, 1969.

Callahan, North. *Daniel Morgan: Ranger of the Revolution.* New York: Holt, Rinehart and Winston, 1961.

Carso, Brian F., Jr. *"Whom Can We Trust Now?": The Meaning of Treason in the United States, from the Revolution through the Civil War.* Lanham, MD: Lexington Books, 2006.

Chernow, Ron. *Alexander Hamilton.* New York: Penguin Press, 2004.

———. *Washington: A Life.* New York: Penguin Press, 2010.

Choppin, Denise Janet. *Godfrey Nims: A History of Colonial New England.* Markham, Canada: Stewart Pub. & Print, 2002.

Clark, Stephen. *Following Their Footsteps: A Travel Guide & History of the 1775 Secret Expedition to Capture Quebec.* Shapleigh, ME: Clark Books, 2003.

Clay, Steven E. *Staff Ride Handbook for the Saratoga Campaign, 13 June to 8 November 1777.* Fort Leavenworth, KS: Combat Studies Institute Press, 2018.

Cohen, Eliot A. *Conquered into Liberty: Two Centuries of Battles Along the Great Warpath That Made the American Way of War.* New York: Free Press, 2011.

Corbett, Theodore. *No Turning Point: The Saratoga Campaign in Perspective.* Norman: University of Oklahoma Press, 2012.

Crockett, Walter Hill. *A History of Lake Champlain.* Burlington, VT: McAuliffe Paper Co., 1937.

Cubbison, Douglas R. *The American Northern Theater Army in 1776: The Ruin and Reconstruction of the Continental Force.* Jefferson, NC: McFarland, 2010.

————. *Burgoyne and the Saratoga Campaign: His Papers.* Norman: University of Oklahoma Press, 2012.

Cumming, William Patterson, and Hugh F. Rankin. *The Fate of a Nation: The American Revolution Through Contemporary Eyes.* London: Phaidon, 1975.

Darley, Stephen. *The Battle of Valcour Island: The Participants and Vessels of Benedict Arnold's 1776 Defense of Lake Champlain.* North Haven, CT: Darley, 2013.

Dearborn, Henry. *Revolutionary War Journals, 1775–1783.* Edited by Lloyd A. Brown and Howard H. Peckham. Chicago: The Caxton Club, 1939.

Desjardin, Thomas A. *Through a Howling Wilderness: Benedict Arnold's March to Quebec, 1775.* New York: St. Martin's Press, 2006.

Di Spigna, Christian. *Founding Martyr: The Life and Death of Dr. Joseph Warren, the American Revolution's Lost Hero.* New York: Crown, 2018.

Duffy, Christopher. *The Military Experience in the Age of Reason.* London: Routledge, 1987.

Duffy, John J., and H. Nicholas Muller III. *Inventing Ethan Allen.* Hanover, NH: University Press of New England, 2014.

Duling, Ennis. "Arnold, Hazen and the Mysterious Major Scott." *Journal of the American Revolution,* February 23, 2016. https://allthingsliberty.com/2016/02/arnold-hazen-and-the-mysterious-major-scott/ (accessed Aug. 30, 2022).

Elting, John R. *The Battles of Saratoga.* Monmouth Beach, NJ: Philip Freneau Press, 1977.

Everest, Allan S. *Moses Hazen and the Canadian Refugees in the American Revolution.* Syracuse, NY: Syracuse University Press, 1976.

Fairfield Museum. "The Battle of Ridgefield: April 27, 1777." *American Revolution & Colonial Life Programs.* https://www.fairfieldhistory.org/wp-content/uploads/BattleofRidgefield.pdf (accessed Sept. 5, 2022).

Ferling, John. *Almost a Miracle: The American Victory in the War of Independence.* New York: Oxford University Press, 2007.

————. "'Oh That I Was a Soldier': John Adams and the Anguish of War." *American Quarterly,* Vol. 36, No. 2 (Summer 1984): 258–275. https://doi.org/10.2307/2712727.

Fischer, David Hackett. *Champlain's Dream.* New York: Simon & Schuster, 2008.

Fleming, Thomas. *1776, Year of Illusions.* New York: W. W. Norton & Company, 1975.

Flexner, James Thomas. *The Traitor and the Spy: Benedict Arnold and John André.* New York: Harcourt, Brace, 1953.

Forman, Sam. *Dr. Joseph Warren: The Boston Tea Party, Bunker Hill, and the Birth of American Liberty.* Gretna, LA: Pelican Publishing, 2011.

Fowler, William M., Jr. *Rebels Under Sail: The American Navy During the Revolution.* New York: Charles Scribner's Sons, 1976.

French, Allen. *The Taking of Ticonderoga in 1775: The British Story.* Cambridge: Harvard University Press, 1928.

Frothingham, Richard. *Life and Times of Joseph Warren.* Boston: Little, Brown, 1865.

Furneaux, Rupert. *The Battle of Saratoga.* New York: Stein and Day, 1971.

Gates, Horatio. "To John Adams from Horatio Gates, 17 July 1776." *Founders Online.* https://founders.archives.gov/documents/Adams/06-04-02-0168 (accessed Aug. 30, 2022).

Gerlach, Don R. *Philip Schuyler and the American Revolution in New York, 1733–1777.* Lincoln: University of Nebraska Press, 1964.

———. *Proud Patriot: Philip Schuyler and the War of Independence, 1775–1783.* Syracuse, NY: Syracuse University Press, 1987.

Golway, Terry. *Washington's General: Nathanael Greene and the Triumph of the American Revolution.* New York: Henry Holt, 2005.

Graham, James. *The Life of General Daniel Morgan of the Virginia Line.* Cincinnati: Derby and Jackson, 1856.

Graymont, Barbara. *The Iroquois in the American Revolution.* Syracuse, NY: Syracuse University Press, 1972.

Greene, Nathanael. "To John Adams from Nathanael Greene, 3 March 1777." *Founders Online.* https://founders.archives.gov/documents/Adams/06-05-02-0053 (accessed Sept. 5, 2022).

Griffith, Samuel B., II. *The War for American Independence: From 1760 to the Surrender at Yorktown in 1781.* Urbana: University of Illinois Press, 2002.

Griswold, William A., and Donald W. Linebaugh, eds. *The Saratoga Campaign: Uncovering an Embattled Landscape.* Hanover, NH: University Press of New England, 2016.

Grumman, William Edgar. *The Revolutionary Soldiers of Redding: Connecticut and the Record of Their Services.* Hartford, CT: Hartford Press, 1904.

Hadden, James M. *A Journal Kept in Canada and upon Burgoyne's Campaign in 1776 and 1777.* Albany, NY: Joel Munson's Sons, 1884.

Haley, Chip Twellman. "'Siege Baby' Was Born at Fort Stanwix as British Bombed." *Rome Sentinel,* September 6, 2020. https://romesentinel.com/stories/siege-baby-was-born-at-fort-stanwix-as-british-bombed,103347 (accessed Sept. 6, 2022).

Hamilton, Edward P. *Fort Ticonderoga: Key to a Continent.* Boston: Little, Brown, 1964.

Hatch, Robert McConnell. *Thrust for Canada: The American Attempt on Quebec in 1775–1776.* Boston: Houghton Mifflin, 1979.

Howson, Gerald. *Burgoyne of Saratoga: A Biography.* New York: Times Books, 1979.

Johnson, James M., Christopher Pryslopski, and Andrew Villani, eds. *Key to the Northern Country: The Hudson River Valley in the American Revolution.* Albany, NY: Excelsior Editions, 2013.

Ketchum, Richard M. *Saratoga: Turning Point of America's Revolutionary War.* New York: Henry Holt, 1999.

Knott, Sarah. *Sensibility and the American Revolution.* Chapel Hill: University of North Carolina Press, 2009.

Laramie, Michael G. *By Wind and Iron: Naval Campaigns in the Champlain Valley, 1665–1815*. Yardley, PA: Westholme, 2015.

Lea, Russell M. *A Hero and a Spy: The Revolutionary War Correspondence of Benedict Arnold*. Westminster, MD: Heritage Books, 2006.

Lefkowitz, Arthur S. *Benedict Arnold's Army: The 1775 American Invasion of Canada during the Revolutionary War*. El Dorado Hills, CA: Savas Beatie, 2018.

Lehman, Eric D. *Homegrown Terror: Benedict Arnold and the Burning of New London*. Middletown, CT: Wesleyan University Press, 2014.

Linklater, Andro. *An Artist in Treason: The Extraordinary Double Life of General James Wilkinson*. New York: Walker, 2009.

Lossing, Benson John. *The Life and Times of Philip Schuyler*. 2 vols. New York: Mason Brothers, 1860.

Lundeberg, Philip K., et al. *A Tale of Three Gunboats: Lake Champlain's Revolutionary War Heritage*. Washington, DC: Smithsonian Institution, 2017.

Luzader, John. *Saratoga: A Military History of the Decisive Campaign of the American Revolution*. El Dorado Hills, CA: Savas Beatie, 2014.

Malcolm, Joyce Lee. *The Tragedy of Benedict Arnold: An American Life*. New York: Pegasus Books, 2018.

Malone, Patrick M. *The Skulking Way of War: Technology and Tactics among the New England Indians*. Lanham, MD: Madison Books, 1991.

Mampoteng, Charles. "The Reverend Samuel Peters, M.A." *Historical Magazine of the Protestant Episcopal Church*, Vol. 5, No. 2 (June 1936).

Martin, James Kirby. *Benedict Arnold, Revolutionary Hero: An American Warrior Reconsidered*. New York: NYU Press, 1997.

Massachusetts Historical Society. "A Bloody Butchery, by the British Troops." https://www.masshist.org/database/viewer.php?item_id=467&pid=2 (accessed Aug. 30, 2022).

McCullough, David. *John Adams*. New York: Simon & Schuster, 2001.

———. *1776*. New York: Simon & Schuster, 2005.

McDevitt, Robert F. *Connecticut Attacked: A British Viewpoint, Tryon's Raid on Danbury*. Chester, CT: Pequot Press, 1974.

McNeill, William H. *The Pursuit of Power: Technology, Armed Force, and Society since A.D. 1000*. Chicago: University of Chicago Press, 1982.

Middlekauff, Robert. *The Glorious Cause: The American Revolution, 1763–1789*. New York: Oxford University Press, 2005.

Mintz, Max M. *The Generals of Saratoga: John Burgoyne & Horatio Gates*. New Haven: Yale University Press, 1990.

Murphy, Jim. *The Real Benedict Arnold*. New York: Clarion Books, 2007.

Nash, Gary B. *The Unknown American Revolution: The Unruly Birth of Democracy and the Struggle to Create America*. New York: Viking, 2005.

National Archives. *Founders Online*. https://founders.archives.gov (accessed Sept. 1, 2022).

Nelson, James L. *Benedict Arnold's Navy: The Ragtag Fleet That Lost the Battle of Lake Champlain but Won the American Revolution*. Camden, ME: McGraw-Hill, 2006.

Nelson, Paul David. *General Horatio Gates: A Biography*. Baton Rouge: Louisiana State University Press, 1976.

Nickerson, Hoffman. *The Turning Point of the Revolution or Burgoyne in America*. Boston: Houghton Mifflin, 1928.

O'Shaughnessy, Andrew Jackson. *The Men Who Lost America: British Leadership, the American Revolution, and the Fate of the Empire*. New Haven: Yale University Press, 2013.

O'Toole, Fintan. *White Savage: William Johnson and the Invention of America*. London: Faber, 2005.

Palmer, Dave R. *George Washington's Military Genius*. Washington, DC: Regnery Publishing, 2012.

Palmer, Peter S. *Battle of Valcour on Lake Champlain, October 11th, 1776*. Plattsburg, NY: Lake Shore Press, 1876.

Pancake, John S. *1777: The Year of the Hangman*. Tuscaloosa: University of Alabama Press, 1977.

Pearson, Michael. "The Siege of Quebec, 1775–1776." *American Heritage*, Vol. 23, No. 2 (Feb. 1972). https://www.americanheritage.com/siege-quebec-1775-1776 (accessed Sept. 2, 2022).

Peters, Samuel. *General History of Connecticut*. New York: D. Appleton & Co., 1877.

Philbrick, Nathaniel. *Bunker Hill: A City, a Siege, a Revolution*. New York: Viking, 2013.

————. *Valiant Ambition: George Washington, Benedict Arnold, and the Fate of the American Revolution*. New York: Viking, 2016.

Phillips, Kevin. *1775: A Good Year for Revolution*. New York: Viking, 2012.

Pippenger, C. E. "A New Eyewitness Account of Valcour Island Resolves the Pringle Controversy." *Journal of the American Revolution*, October 13, 2016. https://allthingsliberty.com/2016/10/new-eyewitness-account-valcour-island-resolves-pringle-controversy/ (accessed Aug. 30, 2022).

Polhemus, Richard V., and John F. Polhemus. *Stark: The Life and Wars of John Stark, French and Indian War Ranger, Revolutionary War General*. Hensonville, NY: Black Dome Press, 2014.

Procknow, Gene. "Personal Honor and Promotion Among Revolutionary Generals and Congress." *Journal of the American Revolution*, January 23, 2018. https://allthingsliberty.com/2018/01/personal-honor-promotion-among-revolutionary-generals-congress/ (accessed Aug. 30, 2022).

Rakove, Jack. *Revolutionaries: Inventing an American Nation*. London: William Heinemann, 2010.

Randall, Willard Sterne. *Benedict Arnold: Patriot and Traitor*. New York: William Morrow and Company, 1990.

————. *Ethan Allen: His Life and Times*. New York: W. W. Norton & Company, 2011.

Reardon, Matthew. "Disastrous Leadership: Lt. Colonel Joseph Harris at the Battle of New London." *Journal of the American Revolution*, December 10, 2014. https://allthingsliberty.com/2014/12/disastrous-leadership-lt-colonel-joseph-harris-at-the-battle-of-new-london/ (accessed Sept. 7, 2022).

Roberts, Kenneth. *March to Quebec: Journals of the Members of Arnold's Expedition*. New York: Doubleday Doran & Company, 1938.

Ronald, D. A. B. *The Life of John André: The Redcoat Who Turned Benedict Arnold.* Havertown, PA: Casemate Publishers, 2019.

Rorison, Arda Bates. *Major-General Arthur St. Clair: A Brief Sketch.* New York: s.n., 1910.

Ross, John F. *War on the Run: The Epic Story of Robert Rogers and the Conquest of America's First Frontier.* New York: Bantam Books, 2009.

Rossie, Jonathan Gregory. *The Politics of Command in the American Revolution.* Syracuse, NY: Syracuse University Press, 1975.

Royster, Charles. "The Nature of Treason." *The William and Mary Quarterly,* Vol. 36, No. 2 (April 1979): 163–193.

————. *A Revolutionary People at War: The Continental Army and American Character, 1775–1783.* Chapel Hill: University of North Carolina Press, 1979.

Scales, John. *Life of Gen. Joseph Cilley.* Manchester, NH: Standard Book Co., 1921.

Scheer, George E., ed. *Private Yankee Doodle.* Boston: Little, Brown, 1962.

Schnitzer, Eric, and Don Troiani. *Don Troiani's Campaign to Saratoga—1777: The Turning Point of the Revolutionary War in Paintings, Artifacts, and Historical Narrative.* Guilford, CT: Stackpole Books, 2019.

Schuyler, Philip. "To George Washington from Major General Philip Schuyler, 1 July 1776." *Founders Online.* https://founders.archives.gov/documents /Washington/03-05-02-0115 (accessed Aug. 30, 2022).

Sellers, Charles Coleman. *Benedict Arnold: The Proud Warrior.* New York: Milton, Balch, 1930.

Shelton, Hal T. *General Richard Montgomery and the American Revolution: From Redcoat to Rebel.* New York: NYU Press, 1994.

Shy, John. *A People Numerous and Armed: Reflections on the Military Struggle for American Independence.* Ann Arbor: University of Michigan Press, 1990.

Smith, Justin Harvey. *Our Struggle for the Fourteenth Colony: Canada and the American Revolution.* New York: G. P. Putnam's Sons, 1907.

Snow, Dean. *1777: Tipping Point at Saratoga.* New York: Oxford University Press, 2016.

Spring, Matthew H. *With Zeal and with Bayonets Only: The British Army on Campaign in North America, 1775–1783.* Norman: University of Oklahoma Press, 2008.

Springman, Kevin T. "Notes and Documents: Thomas Paine's Response to Lord North's Speech on the British Peace Proposals." *The Pennsylvania Magazine of History and Biography,* Vol. 121, No. 4 (Oct. 1997): 351–370.

Standiford, Les. *Desperate Sons: Samuel Adams, Patrick Henry, John Hancock, and the Secret Band of Radicals Who Led the Colonies to War.* New York: HarperCollins, 2012.

Stark, Caleb. *Memoir and Official Correspondence of Gen. John Stark.* Concord, NH: E. C. Eastman, 1877.

Stephenson, Michael. *Patriot Battles: How the War of Independence Was Fought.* New York: HarperCollins, 2007.

Stumpf, Vernon O. *Colonel Eleazer Oswald: Politician and Editor.* Unpublished Dissertation. Durham, NC: Duke University, 1968.

Taylor, Alan. *The Divided Ground: Indians, Settlers, and the Northern Borderland of the American Revolution.* New York: Alfred A. Knopf, 2006.

Thacher, James. *An Army Doctor's American Revolution Journal, 1775–1783.* Mineola, NY: Dover Publications, Inc., 2019.

Thayer, Simeon. *The Invasion of Canada in 1775.* Providence, RI: Knowles, Anthony, 1867.

Thomas, Emory M. *Robert E. Lee: A Biography.* New York: W. W. Norton & Company, 1995.

Trees, Andy. "Benedict Arnold, John André, and His Three Yeoman Captors: A Sentimental Journey or American Virtue Defined." *Early American Literature,* Vol. 35, No. 3 (2000): 246–273.

Tuchman, Barbara W. *The First Salute: A View of the American Revolution.* New York: Alfred A. Knopf, 1988.

Van de Water, Frederic F. *Lake Champlain and Lake George.* New York: The Bobbs-Merrill Company, 1946.

Van Doren, Carl. *Secret History of the American Revolution.* New York: The Viking Press, 1941.

Von Eelking, Max, ed. *Memoirs, and Letters and Journals, of Major General Riedesel during His Residence in America.* Albany, NY: J. Munsell, 1808.

Ward, Christopher. *The War of the Revolution.* New York: Macmillan, 1952.

Washington, George. "From George Washington to John Banister, 21 April 1778." *Founders Online.* https://founders.archives.gov/documents/Washington/03-14-02-0525 (accessed Aug. 30, 2022).

———. "From George Washington to John Hancock, 21 September 1775." *Founders Online.* https://founders.archives.gov/documents/Washington/03-02-02-0025 (accessed Sept. 6, 2022).

———. "From George Washington to Lieutenant Colonel John Laurens, 13 October 1780." *Founders Online.* https://founders.archives.gov/documents/Washington/03-28-02-0282 (accessed Aug. 30, 2022).

Watt, Gavin K. *Rebellion in the Mohawk Valley: The St. Leger Expedition of 1777.* Toronto: Dundurn Press, 2002.

Weddle, Kevin J. *The Compleat Victory: Saratoga and the American Revolution.* New York: Oxford University Press, 2021.

Wells, Bayze. *Journal of Bayze Wells of Farmington.* Hartford: Connecticut Historical Society, 1899.

Wickman, Donald H., ed. "A Most Unsettled Time on Lake Champlain: The October 1776 Journal of Jahiel Stewart." *Vermont History,* Vol. 64, No. 2 (Spring 1996): 89–98.

Wilson, Barry. *Benedict Arnold: A Traitor in Our Midst.* Montreal: McGill-Queen's University Press, 2001.

Wood, Gordon S. *The Radicalism of the American Revolution.* New York: Alfred A. Knopf, 1992.

Wood, William. *The Father of British Canada: A Chronicle of Carleton.* Toronto: Glasgow, Brook & Co., 1935.

Index